I0518154

Constance Santego

Knowledge of a

Soul

Dr. Constance Santego has been practicing and teaching *The Nine Spiritual Gifts, Granted From Spirit,* for over twenty-five years. She lives in British Columbia, Canada, with her husband.

www.constancesantego.ca

Published by
Editor & Interior Layout: Dr. Constance Santego
Book Layout: ©2017 BookDesignTemplates.com
Cover Design: Jennifer Louie
Soft Cover ISBN: 978-1-990062-28-5
eBook ISBN: 978-1-990062-29-2

Created and published in Canada. Printed and bound
in the United States of America
Ordering Information: csantego@gmail.com

ALSO BY DR. CONSTANCE SANTEGO

FICTION
The Nine Spiritual Gifts Series: *(based on actual events)*
Journey of a Soul – (Vol 1 Michael)
Language of a Soul – (Vol 2 Gabriel)
Prophecy of a Soul – (Vol 3 Bath Kol)
Healing of a Soul – (Vol 4 Raphael)
Miracles of a Soul – (Vol 5 Hamied)

NONFICTION
The Intuitive Life, The Gift of Prophecy, Third Edition
Fairy Tales, Dreams and Reality… Where Are You On Your Path? Second Edition
Your Persona… The Mask You Wear
Angelic Lifestyle, A Vibrant Lifestyle
Angelic Lifestyle 42-Day Energy Cleanse
Archangel Michael's Soul Retrieval Guide
Tesla and the Future of Energy Medicine
Scaling Beyond 6 Figures: *Strategies for Health & Wellness Professionals*
Beyond the Mind: *Harnessing the Power of Astral Projection for Creative Awakening*
Bend, Don't Break: *Finding Your Way Back to Abundance*
Ring Therapy: *A Guide to Healing and Balance*
Ring Therapy Pocket Guide
Floraopathy™: *The Art and Science of Vibrational Healing with Essential Oils*

SECRETS OF A HEALER, SERIES:
Magic Of Aromatherapy (Vol I)
Magic Of Reflexology (Vol II)
Magic Of The Gifts (Vol III)
Magic Of Muscle Testing (Vol IV)
Magic Of Iridology (Vol V)
Magic Of Massage (Vol VI)
Magic Of Hypnotherapy (Vol VII)
Magic Of Reiki (Vol VIII)
Magic Of Advanced Aromatherapy (Vol IX)
Magic Of Esthetics (Vol X)
The Reiki Master's Manual (Vol XI)

ADULT COLORING JOURNALS
SERIES - ZEN COLORING:
Quantum Energy and Mindful Living Journal (Vol 1)
Reiki Energy Journal (Vol 2)
Nine Spiritual Gifts Journal (Vol 3)
I Forgive Journal (Vol 4)

SERIES – COLORING PROSPERITY:
Genie-Inspired Mandalas and Wealth Journal (Vol 1)
Entrepreneurial Mindset Reboot (Vol 2)

SERIES – HARMONIC MIND CODE:
Harmonic Mind Code Coloring Journal (Vol 1)

FOR CHILDREN
I am Big Tonight. I Don't Need the Light!

Cast of Characters

Some of the Residents of New York City, USA, and other places.

Alexandra (Lexi) Elizabeth Constantine:
Fashion designer in Upper East Side Manhattan. Daughter of beloved parents—Olivia and Marcus Constantine (Italian). Was a Fiancée to Reverend Edward Julien Hawthorne. Her boss was Sebastian. Friends with co-worker Southern belle, Sherie. Was going to be engaged to Neo, but is in love with Redington.

Susannah Grace Constantine:
Lexi's belated sister and now guardian angel. Lived in Dumbo (Down Under the Manhattan Bridge Overpass). She was an antique collector for Aryeh Jacob Kofman and dated Billy Randazzo.

Olivia Sarah Constantine (Maiden name, Austin): Mother to Lexi and Susannah. Widowed housewife. Parents were from England. She lives in Dyker Heights, Brooklyn, NY. Deceased.

Reverend Edward Julien Hawthorne: Was a mortician and minister of his family's funeral home in Brooklyn. Was a Fiancé to Alexandra (Lexi). Casandra was his secretary. He had an accident and forgot everything. Another soul took over his body at the time of his death and lived as a walk-in.

Sophea (Tamara Reeve): Past Psychic medium and teacher of many of the Spiritual Gifts. Was a Fiancée to Greg Masones. Still owns her grandmother's brownstone in Brooklyn Heights. Now lives in Katmandu, Naples—in a monastery and is a monk.

Detective Ferguson "Red" Redington: Was 1st-grade homicide investigator, Manhattan Bureau – Midtown South Precinct, Shield number 1323, NYPD. Lives in Far Rockaway Beach, Queens, on Long Island, NY. His family comes from England. Now is a FBI agent.

Greg Masones (AKA Julian D'Angelo): At large. Accountant for the Genovese crime family. Italian immigrant. Son of Serena D'Angelo. Was Tamara's fiancé.

Sebastian: Lexi's boss at the fashion house.
Sherie: Lexi's co-worker at the fashion house.
Isabella Jackson: Famous actress. She moved around to wherever her next movie was being filmed. Friends with Lexi, Edward, and

Redington. Girlfriend of belated Hans (now Erland, an Elf) and mother to her beloved son, Aias.

Hans Magnusson (Erland): Lawyer. He lived in Switzerland but was from Sweden. He inherited his family's fortune, and his grandfather was Olof. After he died, he became a walk-in soul to Erland in the Elemental Realm of Alfheim, and still communicates with Isabella.

Aias *(pronounced I-iss)* **Jackson Olof Magnusson:** Son of Isabella and Erland. He was a half-elf with many gifts, the main one being able to heal. Deceased. Became an angel.

Kesia Bango: Gypsy tarot card reader. Daughter of Florence. Ancestral Granddaughter of Tatiana Masones and Clementina (Tatiana's mother). Related to Greg, he is her uncle. Loved Aias.

Luna: Kesia's Wiccan friend from high school. She lives in Jersey Shore.

Doctor Neo Singh: Edward's Neurosurgeon at Brooklyn Neurocritical Care. His Greek mother is Naida, and his East Indian father is Paal. Sister to Evangeline and uncle to her son, Todd.

Evangeline Singh: Neo's sister. Massage Therapist. Her son is Todd, and her fiancé is Jeff.

Delish Chakladar: Acharya Shri Sharma's assistant and devotee at Aias's gurukala (spiritual school) in Puttaparthi India.

Lieutenant Jerome Kennard: New York City fireman. Saved Lexi from the cave and briefly dated her.

Camillo O'Malley: A vulgar-mouthed Scottish man who practices Neuro Linguistic Programming.

Winston Charles Redington: the $2^{nd,}$ Earl of Wrightenton. Redington's father from England.

Countess of Wrightenton, Gabriela: Redington's belated Mother.

Lord Wrightenton, Grayson: Redington's belated older brother.

Lady Wrightenton, Janelle: Redington's belated older sister.

Main Angel of each Novel

Book 1 – Archangel Michael
"Warrior"
Companion Book – Archangel Michael's Soul Retrieval Guide.
Book 2 – Archangel Gabriel
"Messenger"
Companion Book – Your Persona... The Mask You Wear.
Book 3 – Bath Kol
"Daughter of the Voice," the Holy Ghost, and Gabriel
Companion Book – The Gift of Prophecy.
Book 4 – Archangel Raphael
"God Has Healed"
Companion Books – Secrets of a Healer Series.
Book 5 – Archangel Hamied
"Miracles"
Companion Book – Secrets of a Healer, Reiki,
Book 6 – Archangel Raziel
"The Keeper of Secrets and The Angel of Mysteries."

Knowledge of a Soul
The Gift of Knowledge

A Novel
6th in the series, The Nine Spiritual Gifts
'*The Gift of Knowledge*'

Dr. Constance Santego

Vol 6

Dedicated

to all my teachers!

Knowledge of a Soul

The Nine Spiritual Gifts

In the New Testament, my favourite story is
"The Gifts."
Corinthians 1, Chapter 12, Verse 4-11
(Maybe a little differently worded
depending on which Bible you have).

The variety and the unity of gifts
There are many different gifts, but it is always
the same Spirit; there are many different ways of
serving, but it is always the same Lord. There
are many different forms of activity, but in
everybody it is the same God who is at work in
them all. The particular manifestation of the
Spirit granted to each one is to be used for the
general good.
To one is given from the Spirit the gift of
utterance expressing **wisdom**; to another the gift
of utterance expressing **knowledge**; in
accordance with the same spirit to another, **faith**,
from the same Spirit; and to another, the gifts of
healing, through the same Spirit; to another, the
working of **miracles**; to another **prophecy**; to
another, the power of **distinguishing spirits**; to
one, the gift of **different tongues** and to another,
the **interpretation of tongues**. But at work in all
these is one and the same Spirit, distributing
them at will to each individual.
The New Jerusalem Bible

Awaken to the spirit

world, for there lie your
gifts granted by Spirit.

Dr. Constance Santego

Fact:

All biblical references, science, legends, and myths are real *(slightly changed to fit the character.* This novel was written as a story inspired by Spirit, to give you, the reader, a new perspective, a new way to learn, and a new opportunity to empower your life.

Many locations and all characters are fictional.

Prologue

Tamara awoke in a small, austere cell, the kind you might find in an ancient monastery. The cold stone walls surrounded her, their rough texture a stark reminder of her confinement. She lay on a simple cot, covered with a light cotton blanket, her head resting on a pillow filled with what felt like rice or barley. She wore a red robe, the fabric coarse against her skin, and her bare feet felt the chill of the stone floor. Beside her, a small round table held a ceramic pitcher and a large bowl filled with water for washing, the only luxuries in this Spartan environment.

Sitting on the cot's edge, she slowly drank some water using her hands. Afterward, she ventured out of the cell, relieved to find that she was not a prisoner like in her last lifetime. The narrow halls echoed with the serene chants of monks, drawing her toward their source.

A monk, noticing her approach, motioned for her to kneel beside him. She remembered taking a year's vow of silence and how a single tear fell when they had shaved her head. Her days were now filled with prayer, meditation, spiritual lessons, and more prayer.

Once a day, she went out with the other monks to do what they could to help the community and receive food offerings from the local people. This simple, ascetic life starkly contrasted her previous incarnations—some filled with tumultuous passions and others with tranquil wisdom. Each life, with its unique trials and lessons, had been a step on her soul's long journey—a journey toward enlightenment and understanding.

Her current life in the monastery was another chapter in that journey, one that promised deeper spiritual insights and, perhaps, a step closer to the ultimate liberation of her soul. This lifetime was about learning the balance between solitude and service, silence and expression, and the individual soul and the universal spirit.

As Tamara, now called Sophea, settled into the rhythm of monastic life, she often found her mind wandering to the lessons learned in past lives, each a puzzle piece in the vast mosaic of her soul's experience. In this place of quiet introspection and communal harmony, she hoped to find the wisdom to navigate the challenges ahead and fulfill the soul contracts she had made long before this body took its first breath.

This lifetime's journey is a quest not just for personal liberation but for cosmic balance—the eternal dance of souls moving through the tapestry of lifetimes, each learning and teaching, taking and giving in equal measure. Here, in the simplicity of monastic life, Sophea was preparing to take her next step on this grand, celestial journey, guided by the unseen hand of destiny and the clear, resonant voices of the monks in prayer.

4 Dr. Constance Santego

Chapter 1

A cold, brisk wind was coming in from the north. Even though it was only October, you could feel winter was on its way.

Kay Thompson's hood was drawn far over her head, almost covering her eyes. She had pulled the robe around herself even tighter, trying not to let the cold breeze get near her thin body.

It had seemed like days since she last had something to eat and weeks since she had a bath. *What was I thinking? I must be mad trying to find happiness. Well, that is what I thought the man had said, that I would find happiness. I am almost ...*

Days before, she had taken a seminar on personal uplifting and financial improvement.

The motivational class was designed to get people pumped up and ready to improve their lives.

As she was listening to the speaker, a couple behind her kept talking to each other. *Don't they think of anyone else but themselves?*

Their rudeness was really getting under her skin. She shrugged her shoulders several times, hoping they would take the hint. Finally, they quieted down, and she could focus on the speaker.

He was a middle-aged man with dark hair and a mustache, nicely dressed in a casual way. He stood in the center of a large platform a few feet above the seats so all could see him better.

He had a great voice and the talent to speak clearly and motivate the audience. His words made you feel like you "could" change your life and do better for yourself.

As he talked, Kay started thinking about her life and how she needed a change. *I hate being who I am. I don't like how I look anymore—maybe never did—but I hate it even more now. I just turned forty, and life was supposed to be great. The kids were all grown up and almost gone. I had a nice house, a great job, and all the toys, a boat, an RV, etc. We had gone on many wonderful family trips. What could be missing?*

Suddenly, Kay snapped out of her daydream, realizing she had drifted off for a few minutes. The couple behind her had started talking again.

The speaker was still talking about getting your life back and how you had stopped living the life you were meant to live.

"Remember when you were kids," he said, "And life was exciting and fun?"

He continued, "A child's world is very small, usually just a few feet around them. A child notices people or objects that are immediately in their path or very close. A baby's world is even smaller, just a few inches around them. As we age, our space expands. We start to notice and care about our car, house, desk, town, city, province, state, or even our country. One day, it may even be our entire planet."

Kay started to think about her chair space and how she wished it didn't include the two talking behind her.

The two talked about how people could have their own space, even if they were beside another person, how sometimes you want someone in your space, and how other times there are people you don't want anywhere near your space.

Both their conversation and the speaker were starting to overwhelm Kay. The speaker had now shifted to discussing how to control your space.

Kay was getting so mad she couldn't hear anybody anymore. *How could I control any of my space? I can't even control my thoughts, which now want to kill the two behind me*

*because they cannot shut up and let me
concentrate on what the speaker is saying.*

She started to drift off again into her own
thoughts of yesterday.

She had just gotten home from work, and as
she entered the house, you could hear her
teenage children's music blaring from each
room.

After putting her things down, she walked
into the kitchen and started to make dinner, the
same old thing: meat, potatoes, and veggies.

After a long day's work, Kay was always so
hungry…and never had the energy to make
something special or different.

While the food was cooking, Kay opened the
mail to find, to her surprise—*not*—more bills to
pay.

Seeing the bills made her think more about
how anyone can afford to live nowadays. *My
husband, John, has always made good money
working. We could always afford shelter, a nice
place to live, food on the table, and clothes on
our backs. I do the best I can, but with owning
my own business, one never knows when the
money will come in.*

As the kids grew up, Kay and John could
afford to let them try out new sports and
entertainment. Both had their favorite activities.
Jack, their youngest son, was fifteen and into
music, while Kevin, their oldest, was seventeen
and into video games. As they grew from babies
to teenagers, VV Boutique—Value Village—

was their go-to store for clothes. They grew so fast; who could keep up? Designer clothes? Not in this family, especially back then, and with what…good looks and buttons?

Kay's thought changed to a memory of driving by a beautiful home with little kids playing outside.

How do they do it? How do the families live in such beautiful homes and with kids much younger than mine?" John makes much better than minimum wage. We do own a nice car and truck. Sure, we paid full price and have high loans. At least it is a write-off through the company.

It is what she keeps saying to herself to feel better.

I deserve to drive a nice car. I work hard. I so often don't take home a wage, so in my mind, it is justified. I know I will make good money one day, and I love owning my own business.

Again, Kay's thoughts snapped back to the seminar as people in the room started to laugh.

She looked around to see what had happened. The speaker made a funny comment, and everyone laughed at what he said.

She heard him ask his assistants to pass out paper and a pen to each person.

Next, he had everyone move into groups of four or five from the row of seats they were sitting in.

Once in the group, the task was to quickly discuss the group's thoughts on what makes people happy and write the words down on paper.

Kay joined the group in her row, smiled, and said, "Hi."

One of the guys in the group took the initiative and said, "Family and grandchildren make me happy."

Others started to say what made them happy. 'Money, gambling, swimming, hiking, lovemaking, seeing a baby animal start to walk, running, drinking was even one, and the list went on…'

Then, the speaker had everyone write down what made them sad.

Kay's group said things like, "Sad movies, loved ones dying, bad food, not feeling adequate, our looks, no money, war, loss of a cherished item, accidents, incurable disease, and a few more things…"

Next, the speaker said, "How would you make your life better…to mean something? Write down one way you can improve your life."

Some people in Kay's group said, "Give everyone a hug, notice one beautiful thing daily, help someone in need, bite your tongue, smile, do yoga or Tai chi, live, love, laugh."

As everyone at the seminar sat back in their original seats, the speaker came to his close. He finished by saying, "Take what you learned from tonight and make every day a great day, even if you are not feeling up to it. Make sure you smile a little more, laugh even when it might not be funny, put a skip into your step, and start becoming the person of your dreams."

Kay thought to herself, *did I miss that part...Dreams? Did I drift off when he was talking about that part?*

The two behind Kay started talking again as they got up to leave the seminar. As she prepared to leave, Kay quickly glanced at them, wondering how they slept at night. She recalled what the speaker had said about young children only noticing things very close to them. Clearly, Kay and everyone around her weren't close enough to be noticed by these two, who must be immature if they couldn't keep quiet while someone else was talking.

Kay drove home, daydreaming and imagining what life would be like when...

When what? When I have a beautiful home, more money, nicer trips... when...I want, I want, I want...

Kay suddenly remembered a book she had read a long time ago. What did it say? If all you do is think about wanting something, you'll create and attract just that—wanting. You will keep attracting situations that make you want things, but you will never truly achieve or obtain them. You will only achieve the state of wanting.

Pick your words carefully, she thought to herself.

Pick your words carefully.

Kay remembered the speaker from the seminar saying, "Be careful what you think. You might get it."

She remembered some other books she had read. One talked about what you think you create. And another author wrote about "focus" being your destination, just like driving a car. If you start looking left, you will most likely drive to the left.

Kay had attended many motivational seminars and listened to many great speakers.

She remembered one who stated, "Act it, and it will become!" and another, "Dress for success!"

Kay's main thought was, *Man, they make it seem so easy. So, what is the secret to a happy path?*

She thought back to the question she had asked her parents, aunts, and uncles about how they made their money, and to her surprise, no one could really tell her. One of her relatives said, "Luck and lots of hard work and more luck." Another said, "It was different back then. Lower house prices, food, gas, etc., and wages weren't much different from now." Another added, "We didn't need all the extravagance you kids need today."

Kay thought to herself how easy it was for them to say that when they were the ones who let her, and her cousins experience the kind of life they were used to before they went out on their own. Then, they expected the kids to be able to create the same life even when necessities went up in price and wages didn't.

Their level of life is high, but it seems so enjoyable. Maybe it is just me… Do I really need all that stuff, such as a house, holiday home, car, toys, trips, and entertainment? Maybe the golden days were better…you went to work from dust to dawn, came home, read out of the Bible (if you knew how to read), and went to bed. They had no TV, movies, computer, or video games…all they did was work, eat, and be merry. Yeah, right, not in this lifetime.

Kay was unhappy with her life and seemed to watch other people get what she wanted.

Kay made it home safely from the seminar. She went straight to her bedroom, lay down on the bed, and started to cry.

After what seemed like many minutes of crying, she took her driver's license, bank card, and medical card and told John she was going for a walk.

She walked to the nearest neighborhood pub and had a drink, or two, or maybe it was three…but who's counting?

After an hour or so, she walked to the nearest bank and took $500.00 cash out of their savings account.

Saving for what? A rainy day... well, I need a better life. John and the kids will be better off without me holding them back.

Kay walked to the bus station and bought a ticket for the next bus to Vancouver.

She was thinking to herself, *who really cares where it is going?*

She had friends there that she could stay with. Maybe if she had not been buzzed from drinks she had earlier, she would not have made such a rash decision and hopped on the bus.

Kay picked up a brochure left on one of the seats as she got off the bus in Vancouver. It advertised a retreat in the mountains. She took it as a sign from God and paid a taxi driver to take her to the address on the brochure. Two hundred dollars later, she arrived.

Oh well... it is just money. Who needs it anyway? It does not buy happiness...right?

The brochure read:

> Trying to find
> - Yourself, oneness
> - Calm, peace
> - Awakening
> - Inner beauty
> - Enlightenment
>
> To awaken the real person inside of you • All that you can be, you are going to the right place!!!

Kay finished paying the driver and walked into the retreat's office, which happened to be a Buddhist monastery.

The monks were all bald, and the women and men were wearing red robes. When greeting you, they bowed.

After registering, Kay followed the monk, who waved at her and said, "This way to happiness."

She was shown into a room with a shower and was given a robe and sandals.

All her belongings, which consisted of a shirt, jeans, underwear, the three cards she took as identification, and the remaining money, approximately two hundred and eighty dollars, were all taken from her.

The monk said it would be stored for her and showed Kay where to sit.

As she sat down, another monk with a razor came toward her.

What was I thinking...my hair? Well, I went this far; it is only hair, and it will grow back.

A few tears came as she saw her hair fall onto the floor.

After the monk finished, Kay was guided to the shower and told to wash and remove all her makeup, dress, and come into the main hall.

I think I lost my mind, no hair, a red robe, and sandals. I am sure there must be a better way... but...I just left my husband, children, and life. What was in those drinks I had? Why did I drink in the first place? ...oh yeah, I remember, to find happiness.

Kay walked slowly down the big hall, following many monks in the same red robes.

She was instantly in awe when she entered a room with massive double-arched, hand-carved wood doors. It was the most beautiful room she had ever seen.

Facing her, from across the room, was a twenty-foot tall and almost as wide golden Buddha in a sitting position. It reminded her of the little one she remembered polishing at her grandmother's house. She loved to rub its belly for luck when helping her grandmother dust her ornaments.

Everything in the room was so pristine and clean. Red walls with intricate gold designs, flickering glowing candles everywhere, and, to her amazement, rows of many itty-bitty wooden benches.

Kay immediately found out by watching the others that you lift the little bench, kneel, and sit on the wood, which has a slight angle for a seat.

Kay knelt with her legs under her like all the other monks and, to her surprise, found the bench very comfy and supported her bottom end very well as she waited.

She was not told what to do next, so Kay waited and looked around at the other people, wondering what they were doing.

It did not take long for her to figure out what to do since she had been sober now for quite a while.

All the other monks were meditating or praying, and she was meant to do the same.

It had been a while since she was last in any church.

Again, what was I thinking...what am I doing here? What am I supposed to do now?

A few dragged-out hours had passed, and Kay was not used to sitting still for that long in meditation; her legs were beginning to cramp.

Luckily, just as she thought she would have to stand up due to the pain, the monks in front of her started to stand up and leave.

She followed the same waving monk as she had when she came in.

He showed her to her room and said, "Supper will be announced shortly."

Once in the room, she shut the door, sat on the small cot, and began to cry.

Thinking about what she had done—leaving her husband and children behind—she realized she was now bald with a very shiny white head. She decided to get up and run out of the monastery at that moment. She didn't need to sneak out because no one was around to notice. She ran down the road the taxi had brought her up on, not realizing how far the vehicle had driven to the retreat. No matter, she kept running, then slowed to a quick walk.

Looking back quickly over her shoulder as if someone would come after her.

It seemed as if the early night sky had turned into the pitch of black—as if someone had turned a light switch from on to off.

Kay started getting cold and pulled the hood over her head.

She had forgotten that she had left all her clothes and belongings behind in her haste.

Well, I am not going to go back for them now.

All she could think now was, *almost home, I am almost home, I am...*

Suddenly, Kay woke up and realized that she was in her own bed and that it was just a crazy dream.

But to make sure, she got up, touched her head, and looked into the mirror.

Only to find that her hair was just as beautiful as before.

Sophea said, "When I count from three to one, you will be wide awake, remembering all about this past life's experience."

Chapter 2

*K*esia wiggled her toes to come back into full consciousness.

Sophea explained to the three newest monks, "It is the soul's purpose to have experiences on Earth. These experiences achieve the necessary life lessons for a soul to advance to Nirvana."

Kesia raised her hand slightly and asked, "Remind me again what Nirvana is."

"Imagine Nirvana is to the spirit world what Heaven is to us."

Kesia smiled at Lexi and Isabella's smooth-shaven heads. She still couldn't believe Isabella let the monk shave her beautiful black hair and what she said to him as he did, "I've had to play worse roles than this one."

Kesia touched her head and felt how soft it felt as Sophea asked, "Kesia, what knowledge did you get from this past life meditation?"

Kesia took a breath and thought about the meditation.

"I think I am processing shaving my head and becoming a monk."

Lexi and Isabella chuckled as they could relate.

Ignoring the other two's giggle, Sophea changed the subject and asked them, "Who knows the difference between the Tree of Life and the Tree of Knowledge?"

Lexi raised her hand and said, "I know the Tree of Knowledge is spoken about in many cultures. I was taught that Adam and Eve lived in the paradise land known as the Garden of Eden and were forbidden to eat the fruit from the Tree of Knowledge. I don't remember much, though, about the Tree of Life."

Kesia mouthed to Lexi. *I miss my oracle.*

Lexi mouthed back. *You must be going mad without internet and cell service.*

Sophea said as she looked at the three ladies, "Think of the Tree of Life as connecting all forms of creation and the Tree of Knowledge as connecting the heavens and the underworld."

Kesia noticed Lexi's twitch.

So did Sophea. "What?"

Lexi answered, "Just mentioning the underworld sends shivers down my spine. I have had enough experience to know that is one place I can do without ever visiting again."

Isabella, almost shouting, said, "I thought I heard or read somewhere that the Tree of Knowledge represented good and evil."

Sophea responded, "It does in some cultures." Then, she asked the girls, "What is knowledge?"

Lexi said without putting up her hand, "Information. Something we learn."

"True. What else?"

Isabella said quieter, "Facts."

Remembering something from school, Kesia said, "Skills acquired by a person through experience or education." Then she added, "And if you highlight the word experience and click the word doc's thesaurus, knowledge is listed as a choice."

Sophea nodded, "It also means awareness and understanding. But did you know that the Tree of Knowledge represents the laws pertaining to good and evil?"

Lexi spoke up, "I remember from Catechism class the story of Eve taking the apple from the snake, eating it, and giving it to Adam." Then Lexi told the others, "From that moment on, their paradise was tainted."

Enthused learning all about spiritual beliefs, myths, and legends, Kesia asked, "What do you mean by tainted?"

Lexi was about to answer when Sophea said, "Imagine the fruit Adam and Eve ate. You are probably imagining an apple, and an apple most represents knowledge, or at least that is what we gave to our teachers as a gift back in the day. But most theorists believe it was actually a fig. No matter what it was that they ate, the story goes like this. Adam and Eve once resided in a paradise of unparalleled beauty. Each passing moment radiated with bliss and boundless joy. Within this idyllic realm, the concepts of evil and sin were but distant whispers until the fateful day they dared to defy God's command, partaking of the forbidden fruit. Tragically, as their eyes were opened to the complexities and imperfections of the world, the once-vibrant paradise began to lose its luster, gradually fading into mundanity. Knowledge is tricky because it is hard to unlearn once you learn something."

Kesia put her hand up.

Sophea motioned a finger to insinuate that she should wait and said, "Imagine learning that the Earth was flat, and then someone tells you, no, it isn't. It's round. Who do you believe? We had faith in the people that told us in the first place and took their word for it."

Lexi commented, "I can relate. I was told that no Mayans were left in Mexico, but when I went on a tour, the tour guide said that he was Mayan, his father before him, and all the grandfathers before that."

Isabella added, "I remember taking an anatomy class, and another student argued that men had one less rib since one was taken to create a woman and that the teacher was wrong."

Sophea continued, "Isn't it fascinating what we believe to be true when said by someone we consider an authoritative or expert on the subject matter when science can prove that women and men are born with the same number of ribs."

Kesia was still waiting to ask her question, and she noticed how Sophea surprised Lexi by asking her, "What was your life like before you found out that ghosts were real and that the underworld existed?"

Before Lexi could answer, Sophea added, "Or that the spiritual gifts are real and that anyone can learn how to use them?"

"Scary," Lexi said quickly.

"Are you still scared of ghosts, Lexi?"

"Well, not anymore. I love being able to communicate with my sister. But to be fair, I had you to teach me the laws of the spiritual world."

Sophea smiled.

Lexi looked at the other two and said, "Actually, we all have you to thank for teaching us the gift of distinguishing spirits and how to communicate with them."

Kesia added, "And don't forget how to prophesy. I love that one."

"And Aias had the gift to heal," Isabella shared with a tear in her eye.

"And the gift of miracles still amazes me," Lexi added as she started to go into a trance.

"Lexi, stay focused," Sophea demanded. "Stop thinking about Aias and Redington saving you from Marcus."

Kesia watched as Lexi blinked her eyes, trying to shift her thoughts back to Sophea's lesson. She raised her hand again.

"Good question, Kesia," Sophea said.

"I didn't ask anything yet."

"Not out loud."

Chapter 3

$\mathcal{S}$ophea continued the day's study lesson for the three ladies by answering Kesia's question.

"Based on the requirements needed for a soul's personal growth and ascension to Nirvana, five past life levels must be mastered: Newbie, Child, Teenager, Adult, and Geriatrics. These mandatory experiences or acquired knowledge must be achieved before the soul's graduation can be attained."

Kesia asked Sophea, "How did you know I would ask you about past lives?"

Sophea smiled slightly and then said, "The first level is *Newbie*. It is when a soul has only lived one to five lifetimes. These souls come to Earth as plants, insects, or animals. Their experiences are mostly based on instincts of survival and physiological needs. All the essentials are listed on the bottom layer of Maslow's hierarchy of needs."

Lexi asked, "Remind me what Maslow's Hierarchy is."

Sophea started to draw it on the chalkboard, saying, "Kesia, I know that you didn't grow up with chalkboards, but here at the monastery, we believe in the simple things."

Kesia's face showed amazement at Sophea's ability to read minds.

Sophea drew Maslow's Hierarchy on a parchment clipped to the chalkboard.

Turning to face the three, Sophea said as she tapped the lowest level of the triangle, "During these lifetimes, the soul needs to gain knowledge and to experience the physiological needs of survival: breathing, food, water, sex, sleep, homeostasis, and excretion.

"Oh, right," Lexi nodded as she remembered reading about Maslow's hierarchy of needs.

Sophea continued, "When a soul has experienced five to a thousand lifetimes, it is considered a *Child*. During this level of enlightenment, the experiences or knowledge needed for advancement are focused on the physical body. The experiences are based on the 2nd layer of Maslow's hierarchy, daily life: security of body, employment, resources, mortality, the family, health, and property."

Lexi's hand went up.

"Yes, Lexi."

"Does a person's emotions come into play with these lifetimes?"

"Yes, but let's finish the levels first."

"Sorry, of course. Please go on," Lexi said, a little embarrassed.

"The level of *Teenager* is one thousand to five thousand lifetimes. These required experiences are focused on love and vitality. The vital body and the 3rd layer of Maslow's hierarchy: friendship, family, and sexual intimacy.

Adult, is the fourth level of reincarnation, and the soul has lived five thousand to ten thousand lifetimes. These experiences are focused on the Mental body and are the needs of the 4th layer of Maslow's hierarchy: self-esteem, confidence, achievement, respect for others, and being respected by others."

The girls let Sophea finish without interrupting her with any more of their questions.

"The last level is called *Geriatrics,* and a soul needs to experience ten thousand plus lifetimes. These experiences are focused on the supramental body and the 5th layer of Maslow's Hierarchy, all that you want: morality, creativity, spontaneity, problem-solving, lack of prejudice, and the acceptance of facts."

Lexi asked Sophea, "So, just to be clear, the levels our soul needs to experience are called newbie, child, teenager, adult, and geriatrics?"

"Yes, that is correct. Graduation is accomplished when a soul achieves all the required wisdom for the bliss body, 5th level of the hierarchy, and when the soul has made amends for all past life karma."

"The soul graduates?" Kesia asked Sophea.

"Yes, graduation is when the soul is released from the cycle of death and rebirth."

Isabella raised her hand and asked, "Do I understand it correctly? We are here on Earth to have experiences, graduate, and go to Nirvana. Is that correct?"

"Yes."

Kesia asked, "What is Nirvana like?"

Sophea had to take a breath on that one. She didn't have an answer.

After a moment of thought, Sophea said, "Everyone, close your eyes and take a deep breath."

The girls closed their eyes and took a breath.

"Now, imagine a magical ladder you can easily and quickly climb. This ladder will take you to a viewing area. Do so now. Climb your ladder."

Sophea waited a moment before continuing.

"Now that you have reached the end of the ladder, walk over on the platform to the window."

Sophea waited a moment to let the girls imagine they were getting off the ladder and walking to a window.

"What you see is a glimpse of Nirvana. What do you see?"

Sophea could see the three girls' faces change. "What do you see?" she repeated.

Lexi's mouth opened, but no words came out. Kesia looked as if she was in awe. Isabella had a slight smile, but no one answered.

Confused, Sophea said, "Take a deep breath, come down the ladder, and then open your eyes, coming back to this moment in time."

Sophea waited for what seemed like a very long time for the girls to open their eyes. But no one did.

"Take a deep breath and open your eyes," she repeated.

No response.

Thinking of what to do, she said, "Close your eyes from the window. Turn your head."

The girls' faces did not change expression.

Getting worried, for this had never happened before, Sophea picked up a wooden mallet and hit a metal gong.

In the small room, the sound was almost deafening.

The girls instantly snapped out of their meditative state.

"What the?" Kesia said first. "What did you do that for?"

"Yeah, really, Sophea," Isabella said as she rubbed her ears.

Lexi just shook her head.

Sophea was happy that they were awake again and talking to her. "What happened? Why did you not do as I asked and come down the ladder?"

Isabella answered, "Who in their right mind would return to this once you have experienced that?"

Kesia nodded in agreement.

"Tell me," Sophea said. "What did you see?"

Lexi closed her eyes and tried to tell Sophea what she saw. "I can't explain it."

"What about you two? What did you see?"

Kesia tried to say what she saw, "There are no words to describe the vision."

"Bliss," Isabella said. "Pure bliss."

"Bliss? As in perfect happiness?" Sophea asked to clarify.

"Sure, or pure joy," Lexi added.

Sophea asked, "But what did you see to feel that way?"

All three girls couldn't answer.

"Really, you saw nothing?"

"That's it!" Kesia said excitedly. "Nothing."

Sophea asked, confused, "Nothing? You saw nothing, but it was pure bliss?" She had never tried to see Nirvana herself, so she had nothing to compare what they were saying.

All three girls nodded.

Sophea said dumbfoundedly, "Hmm, that is interesting. Well, I guess you now understand what Nirvana is."

Kesia randomly said out loud, "I wonder if that is what happens to some people who go into a lunatic glare?"

"What do you mean?" Sophea asked Kesia.

"I mean, that it is so amazing the feeling I just had that I never wanted to leave. I could have stared out the window for eternity."

"Me too," Lexi agreed.

"Make that three. I could have stayed there also," Isabella nodded.

"I can see why a soul's goal is to get there," Lexi said to the group.

The other two nodded in agreement.

Sophea tried to go on with the lesson, but the girl's attention couldn't be held, so she let them go for the day.

"See you all at prayers," is all she could say as they left.

Chapter 4

"What are we learning today?" Kesia asked as she entered the little teaching room.

Sophea was happy the girls returned to normal after a good night's sleep.

"Reincarnation."

Kesia silently clapped her hands.

Lexi and Isabella smiled at her action.

Smiling, Kesia said, "I don't even need my phone to look that one up."

"You mean oracle," Lexi said jokingly.

Kesia's smile went even bigger, "Transmigration or metempsychosis."

"Show off," Isabella teased.

"Those are big words," Lexi joked.

Sophea added to Kesia's words, "Transmigration means to cause, to go from one state of existence or place to another. And metempsychosis means the supported transmigration at the death of the soul of a human being or animal into a new body of the same or a different species."

"You believe in reincarnation?" Kesia questioned Sophea.

"I do. Millions of people in the world believe that there is a life after this one."

Kesia interjected, "You mean Christians,"

"Not only Christians, but Hinduism, Buddhism, Jainism, Sikhism, Islamic, Judaic, Egyptian, Greek, Shamanism, Druidism, Norse Mythology, Sumerians, Zoroastrianism, and even Voodoo religions."

Lexi commented, "Who knew there were so many people who believe in an afterlife."

"Didn't you grow up believing in life after death?" Isabella asked Lexi.

"You're referring to growing up as a Catholic? Yes, I was taught that God will judge us, and we will either go to heaven, hell, or purgatory."

"What is purgatory again?" Kesia asked.

"A place where sinners go to suffer until forgiven and granted entrance into heaven," Lexi answered her, then added, "It is where one goes to get purified."

"Sounds like fun," Kesia joked.

Lexi defended the reasoning by saying, "Many believe that only a newborn baby is pure enough to get to heaven. That even though we confess our sins to a priest, we still are not cleansed enough after death to be granted instant access to heaven."

Sophea made a sound.

Lexi looked at her. "I know what you are thinking. After my experience with saving my sister's soul, I would have changed my opinion on the matter. I don't know what I believe anymore."

Sophea entered the conversation by saying, "No judgment here, Lexi. I believe that whatever you believe at the time of your death is what will happen to you."

Lexi gave a slight smile to Sophea.

"Today, though, we are going to study past lives," Sophea told the girls.

"How does one study past lives?" Kesia asked.

"Great question," Sophea answered her. You know when you did the meditation, and you were Kay?"

"Ya," Kesia said as she nodded.

"Like that, over the next few weeks, with the use of meditation, we are going to experience many lifetimes and see what we have learned from the past and what we need to learn in this lifetime," Sophea said as she looked at each of the girls.

"Sounds thrilling," Kesia said excitedly. "I liked the feeling of being someone else."

Isabella said matter-of-factly, "Technically, Kay was you."

"I guess," Kesia said as she shrugged her shoulders. "It felt like I was someone else."

Sophea pointed to Isabella, "Why don't you be next? Let's see what past life your meditation reveals."

"I am sure it will be some glamorous life. I think all my lives have been wonderful," Isabella said as she unrolled a mat onto the floor and got comfortable.

Once Isabella was lying on the mat, Sophea started the meditation by saying, "Take three deep breaths."

Sophea watched as Isabella closed her eyes and took three deep breaths.

"Good. Now, imagine you are entering a room filled with many doors. Stand in front of one. Any door. Nod when you have chosen."

Sophea waited for the nod.

Almost instantly, Isabella nodded.

"Good. In a moment, when you open the door, you will walk through, and once you do, tell me what you see. Go ahead and open the door and walk through now."

Isabella squirmed a little, then said, "All I see is dirt."

"Dirt. Okay. Is it in front of you?"

"Yes, all around me. To the sides, above and below." Isabella said, squirming again.

"Is it easy to breathe?" Sophea asked.

"Yes, it seems natural."

"Do you have hands?"

"No."

"Hmm." Sophea thought for a moment. "What are you?"

"A worm. I think an earthworm."

Kesia giggled.

Isabella squirmed again.

"What is your purpose in that lifetime?" Sophea asked Isabella.

"I seem to be breaking down organic matter, like leaves and grass." She squirmed again. "As I move, air and water fill the earth behind me. As I poop, which is called cast, it fertilizes the plants."

"Are you alone?"

"No, there are many of us."

"How many?" Sophea asked curiously.

"Maybe like five hundred thousand in about an acre of land."

"Wow," Kesia said, then put her hand over her mouth to shut up.

Sophea looked from Kesia back to Isabella, "Tell me about life as a worm."

After Isabella took a deep breath, she said, "I see lemon-shaped eggs called cocoons. There are also some hatchlings. They look like mini earthworms but are smaller and paler. There are also some juvenile worms here."

"How can you tell the difference?" Sophea asked.

"They look like the adults but without the saddle."

"What is a saddle?"

"It is a thick, saddle-like ring in the worm's skin. It is where the eggs are formed."

"Do you have a mate?"

After a moment passed, Isabella said, "No, I don't think so. I have both male and female sex organs. Nope, wait, I do need a partner."

"Tell me about the reproduction process," Sophea asked Isabella, now very curious about her experience.

"Oh, this is weird. Another earthworm just gripped me. We created a slime tube on the saddle area and exchanged sperm, which we stored to use later. Then we separated."

"But how does a baby worm form," Kesia said, then slapped her hand over her mouth again.

Lexi just shook her head and smiled at Kesia.

Facing Kesia, Sophea put a finger to her lips, then said, "Tell us more about the egg formation."

"A mucus sheath forms around the saddle and is moved along my body until it comes off my head. As this happens, it picks up the eggs and sperm of the other worm I mated. The mucus sheath forms the cocoon, and the fertilization and growth happen in the cocoon."

"Fascinating," Sophea said. "How old are you?"

"Two years old in human years."

"How long do earthworms live?"

"Some other worms are eight years old, but that is rare."

"Why?"

"Because ahhhhh."

Isabella snapped out of the meditation.

"Holy crap!"

"What happened?' Lexi asked, a bit worried.

"I was eaten."

"Eaten!" Lexi repeated.

Isabella nodded. "That was just creepy."

"What were you eaten by?" Kesia asked.

"A robin."

"A bird?" Lexi asked for confirmation.

"Ya. It was horrible."

Sophea snapped her fingers to return the girl's attention to the moment. "Isabella, take a breath and thank that lifetime experience. Then take another breath and let go of the experience."

Sophea gave Isabella a moment to shift back to the moment before asking, "What was the importance of that lifetime?"

Isabella answered almost immediately, "How important worms are to the world. They perform a very needed role in the ecosystem. See, I told you I live a wonderful life."

Kesia laughed, "Only you would think a worm was a wonderful life."

"Hey, without worms, plants would not grow."

Kesia smiled. "Okay, you have a point, but wonderful?"

Lexi joined the fun, saying, "I bet she had a tiara."

Both girls laughed.

"You can laugh all you want, but I bet your next lifetime won't be as good."

"Will see," Lexi laughed again.

"What did you learn from that past life that would be useful in this lifetime?" Sophea asked Isabella.

"To remember that even the simplest of lifeforms are important."

Sophea asked the girls, "What stage of the soul was that lifetime?"

Kesia's hand shot up, "Newbie!"

"Correct."

Chapter 5

One of Lexi's Past Lives

Looking out the eyes of a man. Lexi knew she was not in New York City, Nepal, or even modern times. It was ancient times, at least five hundred years before Christ was born.

Walking barefoot through the Sierra Nevada de Santa Marta mountains in northern Colombia, Lexi was an indigenous male in his mid-thirties. He had long, messy, greying black hair, a dirty, tanned face, eyes that had seen a lot of misery, and he wore stolen, ripped, and worn-out clothing. He lived in a cave at the base of the sacred mountain.

He had been a newborn baby when he was first brought to Gonawindua, also known as "The heart of the world."

Back then, he was chosen by divination to be trained to be attuned to Aluna, the great cosmic mother. It was a great honor to be taken at birth to live in the sacred caves with the Mamos, the spiritual men—the priests of the tribe.

His birth mother was only allowed to come and nurse him at night. He spent the first nine years of his life in these caves.

Unfortunately, during puberty, he was banned from returning to Gonawindua to complete another nine years of training. That is when his misery began, and his anger at the Mamo Kuncha—the chief Mamo—began.

The cave that now served as his adult refuge bore no resemblance to the nurturing caverns of his youth. Here, his only seat was a crude rock carved by time and necessity, surrounded by a grim array of animal and human bones strewn across the dirt floor.

Driven by hunger, he ventured out to hunt, hoping fortune would bless him with an armadillo, deer, or the hefty paca—a large rodent. Each step through the wilderness was shadowed by thoughts of retribution against Mamo Kuncha. A primal scream escaped his lips into the encroaching dusk, a symbol of his banishment from lands where food and clean water were once abundant. For too long, he had endured this exile.

His meals were the product of a brutal struggle, secured with bare hands or rudimentary tools crafted from branches and stone. Yet, any semblance of comfort was fleeting; the tribe's men periodically stripped him of these meager possessions, claiming them as penance for his past deeds.

It was so long ago he could barely remember the day he was exiled. Then he recalled that coca leaves were chewed for medicinal reasons and to consult with the supernatural. One day, when no one was looking, he took the three leaves that were left as an offering to Mother Earth.

Later that night, as he had seen the mamos do many times during ceremonies, he placed the leaves in his mouth and began to chew. Not knowing what to expect, he was unprepared for what happened next. He transformed into a jaguar.

His pale-yellow fur was covered in spots that transitioned to rosettes on the sides. He was on the hunt, and his bite went directly through the skull of his mammalian prey, between the ears, delivering a fatal blow to the brain.

When he awoke from his drugged state, he was covered in blood. He had killed a young girl from his tribe, ripping her head off. He had no recollection of his actions, but the girl's blood was all the elders needed. He was marked as a dark soul and banned from his tribe, destined to live the rest of his life as a jaguar would.

Starving, he could not take any more of this life. He decided to take matters into his own hands. The Mamo Kuncha was old now and needed to be removed from his position of power. This man had been the one to ban him from the tribe, from finishing his training, from living any normal life. It was time to take back what was taken from him.

In the dark of the night, as silent as the jaguar, he snuck into his old tribe's village and found the double-walled thatched hut that the Mamo Kuncho was sleeping in.

Coming around the side of the hut to the entrance, without taking a breath, he sprang through the door. Only to be hit with a corn-colored powder being thrown from the Mamo Kuncha.

He went through the powered dust and attacked the Mamo Kuncha, killing him.

Swaying as he left, he grabbed at the walls. He wiped at his eyes, for they burned. Whatever the powder was, it was now constricting his throat and lungs. Gasping for air, he tried to make it to his cave but fell to the ground and died a slow death.

Lexi came out of the meditation, shivered, and then shook her shoulders.

"So, what lessons did you learn in that lifetime?" Sophea asked her.

"I am unsure about lessons, but that was a horrible life."

"Why?"

The other two girls listened intently as Lexi told them about her past life experience.

After Lexi finished, Isabella said, "See, being a worm is wonderful compared to that life."

"Agreed," Lexi nodded.

"What emotions did you need to experience in that life?" Sophea asked.

"Well, I guess he was feeling abandoned and maybe hurt. Definitely anger and revenge."

"What do you think the purpose was in that lifetime?"

"I must have agreed to be given away at birth, but as I think about it, I did get nine years of spiritual growth. Even if the rest of my life was horrible."

"Interesting," Kesia said. I never would have thought of something good about that life. But you are right. You did get nine years of spiritual development. That must count for something."

"It does," Sophea nodded, then asked, "What stage of a soul was that lifetime?"

"The second. Child," Keisa said happily.

"Are you sure?" Sophea asked.

Keisa nodded, "Well, he had enlightenment."

"I understand what you are thinking, but he was still in survival mode when he died."

"So, Newbie?" Lexi questioned.

"Yes, good. Who wants to be next?"

Kesia's hand shot up.

Chapter 6

The Group's Joint Past Life

"Before you start Kesia, Let's try something different. Lexi and Isabella, I want you two to join Kesia in the meditation. Let's see who you all were to each other in a past life," Sophea said as she passed out two more mats.

It was dark, really dark. Even the stars were covered by a blanket of thick clouds.

"Shh, they will hear us."

Kesia was a tall African American male, about twenty-one, and was scared for his life.

"Toby, you're not my boss." Isabella was a spoiled little sister, about five years old.

Lexi was a scruffy little terrier named Scrump, whose tail wagged no matter their situation.

"Sissy, stop whining. You'll get us killed this time."

Sissy stuck her tongue out at her brother and pouted as she sat on a rock hidden by a tree.

Scrump hurried over to Sissy and licked her face.

As she petted the dog, a tear fell down Sissy's cheek.

"Oh, stop that. We don't have time for you to act like a baby."

"I'm hungry."

Toby looked at his little sister and then back in the direction he was headed. "I know. Me too."

Looking toward his destination again, Toby lifted his sister and carried her further into the bushes. They had been walking for hours.

"Toby?"

"Ya,"

"Will we ever see Mama again?"

"I don't know."

"But I want Mama."

"I know, me too."

Toby pulled out the last bit of cheese he had grabbed from the fridge as they ran out of the house and gave it to Sissy.

Holding his little sister tighter so she couldn't fall, he maneuvered through the thick bush and over the rough rocks.

A single snowflake touched Toby's eyelash. *Crap, that's all we need, snow. She'll freeze to death if I don't find it soon.*

Hurrying, Toby wished he could find the path, then, he could quickly get to the shack he had built as a kid. At least they would be out of the cold.

Years had passed since he last visited his childhood hideaway, a place shrouded in secrecy. It had taken him two years to construct this hidden refuge. Whenever things turned sour at home or when his father passed out, he would retreat to this secluded spot, venting his frustrations with the relentless pounding of a hammer. It might have been a modest dwelling, but he cherished it deeply.

It had been five years since he had been home. Sissy's birth had been a surprise and a blessing. His parents were getting along, and when he called home, mama always talked as if there were no problems.

He thought that it was safe to come home for Christmas, but he was so wrong. His mom had been lying to him. Things at home weren't better. True, his dad cherished Sissy, but his mama took all the abuse.

Tonight was worse than any night he could remember from his past. Tonight, pop had a gun pointed at Toby's head. *What is it with me? Why do I trigger pop so much?*

Coming back to the moment as Sissy yawned, "Toby, I'm tired."

"Close your eyes. We'll be there soon."

How did I get so lost? I used to know this area like the back of my hand.

He stumbled and almost dropped Sissy, whose head flopped over, but she did not wake up.

Srump, the dog, started to whimper.

"Shh," Toby whispered to the dog.

Scrump's tail hit Toby's leg as he scurried past him and ran ahead.

The moon peaked through the clouds and lit the way. The path was just ahead. Toby could see it.

Twenty minutes later, Toby found his hideout and pulled a key hanging from a chain around his neck. Taking it off with one hand, he tried to unlock the lock. He couldn't. He had to put Sissy down.

She stirred but didn't wake up.

The lock was stuck.

He went around the shack but couldn't find any loose boards he could pull off.

He had built the hideout so no one could get inside. Tonight, that included him.

Grabbing a rock, he returned to the lock and banged on it. All that did was wake Sissy up.

"Toby, where are we?"

"Safe. We are safe."

He tried the lock again. This time, it clicked open.

Hurrying, he removed the lock and opened the door. The inside was just as he had left it: a small table and a broken-back chair, a bucket to collect water from the creek, and some blankets on the ground that he had used as a bed some nights.

Picking up Sissy, he moved her to the bed area.

"Let me clean the dust off first," he told her before she sat down.

"Toby, I'm hungry."

"Here, get yourself warm. Wrap yourself in these blankets."

She did as she was told and wrapped Scrump and herself in the blankets.

Toby went to a board in the wall and removed a panel. Behind was a tin box with a lid. He removed the lid, and inside were some walnuts that he had left there years before. To his amazement, they were still eatable. Breaking the shells open, he tried one and then gave the rest to Sissy.

"I'm thirsty, Toby."

"Okay. I'll be back in a moment." Getting the bucket, he went outside and walked to the creek.

On the way back, he heard a noise. Stopping in his tracks to listen, he heard it again.

The moon illuminated the source of the noise, and for an instant, his heart stopped. Emerging from the bushes was his mama, staggering, her shirt stained with blood.

Running to her, he grabbed her as she fell from exhaustion.

"Mama!" Sissy screamed.

Sophea's voice was heard as she said, "On the count of three, you will open your eyes, take a breath, and return to this moment. One, two, three."

The three girls stretched and opened their eyes.

"So Kesia, tell me about this lifetime," Sophea smiled.

"Well, that was intense."

Lexi nodded as Isabella said, "I'm hungry."

Sophea looked at her funny.

Kesia laughed, "She was always hungry in that past life."

After the girls shared their experiences, Sophea asked, "What was the main lesson in that lifetime?"

Kesia answered, "Survival."

Lexi laughed and said, "As a dog, life was great. I was always happy."

Sophea nodded in acknowledgment of their answers. "So, you all were in a lifetime together, which means you are from the same soul group."

"What does that mean?" Kesia asked. "Are we always together in our past lives?"

Chapter 7

"*A* soul group is a group of people who come into a lifetime together, usually based on shared karma and emotional attachments," Sophea told the girls.

"Shared karma?" Lexi shrugged.

"Many believe that there is a collective karmic memory shared between families, communities, nations, and even across humanity," Sophea answered.

"Remind me what karma is again," Isabella asked Sophea.

"Hinduism and Buddhism believe that depending on the force generated by a person's actions is needed to perpetuate transmigration. That it is the ethical consequences that will determine the nature of the person's next lifetime."

Kesia's hand shot up as she told them, "I read an article once about what Tejal Patel thought about karma. She said, "Karma is a philosophy of how to live our lives so we can truly become the best version of ourselves and live the most fulfilling life we desire."

Sophea looked at Kesia and added, "To put it simply, karma is the memory of our souls, and what we didn't finish in a past life, we come back to finish now. It is your soul's luggage on its trip from life to life."

The girls listened closely to what Sophea said next, "The concept of karma and reincarnation is rooted in various religious and philosophical beliefs, particularly in Eastern religions like Hinduism, Buddhism, and Jainism. While these traditions acknowledge karma and reincarnation, their work's specific details and mechanics can vary.

The idea that karma may cause individuals to reincarnate in a reversed manner, where a parent becomes a child in a subsequent life, is not a universally accepted belief. Different interpretations of karma and reincarnation exist within different philosophical schools and religious sects.

In some beliefs, the gender of a person in a subsequent life may indeed change as a result of karma. It is believed that the experiences and actions of previous lives influence individuals' circumstances and relationships in their current lives.

However, it is important to note that karma is a complex and multifaceted concept, and its workings are not always easily understood or explained. The exact mechanisms of how karma operates and how it influences the cycle of reincarnation can vary across different philosophical and religious perspectives.

It's also worth mentioning that the idea of specific individuals significantly impacting our lives across multiple reincarnations is not a universally held belief. Some interpretations of karma emphasize the broader idea of cause and effect, where our actions in one life generate consequences that we experience in future lives, rather than emphasizing specific relationships between individuals.

Ultimately, beliefs about karma and reincarnation are deeply personal and can vary widely. People find meaning and understanding in these concepts differently, and interpretations can differ based on cultural, religious, and philosophical contexts."

Lexi piped up, "Tell us more about soul groups. That was interesting."

"Sure. Within a soul group, individuals are believed to have strong, energetic bonds and shared purposes or lessons to explore. These souls may take on different roles in each other's lives, such as friends, family members, romantic partners, or even adversaries, to facilitate growth and learning opportunities.

The members of a soul group are often described as having a deep understanding of one another, a sense of familiarity, and a profound connection that transcends time and space. They may experience synchronicities, telepathic communication, or a feeling of resonance when they encounter each other. It is believed that these connections support and guide individuals in their spiritual evolution and help them fulfill their soul's purpose."

"Fascinating," Lexi commented.

Sophea continued, "The idea of matching souls with others who will challenge and balance them is often associated with the concept of soul contracts or soul agreements. These agreements are believed to be made before incarnation, with the intention of experiencing specific lessons, growth opportunities, and shared experiences with other souls. The purpose of these interactions is typically seen as mutual growth and the development of understanding, compassion, and wisdom."

Kesia asked, "What is the difference between a soul group and a soul family?"

Sophea nodded, "According to some spiritual teachings, a soul group refers to a collective of souls that share a common energetic essence or purpose. These souls are believed to have a deep connection and often travel and evolve together throughout various lifetimes and dimensions. They may support and learn from each other as they go through different experiences and incarnations.

On the other hand, a soul family is often described as a more intimate group within a soul group. These are souls that have an exceptionally close bond and affinity with one another. They may have chosen to incarnate together in specific lifetimes to fulfill particular roles, learn specific lessons, or support each other in their spiritual growth."

Curious, Kesia asked, "How many souls make up a soul group?"

"There are primary and secondary soul groups. The first group—your primary group—comprises the souls you interact with most during your incarnation and study time spent in-between lives. There can be anywhere between three to twenty-five souls. Your secondary group is made up of clusters of primary groups and can be made up of thousands of souls."

Kesia's hand shot up again, "Hey, what about a soulmate? Tell us about that."

Sophea smiled at Kesia's enthusiasm, "The essence of a soulmate typically encompasses the following aspects: First, a Profound Connection: A soulmate is someone with whom you share an inexplicable connection as if you've known each other for a long time. It goes beyond physical attraction and involves an emotional, intellectual, and spiritual bond.

Second, Understanding and Empathy: A soulmate can understand and empathize with your thoughts, feelings, and experiences. They intuitively understand who you are and can provide comfort, support, and guidance when needed.

Third, Completeness and Wholeness: Being with a soulmate often evokes a sense of completeness or wholeness. They can fill the gaps in your life, complement your strengths and weaknesses, and help you grow.

Fourth, Shared Values and Goals: Soulmates often share similar values, beliefs, and life goals. They provide a sense of alignment and harmony, supporting each other's aspirations and helping to create a shared vision for the future.

Fifth, Unconditional Love and Acceptance: A soulmate loves and accepts you for who you truly are, embracing your flaws, quirks, and imperfections. They support your personal growth and encourage you to be your authentic self."

Kesia jumped in and asked, "Is a twin flame the same as a soulmate?"

"Many believe "soulmate" and "twin flame" are romantic relationships. While they are related concepts, they carry different meanings.

As I said earlier, a soulmate is someone with whom you have a deep connection and a sense of familiarity. They may be a romantic partner, a close friend, or even a family member. The bond with a soulmate is believed to transcend time and space, and meeting them often feels like reuniting with a long-lost companion. Soulmate relationships are typically characterized by mutual understanding, support, and ease. They can help you grow, learn, and evolve and often play significant roles in your life.

A twin flame is believed to be the other half of your soul. At the beginning of creation, your soul was split into two parts, and each part became a twin flame. Twin flames are said to mirror each other, representing the masculine and feminine aspects of the same soul. Meeting your twin flame is believed to trigger a profound spiritual awakening and transformation. The connection with a twin flame is often intense, passionate, and challenging. It can involve deep emotional and spiritual growth and periods of separation and reunion.

While soulmates and twin flames share a deep connection, there are a few key differences between them: the purpose of a soulmate relationship often focuses on personal growth, companionship, and mutual support. Twin flame relationships, on the other hand, are believed to serve a higher purpose beyond personal growth. They are seen as catalysts for spiritual evolution and transformation.

Soulmate connections are generally harmonious, stable, and comforting. Twin flame connections, however, can be extremely intense, with a mix of passion, love, and turmoil. Twin flames often experience a rollercoaster of emotions and challenges as they work through their individual and shared issues.

Soulmates can be present throughout your life, whereas twin flame encounters are believed to occur at specific times when both souls are ready for the transformative journey. Twin flame relationships may involve periods of separation and personal growth before the eventual reunion."

Kesia's hand went up, but before she could ask, Sophea said, "That is enough for today. You are dismissed. I will see you later in the meditation hall."

Chapter 8

Redington

Redington woke up the next morning by taking a deep breath and stretching his body, toes pointed, and elbows slightly lifted to give his rhomboids—muscles attached to his shoulder blades—a well-needed stretch.

The aroma of Earl Grey tea drifted into his room. Immediately, the memories of yesterday flooded into his consciousness.

Sitting up, swinging his long muscular legs over the edge of his bed, he got up quickly. With a few long strides, he grabbed his housecoat off the hanger in his bedroom closet and went out to find his father, who he knew was in the kitchen making tea, not coffee.

Pausing as he entered, Redington took a breath before he asked, "Did you sleep well, father?"

Lord Winston almost jumped out of his briefs. "Ferguson, you gave me a fright, sneaking up on me like that."

"Sorry, Sir. I will make sure I make more noise next time."

Redington watched as his father raised an eyebrow at his son's remark. "Don't get cheeky, young man."

Ignoring it. *I am a frigen-grown man.* Redington shook it off. "Father, I have to go into the office today. Will you be okay for a few hours?"

Red watched as his father, cup and saucer in hand, walked regally to the kitchen table. Before sitting down to drink it, he placed the tea set on a napkin. "I don't want to ruin the fine woodwork of your table."

Redington brought a coaster over and replaced the napkin with it.

Without looking at Redington, he said, "Son, I would love to come and see your craft." Winston stood up and hurried back to his room without waiting for an answer.

Shocked, Redington tried to say no, but his father was too quick.

A moment later, Winston returned to the kitchen with a top hat and cane, saying. "Remember who you are and the legacy you carry, my son. Let your actions today reflect the honor of our house."

Redington shook his head slightly as he turned to get dressed. *No sense in arguing with him about it. I might as well let him come and see where I work.*

"Chop, chop. We don't want to waste the day," Winston said as he lightly tapped his cane on the floor.

Once in his master bedroom, Redington sat on the edge of his bed and tilted his head. *Damm, it has only been a few hours, and I already want him gone.*

Childhood memories came swooshing in, more bad than good. Well, some might not say bad, but to Redington, they were all prim and proper. He never got to be a kid and just play.

Redington all of a sudden realized why he wasn't married yet. He would have to grow up. *Grow up! Bloody hell, what am I thinking? The fact is, I love my freedom.*

"Ferguson, we are going to be late, son," Lord Winston called out.

"Father, don't get your knickers in a twist. I'm coming."

Redington noticed the gleam in his father's eye when he entered the kitchen.

"Well, don't you look smashing!"

"Thanks, but the suit is a protocol for an FBI agent."

"If you were still in England, you could have joined the MI5, the Secret Service Bureau, and really been part of something."

"Father, here are the facts, MI stands for military intelligence, MI1 is codebreaking, MI2 is Russia and Scandinavia, MI3 is Eastern Europe, MI4 is aerial reconnaissance, MI5 is the British security service, while MI6 is the British Foreign Intelligence Service, MI7 is the press liaison and propaganda, MI8 is a Military Communication Interception, MI9 is undercover operations, MI10 is weapons analysis, MI11 and MI12 aren't worth mentioning, MI13 is paranormal occurrences, MI14 and MI15 are German specialists, MI17 is the Military Intelligence Head Office, MI18 is also not worth mentioning and MI19 is PoW debriefing.

Redington added before his dad could say anything else, "FBI stands for Federal Bureau of Investigation. Father, my work involves investigating federal criminal activity."

His father replied just before he exited Redington's condo, "Ferguson, you are lucky I am not a Carthaginian."

Redington knew that his father had just scolded him without saying anything else. *I might have been better off if you were. Carthaginian parents used to sacrifice their children as an offering to the gods.*

Chapter 9

The next day, Lexi asked Sophea, "Who is the angel of knowledge?"

"Raziel is known as the angel of secrets, or some say mysteries, because God reveals holy secrets to him. He is the angel who knows all the secrets of the universe."

Kesia told the others, "I thought Uriel was the angel of knowledge."

Sophea answered, "Archangel Uriel is the angel of wisdom. You must have knowledge to have wisdom, so I can see why you think that."

"What is the difference between knowledge and wisdom?" Isabella asked.

Sophea looked at the girls and said, "Knowledge is simply knowing something, but wisdom is about the ability to have perspective, insight, and sound judgments. Knowledge is gathered from learning and education, whereas wisdom is gathered from day-to-day experiences. Lao Tzu sums it up as, in pursuit of knowledge, something is gained daily. In pursuit of wisdom, something is dropped every day."

Kesia said, "So, what I am hearing is that knowledge is the information one learns, and wisdom is the ability to use that knowledge in a profound way."

"Wow, that was deep, Kesia," Lexi gasped.

"I wish I could take credit," Kesia confessed. "But no, it is something I remember reading on the internet. Man, I miss using Google."

Sophea shared more about Archangel Raziel by saying, "To hear the creator's guidance more clearly, people ask Raziel to gain deeper spiritual insights and understand esoteric information, be that clairvoyance, alchemy, or divine magic, also known as white magic."

"Do you mean we could ask Archangel Raziel for help right now? To help us understand all that you are teaching us?" Lexi asked Sophea.

"Well, it is knowledge I am teaching, so yes. You could ask for his help if you need it."

"How would one ask Archangel Raziel for help?" Isabella questioned.

"I was taught this prayer," Kesia said to the others. "Beloved Archangel Raziel, I turn to your knowledge and divine enlightenment. I need to see things clearly, hear the truth, feel the creator's wisdom, and know that what I am learning about the secrets and laws of the universe is for the benefit of my higher self. I require your help to make my divine path understood."

Sophea added, "He is also known to be the angel of abundance. When we need help manifesting the life of our dreams, Raziel can help."

"If there are angels to help us with knowledge, are there demons to stop us from gaining knowledge, "Lexi asked.

Sophea answered, "Some say that Belial or Lilith are the demons that block the path to enlightenment." Then she added, "Belial is the proper Hebrew name for Satan."

"But wasn't it Lucifer that convinced Eve to eat from the Tree of Knowledge," Lexi asked. "So, why would he try blocking us from learning more?"

"Good question," Sophea said. "Let's meditate on that. Everyone, take a deep breath and close your eyes. With your next deep breath, go deep within and create your intention to go up through your crown chakra and out into the vast levels of knowledge. Ask Archangel Raziel to help you on this quest for knowledge. The knowledge of truth and the law of education."

Lexi took a deep breath and closed her eyes.

Archangel Raziel, I require your help and clarity on this question of why demons are trying to block us from gaining knowledge of the truth.

A moment later, Lexi received an epiphany.

Lexi received this message as if the information came from a higher being.

Dear child of God, Earth angel, bringer of light and well-being, you are a child of the light, and as such, your quest is to find peace in knowing the unknown. You find yourself gathering information on all levels of understanding. You gather and seek knowledge to gain wisdom. The wisdom to know the difference between truth, fact, and well-being. The gift of knowledge is just that. A gift. A gift of the divine. A gift from the divine. A gift that you will cherish for all time. For it is part of your life purpose to find the understanding of the why. Why is there a Heaven? Why is there a hell? Why does one have to die? Are there other beings in the universe? Are there such things as ghosts? Are there such things as miracles? Are there such things as a God? So many questions that require proof. Science requires proof. But proof is in the minds of the ones who believe. Ones that can see. Ones that have clarity in the unknown. Dear child of the Earth, know that you are right where you need to be. That you are answering your quest and purpose for this lifetime. I know you are loved and cherished for your part in the universe's workings.

Lexi took another breath and knew this message was not just for her to hear. It was for the masses to know and, one day, understand. That is when true wisdom will be accomplished.

As Sophea said, the class was over for today.
Kesia pleaded, "Please tell us more about
Archangel Raziel."

"Tomorrow, I promise."

Chapter 10

Sophea gathered the girls around her, the flicker of candles casting a soft glow on their attentive faces. "Today, we'll delve into the realm of Archangel Raziel." She began, her voice a comforting melody of wisdom. "Known as the 'Angel of Secrets' or the 'Angel of Mysteries,' Raziel holds a revered place in various mystical traditions."

She continued, "In the heart of Jewish mysticism, the Kabbalah, Raziel is not just any angel but a guardian of the divine's most profound secrets and celestial wisdom. It's said that God himself entrusted Raziel with this sacred duty—to be the bearer and protector of the universe's hidden truths.

The legends speak of a time when God disclosed the divine mysteries to Raziel, who then took on the noble role of imparting this wisdom to us, the seekers and sojourners on Earth. Imagine him, girls, as a celestial librarian of sorts, holding the keys to the profound enigmas of creation, the vast cosmos, and the intricate spiritual realms."

Sophea's eyes gleamed with a hint of mystery as she described the book. "Raziel is believed to possess a remarkable tome known as the 'Book of Raziel.' This is no ordinary book, my dears. It's a divine repository containing the universe's ultimate secrets and wisdom. Picture this. After Adam and Eve were cast out from the Garden of Eden, it was Raziel's book that provided them solace and knowledge, offering insights into the heavenly realms and arcane teachings."

She leaned in closer, her voice a whisper of reverence. "But Raziel's influence isn't confined to just one tradition. He's recognized in various mystical paths, even in certain branches of Christian mysticism and the esoteric arts. In these circles, Raziel is seen as a powerful guide, a celestial mentor leading earnest seekers toward the path of hidden knowledge."

Pausing for a moment, Sophea looked at each girl intently. "Remember, as with all spiritual beings, the perceptions and understandings of Raziel's nature and role can vary widely. Different cultures, different seekers—we all see a unique facet of this enigmatic archangel.

As you continue your spiritual journey, consider Raziel a potential ally, a wise guide in the quest for deeper understanding and spiritual enlightenment." Sophea finished with a warm smile, inviting the girls to ponder the mysteries of the Angel of Secrets in their hearts.

Sophea's eyes sparkled with the promise of more mysteries as the girls absorbed Raziel's tale. "Now, let me weave in another strand to this rich tapestry of lore," she said, her voice lowering to draw them in closer. You've heard of Raziel's profound book of secrets, but there's another legend intertwined with the very fabric of human survival and celestial intervention.

In the Sefer Noah, a text wrapped in the enigma of time, there's a tale of Archangel Raphael, known for his healing and mercy. After the great flood, as Noah stepped onto the renewed earth, it was Raphael who presented him with a gift—a 'medical book.' Now, imagine the significance of such a book in the hands of Noah, the father of the new world."

Sophea paused, allowing the gravity of the moment to sink in. "Some say this medical book was none other than the famous Sefer Raziel, the same tome filled with the divine wisdom and secrets of the universe. Now picture this, Noah, holding in his hands the key to not just physical healing but the restoration of the world's spiritual knowledge and balance.

The implications are profound. This wasn't just about healing the ailments of the body but was about offering a guide to rebuilding the world, infused with the understanding of cosmic laws, the harmony of the stars, and the delicate balance of nature. It symbolized a new beginning, a second chance for humanity under the guidance of divine wisdom."

Sophea looked around at the captivated faces of the girls. "Whether it was Raziel or Raphael, the message remains clear. These celestial beings, these archangels, are deeply invested in the journey of humanity, offering guidance, wisdom, and healing when we need it most. The Sefer Raziel, in whichever hands it was placed, represents a bridge between the divine and us, a testament to the shared journey of the cosmos and the human spirit."

As the candlelight flickered, casting shadows that danced like ancient spirits around the room, the girls sat in reflective silence, pondering the deep connections between the divine guides, the ancient texts, and their own spiritual journeys.

Sophea noticed the deep contemplation in the eyes of her students, sensing their readiness for yet another layer of celestial understanding. "Let's delve even deeper into the realm of the archangels and the profound roles they play," she suggested, her voice a gentle guide through the mists of ancient knowledge.

"The term 'apocalypse' often brings to mind destruction and the end of the world. But in its essence, derived from the Ancient Greek 'ἀποκάλυψις apokálypsis,' it signifies something far more enlightening—an uncovering, a revelation of great knowledge." Sophea traced the air with her fingers as if drawing back a veil. "It's a disclosure that brings truth to light, transforming the unknown into the known, the hidden into the seen.

Now, consider Raphael, known for his healing and compassion. In the grand tapestry of celestial roles, he is also recognized as one of the seven angels of the Apocalypse." Sophea let the words hang in the air, a tapestry of thought for the girls to unravel.

"This might seem contradictory at first—how can an angel of healing be associated with the Apocalypse? But remember, the true meaning of apocalypse is not destruction but revelation. Raphael's role in this divine ensemble isn't about bringing an end but rather about revealing profound truths, ushering in healing through understanding, and guiding humanity through transitions that might seem like endings but are, in fact, new beginnings.

Raphael's presence in the Apocalypse symbolizes the healing that comes from facing the truth, from uncovering and understanding the deepest secrets of the cosmos and our souls. It's about the restoration that follows revelation, the growth that comes after transformation."

Sophea leaned back, her gaze sweeping over Lexi, Kesia, and Isabella. "So, when we speak of apocalyptic angels like Raphael, we're not just talking about harbingers of doom. We're talking about divine messengers who bring the light of truth and guide us through the necessary revelations and transitions to lead us toward a greater understanding, healing, and ultimately, our spiritual evolution."

The room felt charged with a new understanding, a sense of connection to something much larger and more profound than ever before. The girls now saw the archangels not just as distant, mythical beings but as integral parts of a cosmic story in which they, too, were participants, navigating the revelations and transformations of their own spiritual journeys.

Sophea, sensing the deepened understanding among the girls, decided to weave the narratives of Raziel and Raphael together, illustrating the interconnectedness of their divine missions. She began, her voice a thread connecting celestial dots, "Now that we've explored both Raziel, the keeper of secrets, and Raphael, the healer and one of the apocalyptic angels, let's consider how their paths intertwine and complement each other in the grand design."

"Imagine the universe as an intricate web, with each strand representing different aspects of divine wisdom and purpose. Raziel and Raphael, two luminous beings, serve as crucial intersections in this web, each carrying out their roles in harmony with the other.

Raziel, with his profound Book of Secrets, is the custodian of divine wisdom, the keeper of mysteries that hold the universe together. His role is to understand and disseminate this knowledge, to ensure it's preserved and passed down through the ages. Now, consider the nature of this knowledge—it's not merely factual but deeply healing, offering insights that can restore the soul and bring harmony to the cosmos.

Here's where Raphael's role becomes beautifully complementary. As a healer and an angel of the Apocalypse, Raphael's mission is to help humanity navigate through the revelations that Raziel's knowledge brings. When truths are unveiled, especially those of a transformative nature, they can be overwhelming and disorienting. Raphael's healing touch ensures that these revelations lead to understanding and growth rather than confusion and despair."

Sophea paused, allowing the significance to sink in. "So, you see, Raziel and Raphael are like two sides of the same coin. Raziel brings the light of knowledge, illuminating the path, while Raphael ensures that we can walk this path with courage and healing. Together, they guide us through our own apocalypses, our personal revelations, and transformations, leading us closer to enlightenment and our ultimate spiritual evolution.

Their partnership teaches us a valuable lesson: knowledge and healing are intimately connected. To truly understand is to heal, and to heal is to embrace the deepest truths of our existence. As you continue on your spiritual journey, remember that Raziel and Raphael are there, offering their wisdom and support, helping you uncover and understand the great mysteries of life and guiding you toward a more enlightened and harmonious existence."

As Sophea finished, the girls felt a newfound appreciation for the archangels' roles in their lives and the universe. They understood that the journey of the soul was not just about seeking knowledge or seeking healing but about integrating both in a dance of divine harmony. Raziel and Raphael, though distinct, worked together within the larger cosmic plan, guiding every soul through its unique journey of revelation and healing.

Chapter 11

Continuing from yesterday's lesson, Sophea, seeing the deepened curiosity in the eyes of her students, decided to expand their understanding even further. She began, her voice a gentle guide, "You've grasped the interconnected roles of Raziel and Raphael,"

The girls nodded their heads.

"But the celestial tapestry is vast and intricate, with other archangels playing their part in the grand design. Let's explore how Michael, Gabriel, Bath Kol, and Hamied also weave into this divine narrative."

Kesia clapped.

"As you know, Archangel Michael, known as the 'Protector' and 'Warrior,' stands as a beacon of strength and defense against darkness. Where Raziel unveils secrets and Raphael heals, Michael provides the courage and protection necessary to face the truths and challenges those revelations might bring. His sword of light cuts through deception and fear, empowering us to stand firm in our quest for wisdom and healing.

Gabriel, the 'Messenger,' acts as the divine herald, bringing crucial insights and announcements to humanity. While Raziel shares the deeper, esoteric knowledge, Gabriel ensures that these divine messages reach those who need them most in a form they can comprehend. He facilitates understanding, helping to translate Raziel's profound truths into actionable guidance."

"Bath Kol, often associated with the 'Daughter of the Voice,' represents the divine feminine and the subtle whisper of truth that resonates in our souls. Where Michael provides protection, and Gabriel delivers messages, Bath Kol encourages us to listen deeply to our intuition and the quiet wisdom within. She complements Raziel's role by helping us internalize and personalize the universal secrets he guards.

And then there's Hamied, the 'Angel of Miracles.' In a world where the knowledge and revelations provided by Raziel can seem overwhelming, and the healing offered by Raphael is a continuous journey, Hamied reminds us of the wonder and unexpected grace that can enter our lives. He works in tandem with the other archangels to create moments of profound transformation and joy, encouraging us to remain open to the miraculous."

Sophea looked at the three girls, her eyes reflecting the flicker of the candles. "Together, these celestial beings form a symphony of divine support. Michael stands guard, ensuring our safety as we explore the depths of Raziel's wisdom. Gabriel makes sure we understand the messages meant for us, while Bath Kol nurtures our inner voice, ensuring we remain true to our most authentic selves. And Hamied, with a twinkle in his eye, reminds us that the universe is a place of wonder, where miracles are waiting around every corner.

As you continue your spiritual journey, remember that you're never alone. Each of these archangels contributes to your path in unique ways, guiding, protecting, and inspiring you as you grow and evolve. They are reminders of the multifaceted nature of the divine, each aspect ready to support you as you uncover your own truths and move toward your own personal enlightenment."

As today's short session concluded, Sophea could tell that Lexi, Kesia, and Isabella felt a profound sense of connection and comfort. The celestial realm no longer seemed like a distant, mystical concept but a present, accessible source of support and guidance, with each archangel playing a part in their spiritual journey. She knew they left the room that night with hearts full of gratitude and souls alight with purpose,

ready to embrace their path with newfound
understanding and courage.

Chapter 12

Redington

*R*edington's morning with his father, Lord Winston, was a snapshot of their complex relationship—one marked by duty, legacy, and unspoken expectations.

As Redington prepared for his day, thoughts of Lexi crept into his mind, offering a brief respite from the tension.

He remembered her smile, and her eyes lit up when she talked about their spiritual journeys. A simplicity and depth to her intrigued him, a stark contrast to the formal world he navigated daily. It wasn't just a crush. It was a yearning for the genuine connection that seemed to elude him in his current life. *What am I thinking? I love being single.*

"Are you thinking of your lady friend?" his father asked.

Stunned that it was that obvious, Redington cleared his throat and picked up some papers on his desk. "Father, I have to go and investigate a murder. I will drop you off at my place and see you after I am finished. It should just take an hour or two."

"I would love to, how do you kids say it, tag-a-long."

Redington didn't think his dad could stomach the realism of his job. "I really think you should sit this one out. It can be gruesome."

"I can handle it. I have butchered many a doe on our lands."

Redington paused, looking into his father's eyes. There was a determination there he hadn't seen in years, a spark of something that went beyond the formalities and expectations that usually defined their relationship. With a reluctant nod, he agreed. "Alright, Father, but please, stay in the car when we arrive."

The drive to the crime scene was filled with an unusual silence. Redington's mind was a tumult of thoughts—his father's unexpected request to join him, the murder case that awaited his expertise, and the lingering thoughts of Lexi. He wondered what she would think of his world, the stark reality of his job. Would it scare her away or bring them closer, bound by the understanding of life's darker shades?

As they arrived, Redington turned to his father. "Please, stay here. I'll be as quick as I can." Lord Winston gave a curt nod, his eyes following Redington as he stepped out of the car.

The scene was as brutal as any Redington had encountered. He worked methodically, pushing aside his personal thoughts and focusing on the victim, the surroundings, and the story that the silent witnesses of crime always told. But as he worked, a part of him couldn't help but feel the weight of his father's presence, the legacy he carried on his shoulders, the expectations he was bound to fulfill.

After completing his preliminary investigation, Redington returned to the car, his mind heavy with the case details. As he drove back, his father broke the silence. "You do important work, Ferguson. I...I am proud of you."

The words, so rarely spoken, struck a chord in Redington. For a moment, the barriers between them softened, and he saw not just the imposing figure of his father but the man behind the title, with his own fears, hopes, and regrets.

"Thank you, Father," Redington replied, the words awkward but sincere. "And, about Lexi - she's more than just a lady friend. She...she understands parts of me that I'm only just beginning to explore."

Lord Winston nodded, a hint of a smile touching his lips. "Then perhaps it's time you explored those parts more, son. Life is too short for maybes and what-ifs."

The rest of the drive was quiet, but a new understanding hung in the air. Redington realized that his path might diverge from the one his father envisioned for him, and that was okay. He was his own man, with his own choices to make. And as he thought of Lexi, her smile, and the journey they were both on, he felt a spark of hope, a desire for a future where duty and personal happiness weren't mutually exclusive.

As he dropped his father off at the door and watched him walk into the condo building, Redington made a decision. He considered Lexi not just a friend but someone he wanted to share more with than just a professional or friendly relationship. It was a small step, perhaps, but one that felt like the beginning of a much larger journey.

Chapter 13

Sophea, noticing the thoughtful expressions on the faces of the girls in the following class, recognized a deeper curiosity stirring within them. "You've come to understand the roles of these archangels, but let's not shy away from the more challenging aspects of our spiritual history," she said, her voice steady and reassuring. "To fully appreciate the light, we must also acknowledge the shadows."

"In the Bible, there's a name that conjures both mystery and unease: Azazel. In Hebrew, עֲזָאזֵל, and in Arabic, عزازيل, this name appears in association with the scapegoat rite." Sophea paused, ensuring the girls were ready to delve into these deeper waters.

"In the dawning days of the world, when humanity was young, and the divine still walked among the mountains and valleys, a being of both awe and warning emerged, known across lands and through time by a single name: Azazel. In the heart of the desert, where the land met the sky in a relentless blaze of heat and light, the people of Israel gathered once a year on Yom Kippur, the Day of Atonement. They performed a sacred ritual, choosing two goats: one to be sacrificed to the Lord and the other, the scapegoat, to be sent into the wilderness to a place associated with Azazel, bearing the sins of the people.

But who was this Azazel? The tale unwinds back to an age even more ancient, recounted in the forbidden chapters of the Book of Enoch. Once a celestial being, an angel of the Watchers, Azazel looked upon Earth with covetous eyes. Leading a faction of angels, he descended, taking human wives and teaching mankind forbidden secrets. He gave them the art of warfare, crafting deadly weapons, and sowing vanity and desire among the people. The world changed, becoming a place of strife, beauty, and pain—a mirror to the complexities of the human heart.

The heavens, in their righteousness, could not ignore the chaos wrought by Azazel. As a testament to his transgressions, he was bound and cast into a deep pit, a warning about the perilous path of disobedience and the danger of forbidden knowledge. Over the millennia, Azazel's name has been whispered through the ages as a symbol of profound struggle, embodying the dualities of wisdom versus temptation and obedience versus curiosity.

Sophea, the wise guide of Lexi, Kesia, and Isabella, shared these ancient narratives with them to highlight the complexities of their spiritual journey. She explained how Azazel's story, particularly toward the end of the Second Temple period, evolved under Hellenization and Christian interpretations. He became known as a fallen angel, introducing humans to forbidden knowledge, a tale that resonates with the serpent in the Garden of Eden.

"In our journey," Sophea said, her eyes reflecting wisdom and caution, "It's crucial to understand that figures like Azazel represent more than a myth. They embody the real conflicts and decisions we encounter in our search for spiritual understanding and growth. While archangels like Michael, Gabriel, Raziel, Bath Kol, and Hamied guide and protect us, Azazel's story reminds us of the challenges in discerning right from wrong and truth from temptation.

His story, a cautionary tale, urges a humble approach to the quest for knowledge, to seek divine guidance, and to be aware of the consequences of actions. It's a reminder that the spiritual path is about understanding light and miracles and the shadows from which they emerge."

~

As the session drew to a close, Lexi found herself enveloped in a profound sense of understanding that resonated deep within her soul. She realized that the celestial realm was far more complex than just a source of light and guidance; it was also a mirror reflecting the intense struggles of the human spirit. The story of Azazel, with its layers of complexity and caution, had significantly deepened her understanding, revealing the multifaceted nature of their spiritual journey.

Under Sophea's wise guidance and with the steadfast support of the archangels, Lexi felt a newfound preparedness to navigate the intricate path that lay ahead. She knew that she and her friends, Kesia and Isabella, were leaving this session enlightened, grounded, and fully aware of the delicate balance they needed to maintain in their quest for spiritual growth. It was a journey of light and shadow, of understanding and vigilance, and Lexi felt ready to embrace it all.

Chapter 14

As Lexi sat in her room in quiet reflection after the session, the ancient stories Sophea shared began to weave into the fabric of her thoughts. She pondered the legendary Gardens of Eden, described in Louis Ginzberg's 1909 book "Legends of the Jews," where beyond the earthly paradise lay the higher Gan Eden. God Himself was said to dwell in this realm, explaining the Torah to its inhabitants.

Lexi imagined the higher Gan Eden, comprising three hundred and ten worlds and divided into seven compartments, each more splendid than the last, tailored to the merit of its residents. The first compartment was for Jewish martyrs, the second for those claimed by the sea, and so on, with each having its unique congregation, from the disciples of Rabbi Johanan ben Zakkai to the innocent youths who had never sinned.

Her mind then drifted to the lower Gan Eden, where the tree of knowledge encircled the tree of life—so vast that a five-hundred-year journey could not reveal its full size. She envisioned the four rivers flowing from beneath these trees: Tigris, Nile, Euphrates, and Ganges, which once watered the world. She thought of Adam and Eve, served by angels, surrounded by animals that understood and respected them.

Lexi's heart lingered on his concept of the journey that souls must undertake after death—passing through the lower Gan Eden to reach the higher, with the Cave of Machpelah as the gateway guarded by Adam himself. Beyond, the cherub with a flaming sword stands watch, annihilating unworthy souls, while the worthy ascend a pillar of fire and smoke to reach the higher realms.

Then her thoughts darkened as she contemplated the fall of man, the serpent's deceit in the earthly Garden of Eden. She recalled the forbidden fruit of the Tree of Knowledge of Good and Evil, the serpent's promise that their eyes would be opened, making them like gods. She envisioned Adam and Eve, banished from the garden to prevent them from eating the fruit of the Tree of Life and attaining immortality, the angelic guard posted at the gates with a flaming sword.

In this moment of introspection, Lexi realized the profound depth of these stories—not as mere myths or ancient texts but as reflections of the eternal human struggle with temptation, the quest for knowledge, and the consequences of our actions. She understood that these legends were not just about the past; they were about her, about all seeking souls, and about the delicate balance between enlightenment and humility.

Taking a deep breath, Lexi felt a renewed sense of purpose and determination. Guided by Sophea's wisdom and the support of the archangels, she knew that her journey was not just about seeking light but also about understanding the shadows, learning from the past, and navigating the complex path toward spiritual growth. And with this knowledge, she felt ready to face the multifaceted nature of her own spiritual journey.

Chapter 15

Sophea's voice gently broke the silence, introducing a new layer to their unfolding tapestry of spiritual understanding. "Let me tell you about a figure from the early Christian desert fathers, a man whose life was a testament to the power of faith and divine calling. His name was Apollonios."

Lexi, Kesia, and Isabella leaned in, captivated by the promise of another profound tale. Sophea continued, "Apollonios was born to pious parents, Aisi and Amani. Before his birth, his parents were childless, but according to some, he had an elder brother, a monk who had passed before Apollonios's birth and appeared to him in a dream, guiding him from the beyond.

At the tender age of fifteen, Apollonios felt a deep calling within his soul. He retired to the inner desert of the Thebaïd in Lower Egypt alongside his kinsman Abib. There, away from the distractions of the world, he sought a life of solitude and contemplation.

For fourteen years, Apollonios lived this solitary life, devoting himself to prayer and fasting. Then, one day, he was granted a Divine Revelation. A voice, clear and resonant, spoke to him: 'Apollonios, by your hands, I will destroy the wisdom of the wise men of Egypt, and I will remove their knowledge, which is not true knowledge. You will also overthrow those who are reputed to be the wise men of Babel and all their service to devils. Now go quickly to the desert, near the habitations of men. There you shall beget for me a holy people, exalted by their good works.

Moved by this divine command, Apollonios ventured closer to the edges of the desert where people dwelled. There, he became a beacon of miracles and wisdom, attracting many who sought spiritual guidance. He became the head of a community of monks, leading them not just in prayer but in living out the profound teachings he received.

As Apollonios grew in his spiritual journey, his fame spread far and wide. People came from all corners to witness the miracles he performed and to sit at his feet, learning the deeper truths of a life dedicated to the divine."

Sophea looked at the girls, her eyes reflecting the flickering candlelight. "In the story of Saint Apollonios, we find a powerful example of the calling each soul has. Like Apollonios, you, too, may feel a deep stirring, a call to a higher purpose. His life reminds us that true wisdom often lies in simplicity, in turning away from the distractions of the world and focusing on the divine voice within us.

As you continue on your spiritual journey, remember Apollonios's example. Consider how you, like him, might be called to overthrow the false wisdom of the world and to lead others toward the truth. His story is not just a tale from the past; it's a living invitation to each of us to seek out our own desert, our own place of solitude and clarity, where we can hear the divine and respond to its call."

Lexi, Kesia, and Isabella sat in silence.

Sophea gazed at Lexi, Kesia, and Isabella, her eyes alight with the wisdom of ages. She spoke with a gentle yet compelling tone, "Consider for a moment the profound journey of Saint Apollonios. His path, though ancient, speaks to us across time, reminding us that each of our journeys is also filled with divine potential.

Like Apollonios, you, too, are called to something greater, something beyond the ordinary boundaries of existence. Your paths are unique tapestries woven with threads of destiny and choice. Within each of you lies the potential to listen deeply, to hear the divine whisper that beckons you toward your true calling."

Sophea paused, allowing her words to settle in their hearts. "Responding to this call isn't merely an act; it's an art, a dance with the divine. It requires you to embrace the grand, unfolding story of your own spiritual awakening. This journey is not always clear or easy, but it is always meaningful."

She continued, "Remember, the divine speaks in many ways—through dreams, intuition, and the quiet moments of reflection. It's in these moments that your path becomes clearer, guiding you to embrace your unique calling. Like Apollonios, you are capable of great things, of touching the divine and being transformed by its grace.

As you walk your paths, hold onto the knowledge that you are part of a greater narrative, a story that is continuously unfolding with each step you take. Embrace your journey with an open heart and a courageous spirit, for it is through this journey that you will discover the true depth of your potential and the beauty of your own spiritual awakening."

Sophea's words hung in the air, a gentle yet powerful reminder of the sacred journey each soul is on.

Chapter 16

As the evening shadows lengthened and the flickering candlelight danced across the room, Sophea turned her gaze to the eager faces of Lexi, Kesia, and Isabella.

Kesia asked, "Why are we having a lesson at night instead of the morning, like we usually do?"

"Tonight," Sophea winked at Kesia, her voice tinged with a hint of mystery. Let's explore a tale that has captivated the Western world for centuries, a narrative that serves as a stark reminder of the price of unbridled ambition. I speak of Faust, also known as Faustus or Doctor Faustus."

The girls leaned in, their interest piqued by the promise of a story both dark and profound. Sophea continued, "Faust wasn't just a character; he was a symbol, a warning. Faust, a German necromancer and astrologer, became infamous for the dire pact he made. Consumed by a hunger for knowledge and power beyond human limits, he sold his soul to the devil.

In exchange for this ultimate sacrifice, Faust received extraordinary powers and a breadth of knowledge that few could fathom. But this came at a cost far greater than he had anticipated. His tale is a testament to the perils of sacrificing one's moral compass on the altar of greed and curiosity."

"Tell us more about the legend," Kesia pleaded.

"In the heart of a bygone Germany, amidst ancient forests and shadowed cobblestone streets, there lived a man whose name would become synonymous with ambition and its price: Doctor Johann Faust. A scholar of no ordinary intellect, Faust's insatiable thirst for knowledge and power drove him to the darkest corners of magic and necromancy.

Faust's story began in a cluttered study filled with dusty tomes and arcane artifacts. Despite his vast learning and the respect it earned him, Faust felt an unquenchable void within. No amount of earthly learning could satisfy the deep hunger in his soul. He yearned for the ultimate knowledge, the secrets of the universe itself, and the power that came with such wisdom.

One fateful night, under a moon veiled by ominous clouds, Faust performed a forbidden ritual, calling forth Mephistopheles, a cunning

demon from the depths of the infernal realms.
The air grew thick with the scent of brimstone,
and the study flickered with eerie lights as the
demon appeared before him.

Mephistopheles, with eyes like burning coals
and a smile that spoke of eons of deceit, offered
Faust a bargain too tempting to resist. In
exchange for his soul, Faust would receive
unparalleled knowledge and earthly pleasures
beyond his wildest dreams for a number of
years. When the time was up, his soul would
belong to the demon.

Driven by pride and desire, Faust agreed. He
signed the infernal contract with his blood,
sealing his fate. The pact granted him magical
powers and secret knowledge, making him a
figure of awe and fear among those who knew of
his dark alliance.

For years, Faust reveled in his newfound
abilities. He conjured spirits, changed his form,
and traveled the world in moments, all while
indulging in earthly delights without care. But as
the end of his bargain drew near, a creeping
dread began to overshadow his marvels. The
once enticing mysteries turned to ashes in his
mouth as the true cost of his bargain loomed
over him.

As the final hour approached, Faust became a
man tormented, haunted by visions of the hell
that awaited him and the eternal torment he had
traded for fleeting power. He desperately sought

ways to escape his doom, delving even deeper into forbidden arts, but to no avail. The pact was binding, and Mephistopheles would not be denied.

In the story's tragic end, as the clock struck the appointed hour, a storm raged like the furies of hell itself. Screams echoed through the night as Mephistopheles claimed what was his. Faust's study lay in ruins, a testament to the catastrophic price of his hubris.

The legend of Faust serves as a timeless warning of the perils of unchecked ambition and the dangers of bargaining with forces beyond human ken. It's a tale that whispers through the ages, reminding us that the quest for knowledge and power, while noble, must be tempered with wisdom and respect for the natural order. For, in the end, the price of violating these sacred boundaries may be nothing less than the soul itself."

Sophea's eyes swept across the girls, ensuring they understood the gravity of the story. "Consider, for a moment, the parallels in our own spiritual journeys. While none of you would entertain such a drastic pact, the tale of Faust urges us to reflect on our intentions and desires. How often have we sought knowledge or power without considering the ethical and spiritual price?

The story of Faust invites us to ponder the balance between our thirst for understanding and the moral boundaries we must navigate. It's a powerful narrative about the consequences of our choices and the importance of aligning our pursuits with a higher, ethical calling."

She paused, allowing the weight of the legend to settle in their hearts. "Faust's legend has endured through the ages because it speaks to a fundamental aspect of the human condition: the constant battle between our higher aspirations and our baser instincts. It reminds us that while seeking knowledge and power is a natural part of our growth, we must always temper our ambitions with wisdom and humility.

As you continue on your path, remember the tale of Faust. Let it be a guiding light, warning you of the pitfalls of unchecked desires and reminding you to seek knowledge and power responsibly, with respect for the divine balance of the universe."

Chapter 17

Continuing from the evening before, Sophea said after the girls got comfy, "To understand our future, we must understand our past. I am going to share with you about the ancient civilizations that shaped the world's spiritual heritage."

As the candlelight cast a soft glow upon the room, Sophea shared the story of a civilization that laid the foundations of human history: the Sumerians.

"Long before the time of Faust, and even preceding the biblical tales of Eden," Sophea began, her voice carrying the weight of forgotten ages, there was a land between two great rivers, the Tigris and the Euphrates, in what you know today as Iraq. This land, called Sumer, cradled an ancient civilization whose echoes still resonate through time.

The Sumerians," she continued, "Were a people of remarkable innovation. They built the world's first cities, like Uruk and Ur, towering ziggurats that reached for the heavens, and they devised the cuneiform script, one of the earliest forms of writing. But beyond their architectural and literary achievements, the Sumerians delved deep into the mysteries of the cosmos."

Lexi, Kesia, and Isabella listened, enraptured by the image of this ancient world. "The Sumerians," Sophea went on, "Worshipped a pantheon of gods and goddesses, each embodying elements of nature and human experience. Through their myths and epics, like the tale of Gilgamesh, they sought to understand the human condition, the balance between the mortal and the divine, and the eternal cycle of life, death, and rebirth. As you walk your spiritual path," Sophea said, turning her gaze to each of her students, "You too are engaging in a quest that the Sumerians began millennia ago. Though long gone, their civilization laid the early seeds of knowledge and spirituality that have sprouted into countless beliefs and practices you see today."

She paused, allowing the significance of this connection to sink in. "Consider the story of Gilgamesh, a king who sought immortality, a narrative that echoes the legend of Faust and his own quest for knowledge and power. Both tales, separated by time and culture, reflect the universal human yearning to transcend our limitations and understand the mysteries surrounding us.

In their quest for meaning, the Sumerians also grappled with the balance between ambition and humility, much like the lessons you've learned from Azazel and the archangels. Their legacy is not just one of historical artifacts and ancient texts, but a continuous thread in the tapestry of human spiritual seeking."

As Sophea concluded her tale, Kesia put her hand up.

"Yes, Kesia."

"Please tell me more about Gilgamesh."

Sophea smiled at Kesia's quest for knowledge, then answered her, "In the ancient city of Uruk, a place of towering walls and bustling markets, there reigned a king unlike any other. His name was Gilgamesh, two-thirds god, and one-third man, endowed with strength and courage but burdened with an arrogance befitting his divine heritage. His subjects revered and feared him, for his great feats were matched only by his authoritarian rule.

The people of Uruk cried out to the heavens for relief, and the gods listened. They created Enkidu, a wild man of the forest, as a counter to Gilgamesh's power. Enkidu, covered in hair and living among the animals, was the embodiment of nature's untamed spirit. A chance encounter with a temple priestess civilized Enkidu, and he ventured into the city to confront Gilgamesh.

Instead of clashing as enemies, Gilgamesh and Enkidu became the closest of friends, their bond forged in the heat of a fierce battle. Together, they embarked on great adventures, challenging the might of monstrous beings and seeking to etch their names in the annals of eternity. Their most notable quest was against Humbaba, the fearsome guardian of the Cedar Forest, a being appointed by the gods to protect the sacred grove. Despite the peril, Gilgamesh and Enkidu vanquished the monster, further cementing their legendary status.

However, their triumphs came at a cost. Enkidu, having insulted the goddess Ishtar by spurning her advances, was struck down by the gods as punishment. His death plunged Gilgamesh into the depths of despair, his grief so profound that it ignited within him a fear of his own mortality.

Determined to escape the fate that befell his friend, Gilgamesh embarked on his most perilous journey yet: the quest for immortality. His path led him to Utnapishtim, the only mortal to have been granted eternal life by the gods after surviving a great flood that wiped out humanity. Utnapishtim shared his story and offered Gilgamesh a test: if he could stay awake for six days and seven nights, he, too, could attain immortality.

Despite his best efforts, Gilgamesh succumbed to sleep, failing the test.

Disheartened but wiser, he returned to Uruk, accepting his mortality. He realized that while he could not live forever, his deeds, the walls of his city, and the epic tales of his adventures would endure through the ages.

The story of Gilgamesh is one of the oldest recorded epics in human history, a tale of friendship, heroism, loss, and the search for meaning in a world governed by capricious gods and the inexorable march of time. It's a story that reminds us of our own limitations and the enduring human quest to understand our place in the cosmos."

As the day's lesson drew to a close, Sophea noticed a contemplative look on Lexi's face, reflecting a deep internal processing of the stories shared. Sensing an opportunity to tie the narratives together, Sophea spoke softly, "You know, Lexi, the story of Gilgamesh, with its timeless themes and existential questions, resonates deeply with our own journey, especially as we unravel the complexities of your spiritual path."

Lexi, Kesia, and Isabella leaned in, their minds open to the weaving of this ancient tapestry into their own lives. "Consider Gilgamesh," Sophea continued, "A being of immense power and knowledge, much like Faust in his own legend. Both sought to transcend the natural limitations of their existence, driven by a desire for immortality and understanding. In their stories, we see reflections of our own quest for spiritual enlightenment and the dilemmas we face along the way.

Like Gilgamesh, you are on a journey marked by trials, friendships, and the pursuit of knowledge. Gilgamesh's bond with Enkidu mirrors the bond you share with each other and with me as we navigate the spiritual wilderness together. His battle against Humbaba represents the obstacles and inner demons you must confront and overcome to grow and progress on your path.

And let's not forget the most poignant part of Gilgamesh's tale—his confrontation with mortality, sparked by the loss of his dear friend Enkidu. This moment of profound grief and subsequent quest for eternal life echoes your own encounters with the archangels, the lessons from Azazel, and the quest to understand the delicate balance between earthly desires and spiritual truths."

Sophea paused, allowing the connections to sink in. "In Gilgamesh's eventual acceptance of his mortality, we find a powerful lesson about the nature of our existence. It's not the literal immortality he sought that defines our legacy but the deeds we perform, the love we share, and the wisdom we impart. Like Gilgamesh, you may not find eternal life in the physical sense, but through your journey, your growth, and your impact on the world and each other, you create something that transcends time.

As you continue to explore the ancient mysteries and the modern complexities of your spiritual paths, remember the lessons of Gilgamesh. Embrace the friendships that strengthen you, confront the challenges that shape you, and seek the knowledge that enlightens you. But above all, understand that the true measure of your journey is not in the years you live but in the depth and richness of your experiences."

Chapter 18

In the serene tranquility of the room Sophea was using for teaching the lessons, where the wisdom of ages seemed to permeate the very air, Isabella found herself drawn into a deep meditative state, guided by the gentle, rhythmic cadence of Sophea's voice. As she drifted further from the material world, a vivid vision began to unfold before her inner eye, a vision of a past life that resonated with the theme of their recent discussions: the quest for knowledge.

Isabella saw herself in a land unlike any she had known in her current life—a place of breathtaking beauty and advanced technology, where crystal spires glittered under a radiant sun, and the sea shimmered with a luminosity that seemed almost otherworldly. She was in Atlantis, the legendary island said to have existed in a time before time, a civilization that had reached the pinnacle of human achievement.

In this past life, Isabella was a scholar and a keeper of the Atlantean libraries, where scrolls of immense knowledge were safeguarded. These libraries were not just repositories of information; they were centers of energy and light, where knowledge was believed to be a living force capable of transforming the soul.

As an Atlantean, Isabella was trained in the use of crystals for healing, telepathy, and accessing higher planes of consciousness. She was part of a society that revered knowledge as the highest form of power, a society that had mastered harmonious living with nature and each other, harnessing the energies of the earth and stars to sustain their way of life.

However, as Isabella explored her past deeper, she sensed a growing shadow. With great knowledge came great responsibility, and not all Atlanteans heeded this sacred duty. She saw how some of her people, intoxicated by their own advancements, began to misuse their knowledge, seeking power over wisdom and control over harmony.

As Isabella's vision continued to unfold, the once-resplendent Atlantis before her began to change. She saw the crystal spires that had once gleamed with hope and promise now reflecting the discord and division among her people. Atlanteans, who had once worked together to harness the energies of the earth and stars, now stood in opposition, their once-unified vision fragmented by greed and a lust for power.

Isabella felt a deep sorrow as she witnessed the leaders and scholars, once guardians of Atlantean wisdom, becoming blinded by their achievements. They pushed the boundaries of their knowledge, experimenting with forces they barely understood and could not control. Once used for healing and growth, their technologies were twisted into instruments of dominance and conflict.

The misuse of knowledge created an imbalance, not just within their society but within the very fabric of nature. The earth beneath Atlantis, which had been nurtured and respected, now trembled with the strain of the Atlanteans' recklessness. The sea that had cradled their island with gentle hands now surged with the fury of betrayal.

As the vision progressed, Isabella felt an ominous tremor beneath her feet. She watched in horror as the great crystal that powered their island, a symbol of their highest achievement, cracked and shattered, its energy unleashed in a devastating wave. The ground split, buildings crumbled, and the sea, once their ally, rose to reclaim Atlantis. Her people, those who had not perished in the initial chaos, scrambled for escape, but there was none to be found. The island, their home, was consumed by the waters in a cataclysm of water and sorrow, lost to the depths in a final, mournful descent.

Tears streamed down Isabella's face as the vision faded, the magnitude of the loss and the profound lesson it imparted etching itself into her soul. She understood now more than ever the delicate balance that must be maintained when wielding knowledge and power. Atlantis was not just a myth or a cautionary tale; it was a visceral, heart-wrenching reminder of what could happen when humanity loses sight of wisdom and moral responsibility in the pursuit of progress.

Emerging from her meditation, Isabella shared her vision with Sophea and her friends.

Sophea listened intently, then spoke softly, "Your vision of Atlantis, Isabella, is a poignant reminder of the double-edged sword that is knowledge. Like the Atlanteans, we, too, are on a quest to understand the secrets that lie beyond the material realm. But your vision warns us that knowledge without wisdom, without ethical consideration and spiritual grounding, can lead to our downfall."

She continued, "The story of Atlantis reflects not just the potential of what we can achieve but also the pitfalls of hubris and the importance of maintaining balance. It reminds us that our search for knowledge must be accompanied by a deep sense of responsibility to ourselves, to each other, and to the world we inhabit."

As the session ended, said to Isabella, Lexi, and Kesia, "I want you to sit in reflective silence, each contemplating the lessons from the lost civilization of Atlantis. I want you to recognize the spiritual journey you are on is not just about acquiring knowledge but about cultivating wisdom, humility, and a profound respect for the interconnectedness of all life."

Chapter 19

As the days turned and the group delved deeper into their spiritual exploration, Kesia found herself increasingly drawn to the mystical and the obscure. One morning, under the guidance of Sophea, she settled into a deep meditative trance, her consciousness reaching back through the ages to a time shrouded in mystery. She found herself in Lemuria, an ancient and lost civilization said to predate even Atlantis.

In her vision, Kesia was a Lemurian healer, living in a society where harmony with nature and the spiritual realm was paramount. Lemuria, often depicted as a paradise of spiritual and emotional enlightenment, was a land of lush landscapes, where colossal, verdant trees stretched up to kiss the sky, and crystal-clear waters sang melodies of the earth's joy.

As a healer, Kesia was attuned to the energies of the world around her. She communicated with plants and animals and understood the whispers of the wind. The Lemurians, in her vision, were a gentle people, their ethereal forms moving with a grace that bespoke their inner peace. They used crystals not just as tools for healing but as conduits for connecting with higher planes of existence and for maintaining the balance of their utopian world.

However, as Kesia explored this past life, she sensed an underlying current of melancholy. The Lemurians, for all their spiritual advancement, seemed aware of the impermanence of their existence. They understood that their way of life, so intricately tied to the natural and spiritual worlds, was susceptible to the same cycles of change that governed all things.

Kesia saw how, despite their efforts to live in harmony with the universe, external forces and internal complacencies began to erode the fabric of their society. Natural disasters, shifts in the earth's magnetic fields, and a gradual cooling of their once tropical paradise challenged the Lemurians. She felt their sorrow as they realized that their time was coming to an end, that their memories and wisdom would be swallowed by the sands of time, leaving barely a whisper of their existence.

As the vision faded, Kesia returned to her own time and place, the impact of her journey leaving her both awestruck and somber. She shared her experience with Sophea and the others, her voice soft but filled with emotion. "The Lemurians," she explained, "Lived with such an incredible connection to all things. They remind us of the delicate interplay between our spiritual pursuits and the physical world we inhabit. Their loss is a poignant reminder that even the most enlightened societies are not immune to the forces of change and the passage of time."

Sophea nodded thoughtfully. "Lemuria, much like Atlantis, serves as a mirror to our own path. It reflects the importance of living in harmony with our surroundings and understanding the broader consequences of our actions. The Lemurians' deep spiritual connection and subsequent loss teach us that while striving for higher knowledge and understanding, we must also remain vigilant stewards of our world and souls."

The group sat in contemplative silence, each pondering the lessons of Lemuria in their own way. Kesia felt a renewed sense of purpose, a deeper commitment to integrating the harmony and balance she'd witnessed in her past life into her present journey. The story of Lemuria, with its profound spiritual connection and its tragic end, had become a part of her, a guiding star on her path to enlightenment and understanding.

Sophea pulled three Lemurian crystals from her pocket in her robe. As she passed one to each of the girls, her voice soft yet filled with a reverence that captured her students' complete attention, she said, "Lemurian crystals are believed to be encoded with the ancient wisdom of the Lemurian civilization, a society that valued harmony, spiritual enlightenment, and a profound connection with the Earth."

She held up a quartz crystal, pointing out its distinguishing features. "Notice the striations or horizontal lines that run along one or more sides. These are known as the 'ladder of ascension' and are thought to hold the Lemurian knowledge. The crystals are usually found loose in sand, not attached to clusters, which is quite unusual. It's as if they were intentionally planted or left behind, waiting to be discovered when the world was ready to receive their wisdom."

Sophea motioned for the girls to feel the crystal and its weight and study its unique markings.

Kesia asked, "Where do these crystals come from?"

Sophea's smile widened at Kesia's unquenchable thirst for knowledge before she responded, "Lemurian crystals, also known as Lemurian Seed Crystals, are primarily found in the Diamantina region of Minas Gerais, Brazil. This area is known for its rich deposits of quartz and other minerals. While Lemurian crystals have been found in other locations around the world, including Colombia, Russia, and the

United States, the most renowned and sought-after specimens typically come from the Brazilian mines."

Kesia nodded as she touched the crystal.

Sophea continued with her lesson, "Lemurian crystals are meditation and healing tools. They are said to enhance one's intuition, aid in spiritual evolution, and connect the bearer to higher consciousness. When used in meditation, they can help you access the vast network of information believed to be stored within them."

She guided them on how to use the crystals. "First, find a quiet space where you feel comfortable and relaxed. Hold the Lemurian crystal in your hand—many prefer to use their non-dominant hand as it's more receptive to intuitive energies. Focus on your breathing, allowing yourself to slip into a meditative state."

Sophea motioned for the girls to get comfy and do as she was instructing. "As you meditate, gently rub your thumb along the striations of the crystal. Some say this helps to 'unlock' the information within. Allow yourself to be open to any thoughts, images, or emotions that arise. The Lemurian crystal is believed to connect with each individual uniquely, imparting wisdom and healing that's most needed at the moment."

Sophea looked at each of the girls, her gaze imbued with a deep understanding. "Remember, the power of any crystal, especially one as special as a Lemurian, lies not just in its physical properties but in your intention and openness to the experience. Approach your work with these crystals with respect, love, and a desire for growth.

As you continue your spiritual journey, let the Lemurian crystal be a guide and a companion. Use it to deepen your meditation, enhance your healing practices, or simply connect with the ancient wisdom it holds. But always, always treat it with the reverence a piece of the Earth's ancient memory deserves."

Chapter 20

Kesia

*K*esia felt a profound connection to the crystal in her hand. She understood that it was not just a tool but a symbol of her spiritual journey, a journey of growth, healing, and the pursuit of deep, universal truth. With Sophea's guidance and the Lemurian crystal's ancient wisdom, she felt ready to explore the depths of her soul and the mysteries of the universe.

As Kesia held the Lemurian crystal, its cool surface pulsating with a gentle yet undeniable energy, her mind began to drift, carried on the waves of her deepening meditation. The room around her, with its soft candlelight and the comforting presence of her friends, faded away. In its place, a vision began to form, a past life memory surfacing from the depths of her soul.

She found herself in a lush, verdant land, where the air buzzed with the pure energy of life itself. Kesia was a healer in this life, living in a small village where the houses were crafted from the earth, and the community lived in harmony with the land. She was known as a wise woman, one who understood the language of plants and the whispers of the wind.

In this past life, Kesia's purpose was clear: to heal and to teach. She spent her days tending to the sick, using her knowledge of herbs and natural remedies to ease their suffering. But more than just physical healing, Kesia provided spiritual guidance. She helped her people understand their connection to the Earth and the divine, teaching them how to live in balance and respect the world around them.

The life lesson she learned in this existence was one of interconnectedness. Kesia saw firsthand how every action, every decision, rippled out into the community and the natural world. She learned that true healing came not just from treating symptoms but from addressing the underlying harmony between body, spirit, and Earth.

However, this idyllic existence was not without its challenges. Kesia's vision showed her a time when her village faced a great crisis, a sickness that spread rapidly and for which there was no easy cure. She worked tirelessly, combining her knowledge with her deep intuition, guided by the very crystal she held in her current life. Despite her efforts, some lives were lost, and Kesia felt each passing deeply, their souls whispering to her of their journey into the beyond.

Through this experience, Kesia's soul learned a profound lesson about the nature of existence: that life is a delicate balance of light and dark, joy and sorrow, and that each soul's journey is its own. She understood that her role was not to prevent every hardship but to provide comfort, healing, and understanding wherever she could.

As Kesia emerged from her vision, the weight of the ancient crystal in her hand, she felt a renewed sense of purpose and connection. She realized that her past life experiences were not just stories from another time but were woven into the very fabric of her being. They were reminders of her enduring soul's journey through lifetimes, each experience shaping her into the person she is today.

With a deep, grounding breath, Kesia opened her eyes, the wisdom of ages shining in her gaze. She understood now more than ever that her path was one of continuous learning, healing, and growth. And with the ancient Lemurian crystal as her guide, she felt ready to embrace whatever lessons the future held.

Isabella

As Isabella held her new Lemurian crystal, the soft luminescence of the room seemed to dim, drawing her inward to a space of profound introspection. The energy of the crystal pulsed against her skin, a rhythmic beat that resonated with her heartbeat, leading her down the corridors of time to a past life that lay submerged in the depths of her soul.

In her vision, Isabella found herself in a realm where the sky shimmered with iridescent colors, a place where the physical and spiritual worlds merged seamlessly. She was a teacher and a guardian of knowledge, living in a community where every individual's talents were nurtured for the greater good. This was Atlantis, in its prime, a civilization that thrived on the harmony between intellectual advancement and spiritual wisdom.

In this life, Isabella's purpose was to guide the young minds of Atlantis, teaching them not just the sciences and arts but also the importance of inner growth and ethical understanding. She was a revered figure, known for her gentle yet profound wisdom and her ability to connect deeply with each soul she encountered.

The life lesson that Isabella learned in this existence was about the delicate balance between knowledge and wisdom. She saw how pursuing knowledge without the guiding light of wisdom could lead to arrogance and eventual downfall. She witnessed firsthand the rising tensions in Atlantis as some began to misuse their advanced technologies and knowledge for personal power, ignoring the ethical implications and the well-being of others.

Her soul experienced the intense sorrow and helplessness of watching a civilization she loved begin to crumble under the weight of its hubris. Despite her efforts to steer her students and community back toward a path of harmony and respect, the forces of greed and power were too strong, leading to the inevitable downfall of Atlantis. As the island sank beneath the waves, Isabella's heart sank with it, mourning the loss of what could have been a utopian society.

Emerging from her vision, Isabella's eyes glistened with unshed tears, the emotional impact of her past life's end still resonating within her. Yet, within that sorrow, there was also a newfound strength and understanding. She realized that her journey was not just about acquiring knowledge but about using that knowledge with compassion, foresight, and a deep respect for the interconnectedness of all life.

With quiet resolve, Isabella looked toward Sophie and her friends, her spirit fortified by the lessons of her past. She understood now that her path was one of continual learning and ethical vigilance, where every step forward was taken with a mindful awareness of its impact on the world. And with the ancient Lemurian crystal as her beacon, she felt ready to embrace her role in this life, teach, guide, and heal with the wisdom of the ages flowing through her.

Lexi

As the day's energy settled into a calm stillness, Lexi clasped her Lemurian crystal, feeling its ancient pulse synchronize with her own. She closed her eyes and took a deep breath, allowing Sophea's guidance and the crystal's vibration to lead her into a deep, introspective state. The room and her companions faded away as she drifted into a profound past life memory, one that would reveal itself to be a cornerstone of her spiritual journey.

In her vision, Lexi found herself in a time and place that felt both alien and intimately familiar. She was in Lemuria, but not the Lemuria she had just learned about. This was a time of its inception, a moment when the continent still whispered secrets of the universe and vibrated with the purest spiritual energy. In this life, Lexi was a sage, a spiritual architect of Lemurian society, one who played a pivotal role in laying down the foundational principles of love, unity, and cosmic harmony.

Lexi's purpose in this ancient lifetime was profound. She was one of the few chosen to receive and interpret the cosmic laws meant to guide Lemuria. She communed with celestial beings, deciphered the language of the stars, and shared this knowledge with her people, teaching them how to live in resonance with the Earth and each other.

The life lesson that permeated her existence was the understanding of the cyclical nature of life and the universe. Lexi learned that every society, every civilization, is part of a larger cosmic rhythm, each with its time to rise and its time to fall. Her heart swelled with love and compassion for all beings, understanding that the physical demise of civilization didn't signify the end but rather a transition into a different form of existence.

However, even in this idyllic world, Lexi's soul encountered profound challenges. She saw shadows creeping into Lemuria as some of her people began to stray from the path, seduced by the illusion of separation and the false allure of power over others. Despite her wisdom and efforts, she witnessed the slow fracturing of the utopia she helped create.

As the vision continued, Lexi felt the impending dissolution of Lemuria. With a heart both heavy and enlightened, she understood that her role was not to prevent the inevitable but to guide as many souls as possible toward spiritual liberation before the end. In her final moments, as Lemuria began to fade from the physical plane, Lexi's soul soared, a beacon of light and love, ensuring that the wisdom and lessons of Lemuria would not be lost but instead scattered like seeds across time and space.

Returning to her present self, Lexi opened her eyes, her face serene yet etched with the profundity of her experience. She shared her vision with Sophea and her friends, her voice a gentle echo of the ancient wisdom she had just embraced. Now, more than ever, she understood that her path was not just about personal growth but about helping to guide humanity toward a deeper understanding of unity and spiritual evolution.

Lexi felt a renewed sense of purpose with the Lemurian crystal in her hand and the ancient memories etched in her soul. She realized that she was not just learning from the past; she was part of a continuum, a living bridge between the ancient wisdom of Lemuria and the future enlightenment of humanity. And with this profound understanding, she felt ready to face whatever her spiritual journey would bring. Her heart and soul were aligned with the timeless dance of the cosmos.

Chapter 21

As the sun dipped below the horizon, casting a warm, golden glow through the windows, Sophea gathered Lexi, Kesia, and Isabella for an evening lesson that promised to expand their understanding of their spiritual selves. The room, filled with the gentle aroma of sage and the soft hum of meditative energy, was the perfect setting for exploring the realms beyond the physical.

"Tonight," Sophea began, her voice as calming as the twilight, "We will explore the higher chakras: the 8th, known as the Soul Star Chakra, and the 9th and 10th, which serve as bridges to your higher consciousness and the universal field. Understanding these will help you deepen your spiritual journey and enhance your connection with the cosmos."

Again, the girls leaned in, their souls open and ready to receive the ancient wisdom Sophea was about to impart. "The 8th chakra, the Soul Star, is located a few inches above the crown of your head. It's not bound to the physical body like the lower chakras but instead serves as a gateway to your higher self and spiritual lineage. When activated and balanced, it allows access to the akashic records, the cosmic library of all your past lives, and the universal knowledge."

As the twilight deepened, casting a serene blue hue over the room, Sophea noticed the spark of intrigue in the girls' eyes when she mentioned the Akashic Records. Sensing their eagerness to delve deeper into this mystical concept, she decided to expand on the topic, understanding that it was crucial for their spiritual development.

"The Akashic Records," Sophea began, her voice steady and soothing. "Are often visualized as a vast cosmic library where every event, thought, word, and intention of every soul is stored. These records are not physical but rather energetic imprints of everything that has ever occurred, existing in the higher realms of consciousness, accessible through the Soul Star Chakra and beyond."

She saw Lexi, Kesia, and Isabella leaning forward, their minds open and receptive. "Imagine," she continued, "That each of your lives is a book in this library. Every choice, every lesson, every moment of joy and pain is inscribed in these ethereal volumes. The Akashic

Records are the collective memory of the universe, the sum of all human experience."

Sophea paused, allowing the magnitude of the concept to settle in their hearts. "Accessing the Akashic Records can provide profound insights and guidance. It's like reading the story of your soul across all its lifetimes. You can understand your karmic patterns, the relationships you've woven through time, and the spiritual lessons that are central to your growth."

She then addressed the practical side of this spiritual endeavor. "To access the records, you must enter a deep meditative state, focusing on your Soul Star Chakra and setting the intention to connect with the Akashic field. It's crucial to approach with a sense of reverence and a desire for wisdom and healing, not mere curiosity. Ask for guidance from your higher self, archangels, and guardians of the Akashic Records themselves."

Sophea's gaze softened. "But be aware, the truths found in the Akashic Records can be intense and illuminating. They're not merely historical accounts but interactive energies. Engaging with them can bring healing and understanding, but it also requires responsibility. The insights gained are meant to guide you toward making positive choices and fulfilling your spiritual potential."

Lexi

In the soft, ambient light of Sophea's room, Lexi, with the Lemurian crystal clutched gently in her hand, closed her eyes and took a deep, steadying breath. Sophea's words about the Akashic Records echoed in her mind, a cosmic invitation to journey into the depths of her soul's history. As she focused on her Soul Star Chakra, a sense of calm transcendence enveloped her, and she felt herself lifting out of the present and into the realm of timeless knowledge.

Lexi found herself in a bustling ancient marketplace, the air thick with the scents of spices and the cacophony of traders and travelers. She was in a body that felt familiar yet distinct—a young woman with keen, observant eyes and a quiet strength about her. This was a past life in a land of desert sands and hidden oases, a place where caravans carried treasures from distant lands and scholars debated in the shade of date palms.

In this life, Lexi was known as Amara, a scribe and a seeker of truths. She had an insatiable thirst for knowledge, much like the Lexi of the present, and spent her days recording the stories of travelers and translating ancient texts. Amara's reputation as a wise and learned woman spread far and wide, drawing scholars and mystics to seek her counsel.

As Amara, Lexi's purpose was to preserve and disseminate knowledge. She believed that understanding the past was key to navigating the present and shaping the future. Her life was a testament to the power of words and the importance of keeping the flame of wisdom alight through generations.

However, this past life was not without its challenges. Lexi, as Amara, faced the struggle of living in a time when women were often denied access to the higher echelons of academic pursuit. She had to fight for her right to learn, to teach, and to be acknowledged. But Amara's spirit was indomitable. She forged alliances, proved her worth time and again, and became a beacon of learning in a world teetering on the brink of darkness.

The life lesson that Lexi absorbed from her time as Amara was profound: Knowledge is not just a personal quest; it's a legacy that one leaves for the world. She understood that her actions, her words, and her teachings would ripple through time, influencing others long after she was gone. This realization instilled in her a deep sense of responsibility to use her knowledge wisely and to contribute to the collective wisdom of humanity.

As Lexi emerged from the vision, the marketplace fading away into the mists of time, she felt a deep connection to Amara and the life she had led. She understood that her own journey of learning and growth was not just about satisfying her curiosity but about contributing to a larger tapestry of human understanding and enlightenment.

With the Akashic knowledge of her past life as Amara fueling her spirit, Lexi felt an even stronger resolve to pursue her spiritual path with purpose and integrity. She knew that the wisdom she gained and shared would be part of her soul's eternal legacy, a chapter in the cosmic library of the Akashic Records that would guide and inspire souls for generations to come.

Isabella

In the serene sanctuary of Sophea's room, as the last rays of the sun disappeared, casting a tranquil darkness interspersed with candlelight, Isabella held her Lemurian crystal and prepared to journey through the Akashic Records. With a deep breath, she allowed her consciousness to drift, guided by the ancient energy of the crystal and Sophea's gentle instructions.

Isabella's mind cleared, and she found herself transported to a mist-shrouded forest, the air filled with a sense of ancient wisdom and a touch of magic. She was in a time forgotten by history books, a place where the veil between the physical and the mystical was thin. In this past life, Isabella was Elara, a guardian of the sacred grove and a priestess dedicated to preserving the delicate balance between humans and the natural world.

Elara lived in a time when people respected the Earth, understanding their role as caretakers rather than conquerors. She was a revered figure, blessed with the ability to communicate with the spirits of the forest, the animals, and the elements. Her role was crucial, for she was the mediator between the human community and the mystical forces that surrounded them.

In this life, Isabella, as Elara, learned the profound lesson of harmony and respect. She understood that every creature, every plant, and every stone had a spirit and a purpose. Her days were spent in rituals, healing, and teaching the younger generations to walk gently upon the Earth, to listen to the whisper of the trees, and to understand the language of the waters.

However, Elara's life was not devoid of challenges. She witnessed the slow encroachment of a different way of life, one that sought to exploit the Earth's resources rather than honor them. A neighboring tribe began to invade her land, cutting down the trees she communed with and hunting the animals she protected. Elara faced the heart-wrenching task of defending her sacred grove and the way of life it represented.

The most significant life lesson Isabella received from her time as Elara was the understanding of interconnectedness. She learned that every action has a ripple effect and that maintaining balance in one's environment is crucial for the well-being of all. Elara's life was a testament to the idea that one must live with intention and consciousness, aware of the impact of one's choices.

As Isabella returned to her present self, the forest and Elara's life fading into the echoes of the past, she felt an overwhelming sense of responsibility and purpose. She realized that her journey, much like Elara's, was about safeguarding and honoring the connections between all forms of life. The lessons from her past life as Elara strengthened her resolve to live with greater awareness and to use her influence to promote harmony and understanding in her world.

With the wisdom of the Akashic Records and the power of the Lemurian crystal guiding her, Isabella felt a renewed commitment to her spiritual path. She knew that her actions and choices were not just for her own growth but were part of a larger, cosmic narrative of healing and balance. Inspired by Elara's legacy, Isabella was ready to embrace her role in this life, carrying forward the lessons of respect, harmony, and interconnectedness that her soul had learned long ago.

Kesia

As the gentle hum of meditation filled the room, Kesia held her Lemurian crystal tightly, its surface warm and alive with ancient energy. Under Sophea's watchful guidance, she closed her eyes and allowed her consciousness to drift into the Akashic realm, seeking the wisdom of a past life that would illuminate her current path.

Kesia's mind floated through time and space until she found herself in an ancient civilization, a place where the stars were not just celestial bodies but guides, teachers, and friends. In this past life, she was Kaya, an astronomer and priestess in a society where the heavens were a map to understanding the human soul and the mysteries of the universe.

Kaya lived in a time when people looked to the stars for answers to their deepest questions. She was revered for her wisdom and her ability to interpret the messages written in the night sky. Her life was dedicated to studying the movements of celestial bodies, deciphering their patterns, and teaching others how to find guidance in the stars.

In this life, Kesia, as Kaya, learned the powerful lesson of perspective. She understood that the world was much larger than her immediate surroundings and that every individual was a part of a vast, interconnected cosmos. Her role was not just to predict and observe but to connect people with the greater universe, helping them understand their place within it.

However, Kaya's life was not without its trials. A great calamity threatened her civilization, a disaster foretold by the stars but ignored by the rulers. Kaya faced the daunting task of convincing the leaders and the people to heed the warnings of the heavens. She worked tirelessly, charting the skies and interpreting the omens, trying to prepare her society for what was to come.

The most significant life lesson Kesia received from her time as Kaya was the importance of understanding and communication. She learned that knowledge was only powerful when shared and that her voice could be a beacon of change and survival. Kaya's life taught her that wisdom required not just interpretation but also action and courage.

As Kesia returned to the present, the vivid memories of Kaya's life still swirled in her mind, and she felt an overwhelming sense of clarity and purpose. She realized that her path was intrinsically linked to the past, that Kaya's wisdom was a part of her, guiding her in her current journey.

With the Akashic knowledge of her past life as Kaya and the Lemurian crystal as her talisman, Kesia felt a renewed sense of commitment to her spiritual path. She understood that her pursuit of knowledge and understanding was not just for her own enlightenment but for the betterment of those around her. Inspired by Kaya's legacy, Kesia was ready to embrace her role in this life, carrying forward the lessons of perspective, communication, and courage that her soul had learned amongst the stars.

Chapter 22

"*As* you delve into your past lives and the lessons they hold," Sophea continued, her gaze sweeping over each of her students, "Your Soul Star Chakra becomes a vital tool. It's through this chakra that you can understand the karmic threads and spiritual contracts that span across your incarnations, gaining insights that are crucial for your growth and enlightenment in this life."

"That was amazing," Kesia divulged. "The power of the crystal with the intention of the eighth chakra and the knowledge of the Akashic records is purely amazing."

"I agree," Lexi nodded.

Isabella sat there in awe before adding, "I wonder how many people would believe what we just experienced?"

1662ɡ2

Sophea smiled warmly at the genuine awe and wonder expressed by her students. "Belief," she said thoughtfully, "Is a personal journey. Not everyone is ready to embrace these truths, and that's okay. Each soul awakens in its own time and in its own way. But for those who are ready, like yourselves, the experiences can be profoundly transformative."

She glanced at each of her students, her eyes filled with a knowing wisdom. "What you've experienced today, through the connection with your Soul Star Chakra and the Akashic Records, is a sacred glimpse into the tapestry of your souls. It's a gift and a responsibility. You're not just accessing information; you're reconnecting with the essence of who you are across time and space."

Sophea stood and began to pace slowly in front of the girls, her hands clasped behind her back. "Consider the karmic threads and spiritual contracts you've encountered in your visions. They're not mere stories or past events but alive within you, influencing your present journey. Understanding them helps you make sense of your experiences, your relationships, and even your challenges."

She stopped and faced them directly, her expression earnest. "By working with your Soul Star Chakra and the Akashic Records, you're engaging in a form of soul archaeology. You're unearthing the wisdom of your past to illuminate your present and shape your future. And as you do so, you're healing not just yourselves but the collective soul of humanity."

Isabella, deeply moved by the words, whispered, "It's like we're part of something much larger than ourselves."

"Exactly," Sophea nodded. "You are. We all are. As you continue on this path, remember that your growth contributes to the world's evolution. Your healing is a ripple in the cosmic ocean, touching lives and souls you may never meet."

The room fell into a contemplative silence, each girl lost in thought, pondering the profound implications of their spiritual journey. The air was thick with the promise of further exploration and the deepening of their understanding. The realization that their quest for knowledge and enlightenment was not a solitary endeavor but a shared journey that connected them to the past, the present, and the future.

"You three are ready for this next lesson. Now, let's ascend to the 9th and 10th chakras. These chakras connect you even further with the divine source and the universe's vast consciousness. The 9th chakra is often associated with the soul's blueprint—the divine aspect that encompasses your soul's true purpose. By engaging with this chakra, you align closer to your destiny, understanding the talents and gifts you are meant to share with the world."

"The 10th chakra," she added, "Extends your connection to the cosmic realms even further, allowing you to access and bring forth divine creativity and manifest your spiritual intentions into the physical world. It's here that your visions, when guided by wisdom and purity of heart, begin to take form."

Sophea paused, ensuring her students absorbed the profundity of these higher energy centers. "In your meditations and spiritual practices, envision these chakras as luminous portals, each opening to a higher plane of existence. As you reach the eighth, ninth, and tenth chakras, imagine them as steps on a celestial ladder, each bringing you closer to your higher self and the universal truth."

"Remember," she concluded, her eyes reflecting the flicker of candles, "The journey through these higher chakras is not just about personal enlightenment. It's about using that enlightenment to heal, teach, and elevate the world around you. Your experiences with the Lemurian and Atlantean civilizations have shown you how knowledge and power, when misused, can lead to downfall. As you access these higher realms of consciousness, carry with you the lessons of the past, and let them guide you to use your spiritual gifts for the highest good of all."

Sophea gestured for Lexi, Kesia, and Isabella to sit comfortably and close their eyes. She dimmed the lights, filling the room with a soft, tranquil energy. "Now, let us begin our journey to awaken and explore the 9th and 10th chakras," she said, her voice a soothing balm to their eager spirits.

"Start by taking deep, slow breaths," Sophea instructed, her own breath audible to the girls as a model. "With each inhale, imagine drawing in pure, cosmic light. Release any tension or thoughts that may hinder your journey with each exhale. Let your body become light and your mind clear."

She allowed a few moments for the girls to find their rhythm, then continued. "Now, focus your attention on the area just above your crown, where your Soul Star Chakra—the 8th chakra— resides. Envision it as a radiant sphere of light, a portal to higher consciousness. Feel it pulsating, connecting you to the wisdom of your past lives and the Akashic Records."

"As you attune to your Soul Star Chakra, imagine it opening, a flower blooming to the sun. With this opening, sense your awareness ascending toward the ninth chakra, located above your head, a beacon of your soul's blueprint. This is the realm where your true purpose lies encoded, waiting for you to discover and embrace it."

"In this space, listen for the tone, the unique vibration that resonates with your soul. This tone is a key to unlocking the knowledge and talents you've carried through lifetimes. As you focus on this sound, let it guide you, revealing insights and abilities that are ready to be awakened and utilized in this life."

"Now, gently shift your focus higher to the 10th chakra, even further above your head. This is where your connection to the divine creativity and universal consciousness becomes even more profound. Visualize this chakra as a gateway to the cosmos, where your spiritual intentions can manifest into reality."

"Here, in the realm of the 10th chakra, allow the divine tone to evolve into a symphony of cosmic creation. Feel yourself as a conduit for this divine energy, ready to bring forth your visions and dreams into the world. Understand that your creative power, when aligned with wisdom and purity of heart, has the potential to manifest wonders."

Sophea's voice was a gentle guide through the celestial landscape. "As you connect with these higher chakras, remember the responsibility that comes with this knowledge and power. Let the lessons of the past, the rise and fall of ancient civilizations, remind you to tread with humility and purpose. You are not just seekers of enlightenment; you are stewards of the Earth and the soul of humanity."

"Take a few more moments to bask in the connection with these higher realms, absorbing the insights and energies that have been revealed to you. When you're ready, slowly bring your consciousness back to this room, to your physical body, but retain the connection and understanding you've gained."

As the girls gradually returned from their meditative journey, they opened their eyes, the room coming back into focus. They looked at each other, a silent acknowledgment passing between them. They had touched something profound, an ancient and eternally relevant cosmic truth. With Sophea's guidance and the wisdom of their own souls, they felt equipped and inspired to continue their spiritual journey, their hearts and minds open to the infinite possibilities that lay ahead.

Lexi

As the flickering candlelight cast soft shadows across the room, Lexi opened her eyes, her gaze distant yet filled with a profound understanding. She took a moment to ground herself back in the present before sharing her experience. The other girls leaned in, their curiosity and anticipation palpable in the quiet space.

"During the meditation," Lexi began, her voice steady but tinged with awe, "I ascended through the chakras, each one opening like a starburst, guiding me higher and higher. When I reached the Soul Star Chakra, it was as if I stepped into a river of light, the currents made of pure knowledge and memories from my past lives."

She paused, collecting her thoughts. "As I connected with the 9th chakra, the realm of my soul's blueprint, I found myself in an ancient library. It was vast, with endless shelves stretching into infinity. Each book was a chapter of my soul's journey, filled with the wisdom of lifetimes. I realized I was not just visiting this place; I was a part of it, a living, breathing aspect of the universal consciousness."

Lexi's eyes twinkled with the memory. "There, I met a guide, a luminous being who knew me more intimately than I knew myself. It showed me a book—my book—and as I opened it, I saw flashes of my past lives. I was a healer in a village, a scholar in a great city, and an artist creating beauty in times of turmoil. Each life was different, yet there was a thread that connected them all—my quest for understanding and my desire to heal and uplift those around me." Lexi took a breath and then continued, "The guide spoke to me, not in words, but in a deep, resonant tone that vibrated through my very soul. It was as if the sound carried the distilled wisdom of each of those lives, reminding me of the lessons I've learned and the gifts I have to offer the world."

Taking another deep breath, "Then, as I reached toward the 10th chakra, I felt an overwhelming sense of unity and creativity. It was like touching the heart of the cosmos, the birthplace of stars and dreams. I understood that my visions and intentions have the power to shape reality and that with wisdom and a pure heart, I can bring forth miracles into the world."

Lexi looked at her friends, her expression serene yet alive with a newfound purpose. "The meditation wasn't just a journey through the chakras; it was a journey through my very essence. I've come back with a deeper understanding of who I am and what I'm here to do. And I know that with this knowledge, I can make a real difference, not just in my own life, but in the world."

As she finished her story, the room was enveloped in a respectful silence, each person reflecting on the profound nature of Lexi's experience.

Isabella

"Isabella spoke next, "As the meditation session came to a close, there was a gentle hum of energy in the room. As I slowly opened my eyes, I felt an expression, one of wonder and deep contemplation."

The other girls watched her, sensing that she had journeyed somewhere profound and transformative.

Sophea nodded encouragingly, prompting Isabella to share her experience.

"During the meditation," Isabella began, her voice soft yet filled with a vibrancy that spoke of her profound experience, "As I ascended through the chakras, I felt as if I was being lifted by an unseen force, a loving energy guiding me upwards. When I reached the Soul Star Chakra, it was like entering a realm of pure light and unconditional love. I felt embraced by the wisdom of my ancestors and the collective knowledge of all my past lives."

She paused for a moment, her eyes reflecting the inner light she had encountered. "But it was when I connected with the 9th chakra, the soul blueprint, that my vision truly began. I found myself in an ancient temple, surrounded by pillars of light that stretched into the sky. In the center was a pool of water, clear and still, and as I looked into it, I saw not just my reflection but the faces of many lifetimes, each one a facet of my soul."

Isabella's gaze became distant, as if she were still seeing the visions that had unfolded before her. "A voice, like a melody, spoke to me from the very essence of the temple. It told me of my soul's journey, of the times I had been a healer, a teacher, and a protector. Each life had its challenges and joys, but the voice reminded me that the purpose of each was to learn, to grow, and to prepare for the life I am living now."

Lightly closing her eyes before she opened them again, "The voice then guided me to the 10th chakra, and as I reached it, I felt an incredible surge of creative energy and a profound sense of connection to all that is. I realized that I am a co-creator with the universe and that my thoughts and intentions have the power to manifest and shape the world around me. It was an overwhelming and humbling realization."

Isabella looked at her friends, her eyes bright with unshed tears of joy. "This meditation, this journey through the higher chakras, it's changed something in me. I feel more connected to my true self, to my purpose, and to the divine source. I understand now that I'm here not just to learn and experience but to use my gifts to make a positive impact."

Kesia

Kesia told of her experience, "As the last echoes of the meditation faded into the room's stillness, I remember slowly opening my eyes and having a profound sense of peace etched across my features."

Her companions watched her expectantly, sensing that she had experienced something deeply moving and transformative.

Sophea's eyes met hers with an understanding smile, encouraging her to share the journey she had embarked upon.

Kesia took a deep, grounding breath before speaking. "During the meditation, as I ascended through the chakras, I felt myself shedding layers of the present, each one falling away to reveal a deeper, more ancient part of my being.

When I reached the Soul Star Chakra, it was as if I stepped into a different dimension—a place where time and space lost their meaning, and all that existed was pure, radiant energy."

Her voice quivered slightly with emotion as she continued. "It was in the 9th chakra, the realm of my soul's blueprint, that my vision began to unfold. I found myself standing in a vast, moonlit clearing, surrounded by towering trees that seemed to touch the stars. I wasn't alone; spirits of my past lives were there, each one a guide, a teacher, whispering wisdom from lifetimes lived long ago."

Kesia's eyes shimmered with unspoken knowledge. "They showed me the tapestry of my soul's journey, the intricate patterns woven from each life I've lived. I was a poet in one life, a warrior in another, and a mystic in yet another. Each existence was vastly different, yet they all shared a common thread—my soul's yearning for understanding and connection, for the sacred union between the self and the divine."

Smiling more to herself than to the others, "As I absorbed the lessons of my past lives, the spirits guided me toward the 10th chakra. There, I felt an overwhelming sense of unity and purpose. It was as if all the knowledge and experience I had gathered were converging into a single point of light, a beacon guiding me toward my true calling in this life."

Kesia looked at her friends, her expression one of serene confidence. "This meditation, this journey to the higher chakras, has given me a glimpse of the vast potential within me—and within all of us. I understand now that my life is not just a series of random events but a carefully orchestrated symphony composed by the universe. And I have a part to play in it, a melody to contribute that is uniquely mine."

As she finished, the room was enveloped in a profound sense of reverence and solidarity. She knew the other girls felt the truth of her words resonate within them, knowing that her experience had not only deepened her own understanding but had also illuminated their paths. She knew they realized that the journey through the higher chakras was a journey of reconnection and remembrance, a way to reclaim the wisdom and power of their souls.

Inspired by Kesia's story, they others felt ready to embrace their own journeys with renewed purpose and passion, guided by the ancient knowledge that had been revealed to them.

Chapter 23

Lexi

As Lexi delved deeper into her spiritual practices in Nepal, the veil between her current life and her past thinned, revealing hidden truths and uncharted paths.

One evening, under the starlit sky, Lexi had a vivid dream where her belated sister, Susannah, appeared to her. Susannah's presence was comforting yet carried an urgency that Lexi couldn't ignore.

Lexi, you must return to New York, Susannah pleaded, her voice a gentle whisper in the dream. *Sebastian, your old boss, and Sherie need you. The legacy you left behind at the fashion house is unraveling, and only you can mend what's breaking.*

Lexi awoke, her heart racing. The dream felt more like a visitation, a message from beyond.

There was a knock at her door as she sat contemplating the meaning.

Sophea had sensed the turmoil within Lexi.

Slightly opening the door, Lexi peeked around it.

"My dear friend, sometimes our spiritual path is not just about moving forward but also about revisiting and resolving the past. Your journey back home might just be the key to unlocking the next step here," Sophea advised, her wise eyes understanding, then turned and walked away without waiting for a response.

As she closed the door and with Sophea's words echoing in her mind, Lexi knew what she had to do. She decided to return to New York to face the world she left behind and the responsibilities she thought were part of a life long gone.

The following day, Lexi sought out Isabella and Kesia to share the decision that had kept her awake most of the night. She found them in the small garden where they often gathered to discuss their experiences and thoughts.

As she approached, the seriousness of her expression quieted their casual conversation. "I had a dream last night," Lexi began, her voice steady but her hands unconsciously twisting the fabric of her robe. "Susannah came to me, urging me to return to New York. There's trouble at the fashion house, something only I can fix."

Isabella's brow furrowed in concern. "But Lexi, you've come so far on your spiritual journey here. Are you sure this is the right thing to do?"

Kesia reached out, her touch reassuring. "We understand the bond with family and past, but this is a huge step. Are you ready to dive back into that world?"

Lexi sighed, the weight of their questions pressing on her shoulders. "I've been asking myself the same things. But Sophea said something that resonated deeply within me. She said that sometimes facing our past is the key to unlocking our future. I believe this is one of those times."

The friends sat in silence for a moment, the gentle hum of the monastery around them. "I'll miss you," Kesia said, her voice thick with emotion. "But I believe in you, and I believe this is part of your path."

Isabella nodded in agreement. "We're here for you, no matter where you are. And who knows, this experience may bring a new depth to your spiritual journey."

Lexi smiled, grateful for their understanding and support. "I'll be back. I don't think my story is finished here yet. But for now, I need to do this. Not just for Sebastian and Sherie but for myself. I need to know that I can face my past and not lose the part of me that I've found here."

With a group hug and promises to keep in touch, Lexi began preparing to leave. As she packed the few belongings that she had on her person when she teleported to Nepal, she felt a mixture of apprehension and determination. This wasn't just a trip across the world; it was a journey into the heart of who she was and who she was becoming.

As the taxi pulled away from the monastery, Lexi looked back at the place that had been her sanctuary, her school, and even her home. She knew she was not the same person who had arrived weeks ago, and she was curious to see how this new version of herself would navigate the complexities of her old life in New York. With a deep breath, Lexi turned her gaze forward, ready to face whatever awaited her, with the lessons of her past and the hopes of her future guiding her way.

Chapter 24

*S*tepping off the plane in New York City, Lexi was immediately struck by the stark contrast between the serene monastery and the relentless pulse of the city she once called home. The loudness of urban life felt alien after her time in Nepal, yet there was no time to adjust slowly. She was here on a mission—to rescue the fashion house she had once been a part of from the brink of disaster.

Foregoing the familiar comfort of Aias's condo, Lexi made her way directly to the fashion house, the epicenter of the crisis. Sebastian's expression was a tapestry of shock at Lexi's bald head and relief at her return, no matter what she had been up to all these months. He detailed the dire situation, a major line crucial to the fashion house's reputation, and revenue was at risk due to a series of missteps and creative disagreements. The collection was disjointed, the team was in disarray, and the clock was ticking toward a catastrophic launch. Sherie, her dear friend and colleague, was caught in the crossfire, her career hanging by a thread.

Armed with a fresh perspective honed by months of introspection and spiritual learning, Lexi dove into the chaos. She approached the collection with eyes that saw beyond the fabric and threads, perceiving the deeper harmony that was needed to bring the pieces together. Her suggestions were unconventional yet intuitive, blending her innate design sense with her cultivated spiritual balance.

Day and night, Lexi collaborated with Sebastian, Sherie, and the team, her presence a calming, unifying force. She guided them through redesigns, realignments, and refinements. The collection began to resonate with a newfound coherence and vision with each adjustment.

As the launch day approached, the team watched in awe as the once-scattered collection transformed into a stunning, cohesive line that perfectly captured the essence they'd been striving for. Lexi's new ability to see the spiritual essence of design and understand each piece's energy and story saved the collection and the future of the fashion house.

As she prepared to return to Nepal, Lexi knew she was not the same person who had left. She had faced her past, embraced her present, and was now ready for whatever future lay ahead. The bond with her old colleagues was restored, and the message from Susannah had guided her to a deeper understanding of her purpose.

Lexi was finalizing her preparations and reflecting on the whirlwind of events that had transpired in New York when her phone buzzed with an unexpected message. It was from Redington, a man who had been occupying her thoughts more than she cared to admit.

The text read:

"Lexi, I heard about the incredible turnaround at the fashion house. I'm unsurprised; your talent and spirit were destined to make a difference. Before you leave, could we meet? There's something important I'd like to discuss with you. - Red"

The message sent a jolt of mixed emotions through Lexi. The thought of seeing Redington stirred a blend of excitement and apprehension within her. They had shared a connection, unspoken yet unmistakable, and part of her longed to explore what it might mean. Yet another part of her was cautious, aware of the complexities such a meeting could entail, especially now when she had rediscovered her purpose and was about to return to her spiritual retreat.

She pondered her response, knowing that this meeting could potentially open doors she wasn't sure she was ready to step through. But the pull of unresolved feelings and the words *"Something important"* resonated with a part of her who knew some paths were meant to be walked and conversations meant to be had.

With a deep breath, Lexi typed her reply:

"Redington, thank you for your kind words. The fashion house was a journey back in time and a step forward for me. I'm leaving for Nepal soon, but I believe you're right; we should meet. Let me know the time and place. – Lexi."

As she sent the message, Lexi felt a sense of calm mixed with anticipation. Whatever Redington wanted to discuss, she was ready to face it with the same courage and openness that had guided her through her recent challenges. This meeting, she sensed, was not just a conclusion to her time in New York but possibly the beginning of a new chapter in her ever-evolving journey.

Chapter 25

As Lexi sat in the quaint café, her fingers absentmindedly tracing the rim of her coffee cup, the bustling sounds of New York City faded into the background. Redington's message had ignited a storm of thoughts, each a flash of concern and apprehension. She knew the world Redington inhabited, one where duty and danger often walked hand in hand, and his urgent tone hinted at a situation far more severe than his job's usual risks.

Her mind raced with possibilities, each more disconcerting than the last. Could it be a case gone awry, tangling Redington in a web of legal and criminal complexities? Or perhaps it was something more personal, a vendetta or a power play in which they were unwitting pawns? The mob's shadow loomed large in her memories, a dark specter of her past that she had hoped never to confront again. The thought that Redington might now be ensnared in a similar peril sent a chill down her spine.

Lexi remembered all too well the feeling of being hunted, the sleepless nights wondering if every shadow concealed a threat. The stakes were always high in their world, and the players were merciless. She considered the connections and alliances that Redington, with his status and influence, might have unwittingly formed, each one a potential risk factor in the intricate chess game of power and retribution.

Her concern wasn't just for Redington's physical safety but also the psychological toll such situations could create. She knew the burden of living in constant vigilance, the way it could warp one's sense of normalcy and trust.

As Lexi pondered these scenarios, her resolve hardened. No matter the nature of the danger, she couldn't let Redington face it alone. Their past, crazy as it was, had forged a bond of mutual respect and understanding. She knew the loneliness of battling one's demons in solitude and refused to let Redington endure that fate.

Yet, even as she steeled herself for what was to come, a part of her mourned the peace she was about to leave behind. Nepal had offered her a sanctuary, a place to heal and grow. The tranquility she'd found there felt worlds away from the chaos she was about to re-enter. But perhaps, she mused, this was just another part of her journey, a test of her strength and a chance to close the chapter of her past that had haunted her for so long. *What am I thinking? I don't even know why he wants to meet.*

As Lexi's thoughts swirled, the café's door chimed, and she looked up to see Redington stepping inside. The moment of truth had arrived, and with it, the first step back into a world she had left but was never truly free from. With a deep breath, Lexi readied herself to face whatever lay ahead, her spirit a blend of apprehension and unyielding determination.

Redington arrived, his face a mask of urgency that Lexi had never seen before. "Lexi, what happened to your hair?"

"Nice to see you too," Lexi commented as she rubbed her newly-grown hair.

"Ah, right. Hi." Shifting his sight to her eyes, he began, his voice low and tense, "Thank you for meeting me. I wish this were under better circumstances."

I knew it. Deep down, my gut was right. Lexi thought as she tried to stay calm.

"It's my father, Lord Winston. We've found ourselves in a precarious situation. He's unknowingly gotten involved with individuals connected to the mob, the same ones you had your dreadful encounter with in the past."

Lexi's heart raced. The memories of her kidnapping flashed before her eyes. She had hoped those dark days were behind her, yet here they were, casting a shadow once more.

"The situation is delicate. They're using my father's influence for their schemes, and now they're threatening to expose him unless certain... demands are met." His jaw clenched, Redington continued, " Lexi, I'm doing everything in my power to resolve this quietly, but I need your help. You understand their operations, and you're the only one I can trust with this."

The café around them faded into a blur as Lexi processed what Redington was asking. Helping him meant diving back into a world she had fought hard to leave behind, a world of danger and deceit. But how could she refuse? Redington and his father were in danger, partly because of their connection to her.

Yet, returning to Nepal and her spiritual journey was crucial for her. She had commitments and a path she was determined to follow, one that promised peace and growth. The dilemma tore at her, a battle between her past and her present, her sense of self-preservation, and her loyalty to a friend in need.

The conflict played out on her face. She confessed, her voice a mix of determination and fear, "Redington, I want to help, but I'm afraid of being pulled back into that world. My life has changed, and so have I. I have responsibilities in Nepal, a journey I need to continue."

Redington implored, his eyes pleading, "I understand, Lexi, and I wouldn't ask if there was any other way. But I'm desperate. You have insights no one else does, and my father's safety, our family's legacy, is at risk."

The weight of the decision pressed down on Lexi. It was a crossroads moment, one that would define her path forward. Could she turn her back on a friend in need, especially when her past experiences might be the key to their salvation? Yet, could she risk her hard-won peace and the spiritual future that awaited her in Nepal?

As Lexi looked into Redington's eyes, filled with a mix of hope and despair, she realized there was only one choice she could live with. She would help Redington confront the demons of her past one more time and hope that this detour wouldn't derail the journey she was meant to take. "I'll help you, Redington. We'll face this together," she said, her voice steady despite the turmoil inside her. "But once this is over, I must return to my path, the path I've chosen for myself."

As they left the café together, a sense of resolve enveloped Lexi. The road ahead was fraught with danger and uncertainty, but it was a road she had to travel, a testament to the strength and courage she had found within herself. This conflict, this dilemma, was not just a crisis to be managed; it was a crucial part of her unfolding story, a story of resilience, loyalty, and the perpetual quest for a higher calling.

Chapter 26

After leaving the café, Lexi and Redington stepped out into the bustling streets of New York, the city's ceaseless energy enveloping them, even as the day had turned into evening. They moved with purpose, their strides matching in unspoken synchrony. Lexi could feel the tension radiating from Redington; it was a mix of resolve and an underlying current of apprehension.

Redington led the way to his car, which was parked a block away. As they walked, the noise of the city seemed to fade, replaced by the gravity of their shared mission. Lexi noticed the subtle tightening of Redington's jaw, the occasional deep breaths he took as if bracing himself for what was to come. His usual composed demeanor was edged with a seriousness that underscored the urgency of the situation.

Once inside the car, Redington didn't immediately start the engine. Instead, he turned to Lexi, his eyes meeting hers with a depth of sincerity. "Lexi, before we go any further, I want you to know how much I appreciate this. I wouldn't have asked if there were any other way. You've already been through so much, and I hate to drag you back into the shadows you fought so hard to escape."

As Redington's words lingered in the air, a chill ran down Lexi's spine. His gratitude and concern pulled her back to a memory she had tried to bury deep within her mind—the night of terror at the auction house when Adramelech, the archdemon, had taken over little Eddie's body and nearly ended her life. It was a night that had changed her forever, a night when the shadows she now faced had first truly revealed themselves to her.

The memory was vivid, almost painfully so. She remembered the eerie chill of the auction house, the way the lights flickered as if responding to an unseen presence. Then there was Eddie, or rather, the entity that had claimed him. His eyes had glowed with a malevolent light, and his voice had twisted into a sinister echo that seemed to scrape against her very soul. Adramelech had spoken in tongues of old, his words a dark symphony of threats and malice.

Lexi had felt an icy grip of fear that night, a fear that went beyond physical danger and touched upon something deeper, more primal. It was the fear of the unknown, of the power that lurked in the shadows of the world, waiting to claim the unwary. She had stared into the abyss that night, and what looked back had left its mark upon her.

But it wasn't just the terror that she remembered. There was also the surge of strength and determination that had welled within her as she stood against the darkness. She had fought not just for her life but for the innocence that Adramelech sought to corrupt. And in the end, despite the odds, she had prevailed. The memory of that victory, hard-won and fraught with danger, filled her with a renewed sense of resolve.

Lexi turned to Redington, her eyes clear and steady."Redington, I remember the shadows. I remember Adramelech and the fear he brought. But I also remember standing up to him, fighting back the darkness. You're right. I've been through so much. But those experiences, as harrowing as they were, they've made me stronger. They've taught me that no matter how deep the shadows, there's always a way to fight back. And that's exactly what we're going to do."

Redington nodded, a look of admiration and gratitude in his eyes. They shared a moment of understanding, two souls brought together by their battles against the darkness, both literal and metaphorical. With Lexi's words hanging between them, ready to confront whatever lay ahead. The memory of Adramelech was a reminder of the dangers they faced but also of the strength they possessed. Together, they stepped forward into the shadows, united in their determination to bring light to the darkest of places.

Lexi placed a reassuring hand on his arm. "Redington, we face what comes together. I'm not stepping back into the shadows. I'm confronting them." Her voice was steady, a testament to the inner strength she had cultivated during her time away.

Nodding with gratitude, Redington started the car, and they began their journey toward the heart of the crisis. The drive was quiet, each lost in their thoughts, mentally preparing for the confrontation ahead. Lexi thought about the monastery in Nepal, the peace she had found there, and how it now felt like a distant dream. Yet, she also felt a new sense of purpose, a drive to resolve the unfinished business that had once threatened to consume her.

As they neared their destination, the landscape changed from the bustling city center to a more secluded area. The buildings grew sparse, the shadows longer. Redington parked the car down the street from an unassuming warehouse, the supposed epicenter of the current crisis.

His voice low, he said, "This is it. We need to be extremely careful from here on out. My father is inside, and I have no idea what we're walking into."

As Redington uttered those solemn words, Lexi felt a familiar stirring in her mind, a gentle but insistent presence that she had come to recognize and cherish. It was Susannah, her belated sister, now an angelic guardian who had guided her through many perils since her passing.

Lexi closed her eyes for a moment, tuning into Susannah's voice, which resonated within her like a soothing melody amidst the loudness of the world. The connection they shared transcended the physical realm, a bond unbroken by death, strengthened by love and the spiritual journey Lexi had embarked upon.

Lexi, Susannah's voice echoed softly in her consciousness. *I'm here with you. Inside that warehouse, the situation is more volatile than Redington realizes. Lord Winston is being held in the back room, his spirit unbroken but his body weary. The men holding him are agitated, desperate, and dangerous. But there is hope.*

Lexi listened intently, her heart pounding with a mix of fear and determination. Susannah continued, her words clear and urgent. There's a side entrance that is poorly guarded and *a remnant of the building's old design. It's your best way in. Move quietly, and you can avoid the main group of thugs. Redington should confront them head-on, a distraction to draw their attention.*

The plan was risky and fraught with danger, but Lexi trusted her sister implicitly. Susannah had never steered her wrong, her angelic insight a beacon in the darkest times. *And Lexi,* Susannah added, her tone taking on a comforting warmth, *remember your strength, the light within you that has overcome so much. Let it guide you now. You're not just saving Lord Winston; you're reclaiming a part of yourself that refuses to succumb to fear.*

Opening her eyes, Lexi turned to Redington, who was watching her with a mix of concern and curiosity. "Redington, there's a side entrance. We need to split up. You create a diversion, and I'll sneak in to get your father. Trust me, I have...guidance."

Redington hesitated, the protective instinct in him battling with the trust he had grown to have in Lexi. Finally, he nodded, understanding her unspoken connection with something beyond his perception. "Be careful, Lexi. We'll meet back here in ten minutes. If anything goes wrong..."

They exited the car, their senses heightened. Lexi could feel the adrenaline coursing through her, a mix of fear and determination. As they approached the warehouse, she noticed the subtle signs of surveillance—cameras discreetly placed, the faint sound of muffled voices. This was the lair of those who thrived in the city's underbelly, and they were walking right into it.

"Nothing will go wrong," Lexi interrupted, her voice laced with a confidence that surprised even herself. "We've got this, Redington. Let's bring your father home."

With a final nod to each other, they moved into action. Redington strode toward the front of the warehouse, his posture radiating authority and purpose. Lexi, meanwhile, slipped into the shadows, her steps silent and sure as she made her way to the side entrance Susannah had described.

As she navigated the dimly lit corridors of the warehouse, Lexi felt another surge of adrenaline and an even more profound sense of clarity. She was not just Lexi, the fashion designer, or the spiritual seeker; she was a woman on a mission, guided by an angel, driven by a deep-seated resolve to protect, to heal, and to fight back against the darkness. This was her moment, a testament to her journey and the power she wielded within. As she moved closer to the room where Lord Winston was held, she knew that nothing would stop her from achieving her goal. Not fear, not the past, not the shadows that had once threatened to engulf her. She was Lexi, and she was unstoppable.

As Lexi neared the back room where Lord Winston was reportedly held, she heard the distinct sound of a deep, weary voice pleading for reason. It was Lord Winston, his tone both defiant and fatigued. The response was a harsh laugh, followed by a threat that made Lexi's blood run cold. She knew she had to act fast.

Meanwhile, at the front of the warehouse, Redington created his diversion. He announced his presence with the authoritative boom of an FBI agent demanding entry. The sound of hurried footsteps and panicked voices told Lexi that the thugs were taking the bait. It was now or never.

With a deep breath, Lexi rounded the corner and found herself face-to-face with two of the men guarding Lord Winston. Without hesitation, she relied on her self-defense training (which Redington insisted years ago that she take), incapacitating them with swift, precise movements. It was over in seconds, and the men slumped to the ground, unconscious.

Lord Winston, bound and bruised, looked up in astonishment. "Lexi?" he gasped, disbelief and relief mingling in his eyes.

"There's no time, Lord Winston. We have to get out of here," Lexi urged, quickly working to untie him. As she did, she explained the plan and the need to move quickly and quietly.

They made their way back through the corridors, Lexi leading Lord Winston with a firm, reassuring grip. They could hear the chaos Redington had incited at the front, buying them precious time. As they neared the exit, Lexi's heart raced with a mix of fear and hope. They were so close to freedom, yet the danger was far from over.

They emerged into the cool night air, the city's distant lights twinkling like stars grounded on earth. Redington was waiting for them, his expression a mix of relief and concern. "You did it, Lexi," he breathed, his gaze taking in his father's battered state.

Together, they helped Lord Winston into the car and drove away from the warehouse, leaving the night's ordeal behind them. As they put distance between themselves and the danger, Lexi allowed herself a moment of relief. They had faced the shadows together and emerged victorious.

But as the adrenaline faded, Lexi felt the weight of the night's events settling on her shoulders. She had returned to the darkness she thought she had left behind and found within herself a strength she hadn't realized she possessed. It was a reminder of the journey she was on, a path of self-discovery and spiritual awakening that was far from over.

As they drove back to the city, Lexi knew that this experience would stay with her, a defining moment in her ever-unfolding story. She had saved Lord Winston and helped Redington, and in doing so, she had saved a part of herself. The road ahead was uncertain, but Lexi was ready for whatever came her way. She was no longer just a fashion designer or a spiritual seeker; she was a warrior of light, and her journey was just beginning.

Chapter 27

As Redington navigated the streets of New York, his jaw set with determination, Lexi couldn't help but feel a twinge of anxiety. Aias's condo had been a sanctuary for her, a place of peace and reflection in the heart of a bustling city. But now, with the shadows of the mob potentially trailing them, it was about to become a fortress, a haven against the dangers they had just narrowly escaped.

Lord Winston sat silently in the back seat, his demeanor a mix of shock and enduring resolve. The ordeal had taken its toll, but his spirit, much like his son's, was unyielding. Lexi glanced at him through the rearview mirror, her heart aching for the pain and fear he must have endured. She knew the feeling all too well, the helplessness and desperation that came with being in the clutches of those who thrived on power and intimidation.

As they pulled up to the condo, Lexi felt a surge of protectiveness. This place was more than just a residence; it was a reminder of Aias, his presence still lingering in the walls and the air. She would do everything in her power to keep it and those within it safe.

Redington turned off the engine and looked at Lexi. "Lexi, I can't thank you enough for this. For everything you've done tonight."

She shook her head, dismissing the need for thanks. "We're in this together, Redington. We look out for each other, and right now, this is the safest place for your father."

Together, they helped Lord Winston out of the car and into the building. The security at Aias's condo was top-notch, a necessity for someone of Isabella's stature and past. Cameras, guards, and state-of-the-art technology all worked in concert to provide a level of safety that was nearly impenetrable—Isabella had paid for the updates and extras, knowing her son was worth every penny.

Once inside, Lexi led them to the living area, a space that was both modern and warm, filled with memories and touches of Aias's personality. Lord Winston settled into a chair, his body finally relaxing as the reality of his safety began to sink in.

"We'll need to stay put for now," Redington said, his gaze sweeping over the condo with a tactical eye. "I'll make some calls, see what can be done about the men who took my father. We need to understand why this happened and ensure it doesn't happen again."

Lexi nodded, her mind already racing with plans and precautions. "I'll contact Susannah and see if she has any other insights."

As the night deepened, the condo became a quiet command center. Phone calls were made, strategies were discussed, and every possible measure was taken to ensure their safety. But amidst the planning and vigilance, there was also a sense of unity, a bond forged through shared danger and mutual trust.

Lexi looked around at her companions, feeling a fierce determination rising within her. They were more than just individuals caught in a web of crime and conflict; they were a team, a makeshift family brought together by circumstance and held together by loyalty and courage.

As they settled in for the night, each lost in their thoughts, Lexi knew that the road ahead would be challenging. But with Redington and Lord Winston by her side, she felt a sense of hope. Together, they had faced the darkness and emerged stronger. And together, they would navigate whatever lay ahead, protecting each other and fighting back against the threats that sought to bring them down. This was their sanctuary, their battleground, and they were ready for whatever came their way.

Sitting on the couch, Lexi finally asked what she had been wondering ever since the café, "Redington, how did Lord Winston get taken in the first place?"

Redington, who had been pacing the length of the room, seemingly deep in thought, stopped and turned to face Lexi. He let out a weary sigh, the lines of tension on his face softening slightly as he prepared to recount the events that had led to his father's abduction. Lord Winston, looking more composed now but still visibly shaken, turned his gaze toward the floor, a silent acknowledgment of the difficult story about to be told.

"It's a bit of a complicated situation," Redington began, his voice laced with frustration and a hint of guilt. "My father has always been a man of influence and power, and with that comes certain... vulnerabilities. Recently, he's been involved in a deal, a legitimate business venture, but it seems that not all parties playing were as honest as he believed."

Lord Winston interjected, his voice carrying the weight of regret. "I thought I was negotiating a beneficial partnership. But I was too trusting, too naive. They seemed reputable, but their intentions were far darker than I could have imagined. They used the deal as a front to gain my trust, to get close."

Redington continued, "When they realized my father wouldn't bend to their more illicit demands, they decided to take a more aggressive approach. They abducted him right outside in public and took him to that warehouse. I was on a murder investigation. He was waiting for me in the car. They thought they could use him as leverage, manipulate him into complying with their demands."

Lexi listened intently, her heart aching for the ordeal both men had gone through. "And you, Redington? How did you find out about this?" she asked, her concern evident in her eyes.

"I was still investigating the crime scene when I received an anonymous tip," Redington admitted, his jaw clenching at the memory. "A text message with the warehouse location and a warning that my father was in danger. I still don't know who sent it, but I didn't have time to question it. I had to act fast."

Lord Winston looked up, his eyes meeting Lexi's. "Ferguson, son, you saved my life," he said with a mix of pride and gratitude. "I can't believe you came for me without a second thought, risking his own safety to bring me back."

The room fell silent for a moment, the gravity of the situation settling over them like a heavy cloak. Lexi reached out and took Lord Winston's hand, offering a comforting squeeze. "You're safe now," she reassured him, her voice soft but firm. "We're all here together, and we're going to make sure nothing like this ever happens again."

Redington nodded in agreement, a determined glint in his eye. "We'll increase security, conduct our own investigation, and get to the bottom of this. No one threatens my family and gets away with it."

As they sat there, united in their resolve, Lexi couldn't help but feel a surge of admiration for the father and son duo. Despite the fear and the danger they had faced, they remained strong, ready to confront whatever challenges lay ahead. And Lexi knew deep inside that she, too, would be there every step of the way, standing beside them as they navigated the murky waters of their current predicament. Together, they were a force to be reckoned with, and no shadow, no matter how dark, could extinguish the light they carried within them.

Chapter 28

The evening wore on, and the weight of the day's events settled heavily upon them. Lexi excused herself and stepped into her bedroom, seeking a moment of solitude. The room, with its lingering sense of presence, was the perfect place for reflection. She closed the door gently behind her and sat on the edge of the bed, taking a deep, steadying breath.

Lexi closed her eyes, allowing the silence to envelop her. In the quiet, she reached out with her heart, calling to Susannah. Their bond, unbroken by death, was a constant source of comfort and guidance. *Susannah,* she whispered, *I need you.*

As if on cue, the air in the room shifted, a gentle cooling spreading through the space. Lexi felt a familiar touch, light as a feather, on her shoulder. She opened her eyes, and though she

couldn't see her sister, she could sense
Susannah's presence, a comforting light in the
darkness.

Lexi, Susannah's voice echoed in her mind,
soft and reassuring. *I'm here, little sister. You're
not alone.*

Tears welled up in Lexi's eyes, a mix of relief
and aching longing. *Susannah, it's all so much.
Redington's father, the danger we just faced. I
feel like I'm being pulled back into a world I
thought I'd left behind.*

Susannah's presence grew stronger, a beacon
of love and understanding. *I know, Lexi. But
remember, you're not the same person you were.
You've grown, healed, and found strength you
never knew you had. This challenge is not a step
back; it's a testament to how far you've come.*

Lexi nodded, drawing strength from her
sister's words. *But what if I can't protect them?
What if I'm not strong enough?*

*You are strong enough, Lexi. You've proven
that time and time again. Trust in yourself and
in the journey you've undertaken. And
remember, I'm always with you, guiding and
watching over you.*

A sense of calm began to settle over Lexi.
Susannah was right. She had faced darkness
before and had emerged stronger each time. This
was just another step in her journey, another
challenge to overcome.

"Thank you, Susannah," Lexi murmured,
feeling a renewed sense of purpose. *I won't let*

fear hold me back. I'll do whatever it takes to protect Redington and his father. And I'll keep moving forward on my path.

As the connection faded, Lexi felt a gentle squeeze, as if Susannah was reassuring her one last time before departing. She stood up, wiped away her tears, and stepped back into the living room where Redington and Lord Winston were discussing their next steps.

They looked up as she entered, and Lexi met Redington's gaze with a newfound determination. "I've just spoken with Susannah," she announced, her voice steady. "We're going to get through this. And I have a few ideas on how to start."

As they gathered around, Lexi began to outline her thoughts, her strategies born from a blend of her spiritual insights and practical knowledge. Together, they began to plan, a united front against the shadows that threatened them.

And as they worked into the night, Lexi knew that they were not just planning a defense; they were weaving the threads of their shared destiny, a tapestry of courage, loyalty, and an unbreakable bond that would see them through the darkest of times. With Susannah's spirit watching over them and the strength they found in each other, there was nothing they couldn't face. This was their fight, and they were ready to stand together, come what may.

As the night deepened and their plans took shape, Lexi, Redington, and Lord Winston realized that they were at the beginning of a complex and potentially dangerous path. Lexi felt a weight of responsibility on her shoulders but also a fire of determination in her heart. She knew they were not just fighting for Lord Winston's safety but also battling the darker forces that had long plagued the edges of their lives.

Lexi stood up, stretching her stiff muscles after hours of strategizing. "We need to be proactive," she said, her eyes scanning the room, taking in the determined faces of Redington and his father. "We can't just wait for them to make the next move. We need to find out who's behind this and why. And most importantly, we need to ensure they can't harm anyone else."

Redington nodded in agreement, his face a mask of resolve. "I've got contacts in the FBI who can help us dig deeper into this. We'll need to be careful, though. If these people were bold enough to abduct my father in broad daylight, they're not going to be scared off easily."

Lord Winston, who had been listening quietly, spoke up, his voice firm despite the ordeal he'd been through. "And I have resources of my own. Friends in high places who owe me favors. It's time to call those in. We need all the help we can get."

The trio knew that their journey ahead would be fraught with challenges. They were up against a shadowy enemy, one that lurked in the murky intersections of the legitimate business world and the criminal underworld. But with Lexi's spiritual insight, Redington's investigative skills, and Lord Winston's connections, they had a fighting chance.

As they wrapped up their meeting, Lexi's thoughts turned to the spiritual aspect of their struggle. "We should also consider protecting ourselves on a spiritual level," she suggested. "I've learned a few things in Nepal that might help shield us from negative energies and intentions."

Redington, who had always been more pragmatic, couldn't deny the strange and inexplicable events he'd witnessed since meeting Lexi. "I'm open to anything that gives us an edge," he conceded. "What did you have in mind?"

Lexi explained about protective rituals and talismans, about setting intentions and calling on higher powers for guidance and protection. As she spoke, the room seemed to fill with a sense of calm and strength, as if her words were weaving a protective web around them.

They agreed to start the next day by fortifying themselves spiritually and then moving on to the more practical aspects of their plan. They would reach out to their contacts, gather information, and start piecing together the puzzle of who was behind the abduction and what they wanted.

As they said their goodnights and retired to their respective rooms, Lexi felt a mix of apprehension and hope. The road ahead was uncertain, filled with potential dangers and pitfalls. But they were not facing it alone. They had each other, and they had the unseen support of forces both in this world and beyond.

In her room, Lexi took a moment to meditate, center herself, and connect with the peace she had found in Nepal. She called on Susannah's spirit, on the wisdom of her teachers, and on the strength of her own soul. "Guide us and protect us," she whispered into the silence.

As she drifted off to sleep, Lexi felt a profound sense of connection, not just to the people in the condo with her, but to a greater tapestry of existence, one that wove through time and space, through light and darkness. They were a part of something larger, a story of courage and resilience, of light pushing back against the shadows. And whatever tomorrow brought, they would face it together, with hearts brave and spirits unbroken.

Chapter 29

*L*exi found herself in a haze of vibrant colors and sounds, her mind a whirlpool of half-formed memories and sensations. She was no longer in her apartment in Manhattan, nor was she the successful fashion designer she knew herself to be. Instead, she was Lex—a teenager with fiery red hair, freckles dotting her face, and living a life far removed from the complexities of her current reality.

In this dreamscape, Lex attended a bustling high school nestled in a small, vibrant town. Her days were filled with the typical dramas of teenage life friendships, rivalries, and burgeoning romances. Yet, this world was slightly off-kilter, a shade different from the typical American town.

Lex's closest friends in this dream were two people who, in her waking life, would seem out of place in her teenage world: Mr. Reddington, her history teacher, known for his stern demeanor and piercing blue eyes, and Mr. Edwards, the school principal, whose stately posture and reserved mannerisms belied a surprising sense of humor.

These characters in her dream mirrored her real-life acquaintances: Detective Redington and Reverend Edward. However, in this dreamscape, they played roles that were intimately entwined with her daily life as peers and guardians rather than as complex figures of love and authority.

One day, Lex, Mr. Reddington, and Mr. Edwards found themselves grouped together for a school project. They were to document the history of their little town, which involved exploring old buildings, gathering stories from the elderly, and even unearthing artifacts buried under the town's ancient oak tree, rumored to be as old as the town itself.

As they delved into the town's past, Lex felt the weight of history in her hands. An old diary they found beneath the tree detailed a love story between the town's founder and a mysterious woman who seemed to vanish like a wisp of smoke. The handwriting in the diary eerily mirrored her own, and the founder's fiery resolve and adventurous spirit felt disturbingly familiar.

In the midst of this historical adventure, tensions arose. Mr. Reddington and Mr. Edwards, who in her dream were father and son, began to reveal personal histories that paralleled the town's stories of conflicts and reconciliations. Mr. Reddington's protective nature over Lex clashed with Mr. Edwards' more philosophical approach to letting her explore her boundaries.

The project culminated in a presentation at the town hall, attended by faces both young and old. As Lex narrated the love story from the diary, a tale of lost chances and eternal waiting, she couldn't help but glance at Mr. Reddington and Mr. Edwards. Their expressions were unreadable, but she felt a profound connection as if the story she told was theirs, woven into the very fabric of their beings.

That night, Lexi dreamt within her dream. She saw the town's founder and the mysterious woman under the ancient oak tree, their hands almost touching, their gazes locked. The founder was a spitting image of Mr. Reddington, and the woman had her eyes—green, vibrant, and full of unspoken love.

Lexi awoke from her dream with a start, the morning sun casting a warm glow across her room. The emotions and images from her dream lingered, a mosaic of feelings and faces that felt both alien and incredibly familiar.

As she prepared for her day, the dream's echoes mingled with her reality. Detective Redington's concerned calls, reminders of Reverend Edward's cryptic messages about choices and paths, all seemed to be dialogues from her dream, blurring the lines between her past life memories and her present.

In this dream, Lexi didn't just relive a teenage past life; she uncovered layers of her soul, revealing connections that transcended time and space, hinting at the eternal dance of relationships and roles reborn.

Thus, in her seemingly whimsical dream of a past life, Lexi explored the themes of vitality and connectivity, the intertwining of souls through ages, manifesting in the present in new forms and stories. Through this, she gained insights into her current trials and the reassurance that some connections are indeed destined, repeatedly reborn to converge, diverge, and converge once more in the kaleidoscope of lives.

Chapter 30

In the early hours of the morning, as the city was just beginning to stir, Lexi rose from a restless sleep. She moved quietly through the dimly lit condo to a space she had set aside for meditation and spiritual work. The events of the past days weighed heavily on her, but she found a sense of purpose and clarity in the rituals she was about to perform.

Lexi spread a small, intricately woven mat on the floor, its patterns reminiscent of the ones she'd had used in the monasteries of Nepal. She then placed several items before her: a small bowl of water to represent purity and life, a feather to symbolize air and the freedom of the spirit, a candle for fire and enlightenment, and a stone for the earth and grounding.

Sitting cross-legged on the mat, Lexi closed her eyes and took several deep breaths, centering herself and reaching inward to the calm core of her being. She then began to chant softly in Sanskrit, the ancient words flowing from her like a gentle stream, filling the room with a sense of peace and sanctity.

As the chant continued, as she remembered what Luna had taught her, Lexi picked up the bowl of water and, dipping her fingers into it, flicked droplets in the four cardinal directions, blessing the space and those within it. She then lit the candle, watching as the flame took hold, its light pushing back the shadows. The feather she held lightly, waving it through the air to cleanse and purify the energy around her. Finally, she placed her hands on the stone, feeling its solid, grounding presence.

With the elements acknowledged and the space sanctified, Lexi began a more personal ritual, one she had learned from a wise teacher in Nepal, Sophea. She visualized a protective bubble of light surrounding the condo, a shield against any negative energies or intentions. She imagined it strong and bright, impenetrable to anything that might wish them harm.

As she chanted, Lexi also called on the higher powers she had come to trust, asking for their guidance and protection. She pictured Susannah's spirit, her guardian angel, watching over them and felt a sense of reassurance and love.

The ritual was completed, and Lexi opened her eyes, the candle still burning brightly before her. She felt a renewed sense of strength and determination. They were entering a battle on multiple fronts, against visible enemies and invisible ones, but they were prepared. They had taken steps to protect not just their physical bodies but their spirits as well.

After completing her protective rituals, Lexi felt a deep pull toward further spiritual counsel. She understood that the challenges they faced were not just physical threats but battles of a deeper, more esoteric nature. It was the perfect moment to seek guidance from a higher source, one intimately connected with the theme of her current journey—the quest for knowledge. Lexi decided to call upon Archangel Raziel, the keeper of divine secrets and mysteries, whose insight could be invaluable in navigating the complex web they found themselves entangled in.

In her hands, she held a small, clear crystal, a conduit for her intentions and a symbol of clarity and connection.

Closing her eyes, Lexi focused her mind and heart on Archangel Raziel. She envisioned the archangel as a luminous figure surrounded by a soft, rainbow light, the color often associated with deep wisdom and spiritual insight. She whispered a heartfelt invocation, her words a bridge between her soul and the higher realms.

"Archangel Raziel," Lexi began, her voice steady and sincere, "I call upon your wisdom and guidance in this time of need. We are faced with challenges and threats that go beyond the physical, touching the very essence of our souls. I seek the knowledge and understanding that you guard, the divine secrets that can illuminate our path and guide us to the truth."

As she spoke, Lexi felt a subtle shift in the energy around her, a sensation of deepening connection and an almost palpable presence of something ancient and wise. She continued, her heart open and ready to receive the guidance she sought.

"Help us to see beyond the surface, to understand the hidden forces at work, and to discern the best course of action. Grant me the clarity to recognize the lessons from my past lives that can aid us now and the foresight to navigate the future with wisdom and courage. Archangel Raziel, be our guide and protector as we journey through the unknown, seeking the light of truth in the shadows that surround us."

Lexi sat in silence for several moments after her invocation, the crystal in her hands warming slightly as if resonating with her plea. She opened herself to any signs, feelings, or thoughts that might emerge, trusting that Raziel's guidance would come in the form needed.

After some time, a sense of calm assurance settled over her. While she didn't receive a direct message or vision, she felt an inner conviction that they were not alone in their struggle, that the wisdom and knowledge they sought were within reach, and that they were being guided by a force far greater than themselves.

As Lexi opened her eyes, the room seemed a little brighter, the sunlight a bit more radiant. She stood, her spirit fortified by the ritual and the sense of connection she had experienced. With a renewed sense of purpose and confidence, she was ready to rejoin Redington and Lord Winston, to share with them the strength and insight she had gained, and to continue their collective quest for truth and safety.

As Lexi extinguished the candle, a knock came at the door. It was Redington, ready to discuss their plans for the day. Lexi stood, the peace of her morning ritual still surrounding her like a cloak. "Good morning," she said, her voice steady and calm. "I will be out in a moment."

Chapter 31

Before she spoke, her mind revisited the lessons from Sophea, the echoes of her past lives, and her recent entanglement with the mob. Each memory and experience seemed like pieces of a vast, cosmic puzzle waiting to be understood and assembled.

"Redington," Lexi began, breaking the silence that had enveloped the room, "I've been thinking about the connections we've encountered, the dangers we've faced, and the path that lies ahead. I believe there's more to this than mere coincidence. It feels like...like we're being guided toward something greater, something that transcends our understanding."

Redington, who had been lost in his own thoughts, turned to face Lexi. His eyes, usually so sharp and focused, now reflected a depth of introspection. "I've felt it too," he admitted. "Ever since we encountered the mob, and with my father's abduction, it's as if we're being pushed toward a destiny that's been written in the stars."

Lord Winston, who had been quietly listening from another room, spoke up, his voice steady despite the recent ordeal. "My dear children, I dreamt last night that the world is far more intricate and interconnected than we can fathom. Our lives, our choices, and the paths we tread are all threads in a divine tapestry. And sometimes, those threads lead us into the shadows so that we may find the light."

The words of Lord Winston resonated with Lexi, and she felt a surge of determination. "Then we must be vigilant, not just in our actions but in our spirits. Sophea taught me about the power of knowledge, the strength in understanding our past, and the wisdom it brings to our present. I think it's time we seek guidance from a higher power, from Raziel."

Redington shook his head, his resolve not mirroring Lexi's. "I wish I agreed. Let's say I did. If we're to navigate this labyrinth of mysteries and dangers, you say we need insight that goes beyond the ordinary. That we need the wisdom of the ages, the kind that Raziel, the Keeper of Secrets, can provide?"

Lexi chose her words carefully, "Yes. I know that you still are hesitant about the unknown, but I trust the celestial world, more so now than ever before."

Lord Winston looked at Redington and said, "It can't hurt. Let her do whatever she must do to make this right."

And so, under the illusion of his father, Redington agreed, "Who am I to argue? You would think by now I would be used to all this woo-woo stuff. But to be honest, it still freaks me out."

"Woo, woo," Lord Winston echoed. "Archangel Raziel is not only a Christian angel, but many other religions believe in him as well."

"Such as," Redington challenged.

"Judaism, Islam, and Esoteric," Lord Winston said with an authoritative tone.

"How would you know that?"

"Your mother. She loved angels and all that they represented."

Redington didn't comment.

Lexi decided this was a good time to invoke the presence of Archangel Raziel, to illuminate their path, and to reveal the knowledge hidden within the soul of their story.

"Come sit, you two. Let me tell you all that I have learned about Archangel Raziel," Lexi said as a flicker of excitement crossed her features. "In Nepal, I was studying about Archangel Raziel. He's known as the angel of mysteries, the keeper of secrets." She paused, gauging their interest before continuing. "Raziel looks somewhat ethereal—imagine a wise figure with a white beard, like Merlin, but his aura is like a rainbow, very vivid and striking."

Winston, who had settled into a chair with his tea, listened intently, his interest piqued.

"His wings are either silvery or sky blue, and he usually appears in armor, carrying a ring of ancient keys and an old book that contains profound secrets of the universe," Lexi explained, her eyes alight with the passion of her subject. "This book is said to have been thrown into the sea and later retrieved, filled with insights into both celestial and earthly realms."

Redington, intrigued, asked, "How does one interact with an archangel like Raziel?"

Lexi, encouraged by his genuine curiosity, detailed further. "Through meditation and specific prayers, you can seek Raziel's guidance to understand the mysteries of the universe. He helps with past-life regression, dream interpretation, and even guides you in connecting with the natural elements—fire, air, water, earth, metal, and ether."

She recited the prayer she learned in Nepal, her voice soft but clear, "Archangel Raziel, I am ready to awaken to the mysteries of the universe. I ask for your rainbow light to wash over me and cleanse me of anything that would hold me back from your glory. Please allow the flow of miracles into my life. Amen."

Winston's eyes reflected a spark of wonder, a rare glimpse into the depth of his contemplative spirit. "It sounds like Raziel's teachings could offer much guidance, especially in understanding the complexities of our existence and the spiritual dimensions that often elude us."

Redington nodded, his analytical mind finding a new respect for the spiritual elements Lexi described. "I am trying Lexi, I am," he admitted. "If I could figure out a way to have such forces potentially be useful even in my line of work, deciphering the enigmas we encounter would be a real asset."

Lexi closed her eyes and took a breath. *God, grant me the serenity to accept the things I cannot change, the courage to change the things I can, and the wisdom to know the difference.*

Chapter 32

As the city awoke to the familiar harmony of urban life, Lexi, Redington, and Lord Winston gathered in the living room of Aias's condo, a space that had become a sanctuary of sorts in the eye of the storm they found themselves in. The previous night's revelations had left them with more questions than answers, and they knew it was time to delve deeper into the enigma surrounding the mob's intentions.

Redington, with a steely resolve in his eyes, turned to his father. "Father, we need to understand everything that happened in the warehouse. Any detail could be crucial."

Lord Winston, his demeanor a blend of aristocratic composure and the weariness of a man who had stared into the abyss, nodded in agreement.

He began recounting his experience, the cold touch of his captors' hands, the stark, dimly lit confines of the warehouse, and the conversations he overheard. "They were speaking in hushed tones about an ancient power, something that could change the balance of not just the criminal underworld but the entire world. They mentioned a 'key' that I supposedly had knowledge of due to our family's lineage."

Lexi, who had been silently listening, interjected, "Oh my God, I think I know what they were referring to. I learned about artifacts in Nepal."

Redington and Lord Winston exchanged a glance, a silent acknowledgment of the gravity of the situation.

"Don't leave us in suspense," Redington replied with a bit of attitude.

After giving Redington a look as if to say careful, buddy, Lexi continued, "In Nepal, I learned about artifacts that are not just physical objects but conduits of spiritual power and knowledge. If the mob has learned about such an artifact and believes it can be exploited for power..."

At that moment, Lexi felt a gentle yet profound presence in her mind, the newer but now familiar touch of Archangel Raziel. She closed her eyes, focusing on the celestial guidance. Raziel's voice, like a whisper of wind through the leaves, spoke of an ancient artifact that was indeed a key to vast, untapped knowledge and power. It was something that, if fallen into the wrong hands, could wreak havoc on a scale they couldn't imagine.

Opening her eyes, Lexi relayed Raziel's message. "We're not just dealing with a criminal enterprise; we're facing a threat that could destabilize the spiritual and physical realms. We need to find this artifact before they do."

Redington, his mind racing with the implications, added, "If they're after something they believe to be this powerful, they won't stop at anything. We need to be one step ahead." He turned to his father, "Is there anything in our family's history, any legend or artifact that's been passed down that you know of?"

Lord Winston, his brow furrowed in deep thought, slowly began to nod. "There is an ancient tale, a legend of a key passed down through our lineage. It was said to unlock 'the wisdom of the ages.' I always thought it was just a myth, but perhaps..."

In the quietude of Aias's condo, transformed into a haven of hushed conversations and clandestine plans, Lord Winston's revelation hung in the air like a specter from the past, beckoning them toward an enigmatic legacy that was intertwined with their very fate.

Lord Winston, his voice a timbre of remembrance and reverence, continued, "This tale has been part of our family lore for generations, often spoken of in hushed tones by the firelight during family gatherings. It speaks of an ancient key, forged in a time when the world was younger, and the veil between the earthly and the divine was thinner."

He paused, his gaze distant, as if visualizing the saga he was about to unfold. "The key, known as the 'Aeternitas Clavis,' which translates roughly from Latin to 'Eternal Key,' was said to be crafted by a conclave of sages, mystics who had unlocked the secrets of the universe. It wasn't a key in the literal sense but a symbol of unlocking the boundless wisdom of the ages, the accumulated knowledge of civilizations long vanished and realms beyond our comprehension."

Redington was shocked; he hadn't heard of this tale before. "Why do I not know of this?"

"You left England before I could pass on any of our legacy." Lord Winston sat up straighter and took a breath before he continued. "The sages knew that such power was not meant for all, for in the wrong hands, it could lead to ruin and devastation. So, they entrusted it to a lineage of guardians chosen for their wisdom, integrity, and understanding of the balance between knowledge and responsibility. Our family, according to the legend, is descended from these guardians."

Lexi and Redington listened intently, the magnitude of Lord Winston's words not lost on them. Here was a narrative that transcended time, a responsibility passed down through bloodlines, now resting unknowingly on their shoulders.

Lord Winston leaned forward, his eyes alight with the fire of ancestral pride and a hint of trepidation. "The Aeternitas Clavis was said to grant its bearer access to the Akashic Records, the cosmic library of all that was, is, and will be. It could reveal the past lives of souls, the hidden truths of the universe, and the paths yet to be walked. But it also required an unparalleled purity of intent and strength of spirit, for the knowledge it bestowed was as dangerous as it was enlightening."

"Oh my God! I just learned about the Akashic Records while I was in Nepal," Lexi exclaimed. "Please, Lord Winston, tell us more."

"Over the centuries, the key was lost to time, its tale fading into the realm of myth and legend. Some say it was hidden away by the last guardian, who foresaw a time when the world would need its wisdom again. A prophecy was whispered, speaking of a period of great turmoil, where the key would emerge once more, and its guardians would be called upon to prevent the dawn of an age of shadows."

Redington, his mind racing with the implications, connected the dots. "The mob, they must have stumbled upon this legend, perhaps through an ancient text or a traitorous whisper. They believe that by obtaining the key, they can control the wisdom of the ages, wield power that has been hidden for millennia."

The pieces of the puzzle were beginning to fit together. The mob's interest in Lord Winston, the artifact's description, and the legends tied to his family's history. It was more than mere coincidence; it was fate intertwining their paths with a narrative that spanned back through the ages.

Lexi felt a shiver run down her spine, the weight of destiny pressing upon her. "If the mob is after this key, then it's not just a fight against crime; it's a battle for the future itself. We must find the Aeternitas Clavis before they do." She closed her eyes briefly, seeking the comfort and guidance of Archangel Raziel. *Raziel, keeper of secrets and divine wisdom, guide us in our quest to protect the key and the knowledge it holds.*

Redington, ever the strategist, began formulating a plan. "We definitely need to find this key, understand its power, and, most importantly, keep it from falling into the wrong hands. Lexi, let's hope your knowledge and connection with Raziel will be invaluable."

Lexi nodded, a sense of purpose igniting within her. "We'll need to be careful and use every resource and ally we have. This isn't just a fight against a mob; it's a battle to protect the very fabric of knowledge and power."

As they sat around the coffee table, a makeshift war council, each felt the weight of their chosen quest. They were no longer just individuals with separate paths; they were a united front against a looming darkness. Lexi, with her spiritual insights and connection to Raziel; Redington, with his tactical mind and investigative skills; and Lord Winston, with his lineage and knowledge of ancient lore.

Together, they stood at the precipice of a journey that would test their courage, wisdom, and the very depths of their souls. The road ahead was fraught with danger and mystery, but with the guidance of Raziel and the bonds they shared, they were ready to face whatever lay ahead. The quest for the artifact was more than a mission; it was a calling, a duty to safeguard a legacy of knowledge and power that had chosen them as its protectors.

Chapter 33

"*R*edington, I was wondering how we were so easily able to get your father out of the warehouse?" Lexi asked when they were alone.

Red looked at Lexi, "To be honest, I was wondering about that myself."

"Even with my self-defense training, there really is no way that I should have been able to defeat the guys holding your dad. They should have had guns or something. They are mobsters."

Red chuckled, thinking about Lexi fighting off two big thugs when a wind gust could blow her away. "I don't know what I was thinking about getting him without backup. I think I went insane for the safety of my father. After losing all my other family members, I just can't lose him now that we are on talking terms again."

Lexi nodded. "Do you think they wanted us to come and get him?"

Red took a moment to answer, "Hmm, I think you might be on to something." Redington's brow furrowed as he considered Lexi's question, the gears in his mind visibly turning. "You know, it's not just that they didn't put up much of a fight, it's also the timing of it all. The moment we decided to move, everything just fell into place a little too conveniently."

Lexi leaned forward, her intuition piqued by the oddity of their rescue. "It's like we were meant to find him like we were led there. Maybe it's not just about your father. Maybe it's about us, about drawing us out for some reason."

Redington nodded, his thoughts aligning with hers. "If that's the case, then there's a bigger game at play here. We were reacting, not dictating the moves. It's a classic strategy— maneuver your opponent into the position you want them without them realizing it."

Lexi's mind raced with the implications. "So, if we were lured into a trap or some kind of test, then the question is, who's behind it, and what do they really want?"

"That's what we need to find out," Redington said with determination. "And we need to understand what this 'Aeternitas Clavis' is all about. It might be the key to understanding their motives."

He stood up, pacing the room as he gathered his thoughts. "First, we need to dig deeper into this legend of the key. If it's as powerful as they believe, it could be a dangerous weapon in the wrong hands. And second, we need to be more strategic, anticipate their moves, find out who's pulling the strings."

Lexi watched him, admiring his resolve. She knew that together, they had a fighting chance to unravel this mystery. "I'll reach out to Susannah and see if she or Raziel can provide any insights into the key and its history. Maybe there's something in my past life experiences that can help us."

Redington stopped pacing and looked at her with a look of determination in his eyes. "And I'll start an off-the-books investigation. I have contacts who might shed some light on who's really behind this. We'll play their game but on our terms."

Lexi found a quiet corner in Aias's condo, away from the worries and conversations of the outside world. She settled into a comfortable position, closed her eyes, and focused on her breathing, allowing the rhythm to guide her deeper into a meditative state. In this tranquil space, she called out from her heart, *Susannah, I need your guidance.*

The air around her seemed to shimmer, and a gentle presence filled the room. Susannah's voice, soothing and familiar, responded, *Lexi, I'm here. What troubles you?*

Lexi opened her heart even more to her sister, sharing her concerns about the 'Aeternitas Clavis' and the mysterious circumstances surrounding Lord Winston's abduction.

Susannah, we need to understand what this key is,. It's more than just a legend; it's at the heart of everything happening. Can you ask Archangel Raziel for his wisdom?

Susannah's presence grew stronger, a comforting warmth enveloping Lexi. *I will seek Raziel's counsel. He holds the secrets of the divine and the knowledge of the ages. Wait here, dear sister.*

In the silence that followed, Lexi focused on the connection she shared with Susannah, a thread of light that transcended the physical realm. Time seemed to stretch and fold in on itself until, finally, Susannah's voice returned, carrying a weight that spoke of ancient truths and celestial insights.

Raziel has heard our plea, Susannah announced. *The 'Aeternitas Clavis' is indeed an artifact of great power, one that can unlock the wisdom of the ages, as the legend suggests. It was created in a time long forgotten, intended as a tool for enlightenment, to guide the worthy on their path to understanding the mysteries of the universe.*

Lexi absorbed the words, a mix of awe and apprehension filling her. *But such power can be dangerous, can't it? Especially if it falls into the wrong hands.*

Yes, Susannah affirmed. *Raziel warns that the key must be used with the purest of intentions. In the wrong hands, it could lead to catastrophe, allowing one to manipulate the fabric of past and present to alter the course of history for selfish ends. It's not just knowledge the key offers but the power to shape reality.*

The gravity of the situation settled over Lexi like a shroud. *Then, we must find it before the mob does. We need to protect it and ensure it's used for the greater good.*

Susannah's voice softened, a sister's love and concern shining through. *Lexi, Raziel will guide and protect you. You three are not alone in this. The heavens are watching, and the light will always find a way to shine through the darkness. Trust in your path and in the friends and allies you have beside you.*

With those words, the presence of Susannah began to fade, leaving Lexi with a renewed sense of purpose and determination. She opened her eyes, the room coming back into focus. She knew what she had to do. With the guidance of Archangel Raziel and the support of her friends, she would face whatever challenges lay ahead. The journey to uncover the truth about the 'Aeternitas Clavis' was just beginning, and Lexi was ready to play her part in the unfolding story.

Chapter 34

In a dimly lit room, Marko Calponi sat at an ornate mahogany desk, his fingers steepled in thought. The room was a testament to his power, adorned with lavish furnishings and artifacts that spoke of wealth and influence. But today, his mind was not on his empire or his wealth; it was consumed by a singular, tantalizing goal: the 'Aeternitas Clavis.'

Marko had always been a man who believed in the tangible—money, power, respect. These were the things that mattered in his world. But the discovery of something as enigmatic and potentially powerful as the 'Aeternitas Clavis' had ignited a fire in him. It was a key to knowledge beyond his wildest dreams, a tool to unlock the very fabric of reality and bend it to his will.

As he pondered the possibilities, a trusted gang member entered the room, his footsteps echoing in the silence. "Boss, the preparations are complete. We've secured the location you requested for the artifact's retrieval."

Marko nodded, his expression unreadable. "Good. And the girl, Lexi, and that FBI agent, Redington? What do we know about their involvement?"

The mobster shifted uncomfortably. "They're closer to the truth than we anticipated, sir. They've been asking questions, digging into the key's history. It seems they've got some kind of spiritual backing, too—rumors of angelic guidance or something."

A cold smile spread across Marko's lips. "Angelic guidance, you say? How amusing. It doesn't matter. Let them scurry about with their guardian angels. They won't understand the key's true power, not like I will."

He stood, his presence commanding the room. "We proceed as planned. Once the 'Aeternitas Clavis' is in our possession, we'll control not just the streets, not just the city, but the very threads of history. Lexi, Redington, and whoever else stands in our way will be mere footnotes in the new world I'll create."

The mobster nodded, a sense of unease creeping into his bones. He'd seen what happened to those who opposed Marko Calponi, and he had no desire to share their fate.

"Understood, boss. We'll make sure everything goes smoothly."

As his man left the room, Marko turned to gaze out the window at the sprawling city. He had risen from the gritty streets to become a kingpin, feared and respected by all. But the 'Aeternitas Clavis' offered something more, something grander. It was a chance to ascend from kingpin to a god among men.

In the shadows of his ambition, Marko Calponi plotted and planned, unaware that forces beyond his comprehension were aligning against him. Lexi, Redington, and their celestial allies were already moving pieces into place, setting the stage for a confrontation that would determine the fate of the 'Aeternitas Clavis' and the very fabric of reality itself. But for now, Marko basked in the illusion of his invincibility, dreaming of the power and glory that lay just within his grasp.

Chapter 35

*L*exi stood by the large window of Aias's apartment, gazing out at the bustling streets of New York City. The city's energy was electrifying, but today, it did little to soothe her anxious mind. She had spent the last few days studying anything and everything she could find on the ancient *'Aeternitas Clavis.'* The information she found had been minimal—but they had figured out that the next real clue lay in London.

"Are you ready?" Redington's voice broke through her thoughts. He stood in the doorway, a determined look on his face. "The flight is booked, and the car is waiting downstairs."

Lexi nodded, grabbing her bag and taking one last look at the apartment. "Let's go," she said, her voice resolute.

The ride to JFK Airport was a blur. Lexi's mind raced with thoughts of the mission ahead.

Redington, sitting beside her, was a comforting presence. His calm demeanor always had a grounding effect on her, even in the most chaotic situations.

As the three of them boarded the private jet arranged by Lord Winston, Lexi felt a mixture of excitement and apprehension. The journey to London was not just a physical one—it was a step deeper into the mysteries that had enveloped their lives. The stakes were higher than ever.

Lexi knew that Redington had set about setting up a team to meet us in London.

Lexi turned to Redington, "Anxious about going home?"

Redington looked at her and took a breath, "Not anxious, but I thought I had left that life behind me."

Lexi nodded and looked away, closing her eyes.

The flight was long but uneventful.

Upon landing at Heathrow Airport, they were greeted by a discreet but efficient driver who whisked them away to their destination. The streets of London, with their historic charm and modern vibrancy, contrasted sharply with the frenetic pace of New York. Lexi couldn't help but feel a sense of awe as they drove past iconic landmarks like the Tower of London and Buckingham Palace.

~

A sense of ancestral legacy seemed to whisper through the air. Redington gazed out the vehicle's window, his home soil below him, feeling the weight of his heritage and the responsibility it carried.

The drive to Wrightenton Manor was scenic, passing through rolling hills and quaint villages, each view a stark contrast to the bustling streets of New York City they had left behind.

As the manor came into view, its grandeur and age immediately apparent, Redington felt a familiar tug in his chest—a connection to this place that was both comforting and daunting. They were welcomed by the household staff, who were discreetly efficient, sensing the seriousness of their arrival.

Lord Winston led them directly to the study, the heart of many family decisions. "This is where we'll plan our next steps," he stated, his voice echoing slightly in the high-ceilinged room.

As night fell over Wrightenton Manor, the trio understood that this was more than just a return to a family home. It was a step into the unknown, a dive into the depths of history and their souls. They were not just seeking an artifact; they were seeking answers to questions that span lifetimes and legacies.

Redington found himself in a rare moment of quiet introspection. He sat in his father's study, a room that always seemed to encapsulate the essence of his childhood. Surrounded by the familiar scent of old books and the soft creak of leather, he allowed himself a moment to escape from the present's complexities.

His gaze drifted to a photograph on the desk, one of a much younger version of himself, with a mischievous glint in his eyes that he almost forgot he once possessed. The image triggered a flood of memories, each a jigsaw piece of the boy he used to be.

He remembered the vast gardens of his family estate, a realm of endless adventure where he and his siblings played hide and seek, their laughter echoing through the air like music. He recalled the strict regimen of tutors and the expectations of excellence, a weight he learned to carry with the grace taught by his mother.

But there was a shadow to these memories, too. The loneliness of a child born into a world of protocols and duties, where every action was a step in a dance he didn't choose. He remembered the cold, distant figure of his father, a man more myth than flesh, and the way his mother's eyes sometimes held a sadness he couldn't understand.

As he sat there, Redington realized how these moments, both bright and dark, shaped him. The joy and the pain forged his resolve, his sense of duty, and the protective shell he learned to wear. Yet, amidst these reflections, there was a tinge of regret, a wish that perhaps things could have been different, that he might have known a simpler, more carefree love and acceptance.

But as the shadows lengthened in the room and the dust motes danced in the slanting sunlight, Redington felt a softening in his heart. He understood that these memories, while a part of him, didn't define him. He was more than the lonely boy in the photograph; he was a man who's seen darkness and chosen to walk in the light.

With a deep, almost imperceptible sigh, Redington stood up and straightened his jacket as if to shed the weight of the past. He looked once more at the photograph, then turned away, ready to face the future, whatever it may hold, with the strength forged from the joys and trials of his childhood.

Chapter 36

Wrightenton Manor was set up as a bit of a fortress. The vast land and property owned went on for miles. One would be able to see anyone coming.

Redington had phoned ahead and had brought in more guards and had warned the authorities of the possibility of gangsters coming from the US.

What he didn't expect was that Marko Calponi had the guts to call and ask his father to hand over the 'Aeternitas Clavis.'

Redington could hear his father's side of the conversation.

"If I had any idea what that was, I still wouldn't hand it over," Winston said as he hung up.

"Father, what else did he say?" Redington ask.

Looking at Lexi and Redington, Lord Winston answered, "That if I didn't hand it over, the blood would be on my hands."

Lexi gasped.

Redington knew all too well how brutal Marko Calponi could be. "Well, at least now we know for sure who is behind this."

Lexi piped up, "We still need to figure out what the key—the 'Aeternitas Clavis' is."

"Father, I think it is time to show me those hidden hallways."

Lord Winston stood up and walked over to the ornate fireplace, with its grandeur statues of greyhounds on either side.

Lexi excitedly said, "This feels like I am in a Dan Brown movie."

Lord Winston turned to her and asked, "Did the movie end well?"

Surprised that he had not heard of Dan Brown, Lexi answered, "His books were amazing. I guess that they did end well, but not as one would think."

Lord Winston twisted the nose of one of the dogs and then walked over to a book on a shelf and lifted it up. Under the book was a button that he pushed. Then he walked over to a panel on the opposite wall and lightly touched it.

The panel opened to reveal a narrow staircase that descended.

Lord Winston disappeared down the stone steps. Redington and Lexi followed quickly behind him.

Moments later the sound of the panel moving back into place could be heard.

"Now that was cool," Lexi said as she followed Redington down the staircase.

Redington found the staircase to be a bit of a tight squeeze for his size and was happy to step off the last step into a large chamber. *How did I not know about this room as a child?*

Redington kept following his father through corridors and could see that there were other rooms filled with artifacts and precious art.

The chamber they stood in was lined with shelves that held scrolls, books bound in leather, and peculiar gadgets that seemed centuries ahead of their time. The air was thick with the must of ancient knowledge.

"Father, what is all this stuff?"

Lord Winston turned and walked through one of the doorways. After Redington and Lexi were in the room, he answered his son's question. "Many of these items have been passed down from generation to generation. To be honest, I am not sure what everything down here is like."

Lexi dusted off an old wood crate to read the words on it. "You have got to be kidding me."

Redington came over, "What did you find?"

Lexi brushed away the remaining dust, revealing the inscription more clearly. Her voice trembled slightly as she read aloud, "Aeternitas Clavis—1795."

Redington's eyes widened in disbelief. "That's... that's what Calponi is after?"

Lord Winston approached, his face drawn with concern. He inspected the crate more closely. "It seems this old legend within our family was more than just a bedtime story. This key," he gestured to the crate, "Supposedly opens something of great power, something ancient."

"But what exactly does it unlock?" Lexi inquired, her curiosity piqued as she looked around the room filled with arcane artifacts and old manuscripts.

Winston sighed, running a hand through his hair. "Legend says it opens the 'Vault of Veritas,' a hidden repository that contains wisdom lost through the ages—truths that could shift the foundations of our understanding of history and science."

Redington looked around and found a prybar. He opened the crate.

All three looked inside.

Nothing, it was empty.

"Fantastic!" Redington yelled. Redington, trained to stay calm in the face of the unknown, found his pulse quickening. "No key to open the vault. Of course, why would it be that easy? And my guess is, Calponi believes that we have the key and know where the vault is, and whatever is in that vault can give him power."

"I believe what you are saying is true," Winston confirmed grimly. "But no matter if we have it or not, it must never fall into the wrong hands. The consequences would be disastrous."

Lord Winston moved to a large map on the wall, its edges yellowed with age. He pointed to a spot marked obscurely with ancient script. "Here lies the supposed location of the vault. It's not just the key; one must also know where to use it."

Redington looked thoughtful. "We need to secure everything here. And we need a plan. If Calponi's bold enough to directly threaten you, Father, it's only a matter of time before he makes a move."

Lord Winston nodded in agreement. "We'll increase the manor's security even more. Meanwhile, I think it's crucial we decipher more about this key and the vault. Lexi, your knowledge of historical artifacts could be invaluable here."

Lexi, still somewhat in awe of the cinematic turn their life had seemingly taken, nodded enthusiastically. "It was Susannah who knew about all this stuff, but I'll start with these texts. There has to be a reference to the 'Aeternitas Clavis' or the vault somewhere here."

The trio spent the next few hours poring over the contents of the chamber. Lord Winston and Lexi examined every item that could give them more clues about the vault, while Redington coordinated with his contacts to ensure their safety and gather more information about Calponi's movements.

As evening turned into night, they had mapped out a rough plan. The 'Aeternitas Clavis' would stay hidden in the manor under guard while they worked to unlock its secrets and prepare for any attempt by Calponi to seize it.

"Whatever happens, we're in this together," Redington said, his hand resting reassuringly on Lexi's shoulder. Lexi nodded, her resolve hardened by the gravity of the situation.

"Let's hope we're ready for whatever comes our way," Lord Winston added, his voice a mix of determination and concern as he looked at his son and Lexi, both ready to defend a legacy of centuries-old secrets.

Together, they returned to the upper levels of the manor, the hidden staircase closing behind them with a definitive thud, sealing away the ancient mysteries just as night enveloped the world outside.

Chapter 37

$\mathcal{R}$edington escorted Lexi to one of the many guest rooms.

The hallways were adorned with fancy woodwork and velvet wallpaper decorated in paisley designs. Lexi was in awe of all the family portraits portrayed on the walls.

As she walked by one, she thought she saw it move. Pausing, she backed up. Looking closer, she noticed an emblem similar to the one on the crate. "Redington, what is this painting of?"

Redington turned back to see what she was referring to and quickly came up to where Lexi was standing. The painting she was intrigued by depicted an elaborate scene of a grand ceremony, with several figures dressed in ornate robes gathered around a large, intricately carved chest. The chest bore the same emblem that was on the crate—a complex array of interlocking circles and arcane symbols.

Redington studied the painting, a hint of surprise in his expression. "This is an old family portrait, but not in the traditional sense. It represents the founding members of the Wrightenton lineage participating in the sealing of the 'Vault of Veritas.' The chest in the painting is symbolic of the vault. This emblem," he pointed to the similar design on the crate and in the painting, "Represents the key's guardianship passed through generations."

Lexi's eyes widened with realization. "So, the 'Aeternitas Clavis' is not just a key to a physical location but also a legacy of your family's role as protectors of whatever knowledge the vault holds?"

"Exactly," Redington confirmed. "And each generation has the duty to protect and, if necessary, to seal the vault anew. It seems it's my turn, potentially yours, to ensure its safety now."

Lexi's mind raced with the implications of her involvement as they continued walking through the hallway. They arrived at the guest room. Redington opened the door for her, gesturing inside. The room was tastefully decorated with antique furniture that complemented the ornate styling of the manor.

"This will be your room," Redington said, "I hope you find it comfortable."

Lexi stepped inside, her gaze immediately drawn to a small writing desk by the window overlooking the manor's expansive grounds. "It's beautiful, thank you," she replied, still processing everything she had learned.

Redington lingered at the door, seemingly hesitant. "Lexi, I... If you have any questions or need anything, my room is just down the hall."

She nodded, appreciating his concern. "Thank you, Redington. I might take you up on that, especially with everything happening."

He gave a small smile, then added, "We'll start early tomorrow. Try to get some rest tonight."

As Redington closed the door behind him, Lexi's gaze fell back to the emblem in the painting. Her mind was full of questions about the 'Vault of Veritas,' the key, and what secrets it might hold. She felt a deep sense of purpose intertwined with the danger of guarding such profound knowledge. The weight of history was palpable, and as she unpacked her things, she felt an ancestral pull toward the mysteries she was about to explore.

Settling into the room, Lexi decided to spend the evening reviewing her notes and the photos she had taken of the artifacts in the underground chamber. She was determined to uncover anything that might help them understand more about the vault and prepare for whatever challenges lay ahead with Calponi. Her last thoughts before sleep were of the painting and the emblem, a symbol now laden with meaning, a beacon guiding her into the depths of the Wrightenton legacy.

Chapter 38

As the clock chimed midnight, the gentle breeze fluttered through the guest room curtains where Lexi had settled for the night. Her mind, a whirlwind of ancient secrets and cryptic legacies, found no rest as she tossed and turned. The 'Vault of Veritas' and its mysteries loomed large in her thoughts, a puzzle begging for resolution. As sleep finally claimed her, her restless mind conjured a vivid dreamscape, a corridor lined with the echoes of the past.

In the quiet stillness of the night, a translucent figure materialized at the foot of her bed. The ghost, a dignified man clad in the garb of the late Victorian era, regarded Lexi with a somber, penetrating gaze. His presence, while unexpected, exuded a calming warmth.

"Good evening, Miss Alexandra," he began, his voice a distant echo that filled the room. "I am Edmund Wrightenton, your companion's ancestor. I've come to provide enlightenment amidst your quest for the 'Aeternitas Clavis.'"

Lexi, finding herself surprisingly composed in the presence of the apparition, nodded for him to continue.

"Long ago, our family was entrusted with a profound responsibility," Edmund continued, pacing slowly by the window. "The 'Vault of Veritas' is not merely a repository of arcane knowledge but a safeguard against chaos. Within its depths lies an artifact known as the 'Cosmos Dial' —a device capable of altering the very fabric of reality by manipulating cosmic energies."

Lexi's eyes widened in awe and disbelief. "Altering reality? How is that even possible?"

Edmund paused, his eyes reflecting the moonlight. "The Cosmos Dial was created in an age long forgotten, intended to balance the fundamental forces of nature. However, in the wrong hands, it could cause catastrophic disruptions. The 'Aeternitas Clavis' you seek is the only key to the vault where the Dial is kept, sealed by my forefathers to prevent misuse."

"Why tell me this?" Lexi asked, her curiosity piqued.

"Because, Miss Alexandra, the path to safeguarding the Dial must now be undertaken by new guardians. And I believe you, alongside my descendants, are destined for this task. You possess the unique courage and wisdom necessary to navigate the challenges ahead."

Edmund moved closer, his form becoming more ethereal. "But heed this warning—the key not only opens doors to great power but also to great peril. Calponi's intentions are dark, and he must not reach the Dial."

Lexi processed his words, her resolve strengthening. "How can we find the key and protect the Dial?"

"The answers lie within the history of our family. Look at the origins of the Wrightenton lineage. There, you will find the clues you need to locate the 'Aeternitas Clavis.' Remember, everything required to understand the key's location has been preserved for generations through symbols, lore, and artifacts contained within these walls."

As dawn's first light began seeping into the room, Edmund's form faded. "Be vigilant, Alexandra. The burden of centuries now falls to you and Redington. Protect the vault, and trust in the legacy of those who have guarded it before you."

With those final words, Edmund Wrightenton vanished as quietly as he had appeared, leaving Lexi in the soft glow of morning. She sat up, energized and determined, her mission clear. The ghost's visit had not only given her a deeper understanding of the 'Aeternitas Clavis' but also a renewed purpose to protect the profound secrets it unlocked.

As she closed her eyes to get a few hours of sleep before her busy day, Lexi knew the first step of her journey with Redington would be to delve into the Wrightenton family archives—searching for any reference to the Cosmos Dial and the mysterious origins of their guardianship. The quest for the 'Vault of Veritas' was not just about protecting an ancient artifact anymore; it was about preserving the balance of reality itself.

Chapter 39

As Lexi fell asleep, she dreamed that the wind was howling through the ruins of an ancient temple. Redington, Lexi, and the Secret Service men trod carefully over moss-covered stones. Their flashlights cast long shadows against the crumbling walls, etched with forgotten symbols that whispered of old powers.

"We're close," murmured Redington, his voice barely audible over the gusting wind. "The manuscript mentioned a hidden chamber beneath the statue of Thoth."

Lexi nodded, her eyes scanning the dark corners of the temple. "This place feels... alive as if it's watching us."

As they approached the massive statue, Amira, the team's historian, brushed her hand against the hieroglyphs. "These markings are not just decorative," she explained. "They tell a story—a prophecy perhaps, about the Aeternitas Clavis."

The team gathered around as Amira pointed to a series of intricate symbols that depicted the heavens aligning with the earth. "According to legend, the Clavis holds the power to unlock not just physical barriers but the very fabric of reality," she said, her voice tinged with awe.

The group's attention turned to a small, almost imperceptible seam at the base of the statue. Working together, they pushed against the cold stone. It moved slowly, grinding against the ancient floor, until it revealed a narrow staircase spiraling downward into darkness.

"With every step, we tread deeper into history itself," Redington said, leading the way down. The air grew cooler as they descended, the narrow beam of their lights bouncing off damp walls.

At the bottom of the stairs, they entered a small chamber. The air was thick with the scent of earth and age. In the center of the room, encased in a crystal sarcophagus, lay a gleaming object—the Aeternitas Clavis. It was more magnificent than they had imagined, crafted from an unknown metal that shimmered with an ethereal light.

Amira approached cautiously, her hands trembling slightly. "It's said that the Clavis was created during a celestial convergence," she whispered, her eyes fixed on the artifact. "It was a time of great peril and greater hope. This artifact was crafted as a bridge between worlds, a balance between shadow and light."

The chamber seemed to resonate as she spoke, a low hum vibrating through the stone. The Clavis began to glow softly, responding to her words.

Lexi wondered aloud, "Could it be responding to our presence?"

Redington stepped closer, his expression solemn. "Or perhaps it recognizes the lineage of those destined to uncover it. There's more to this story, and I believe it's intertwined with our own pasts."

The team stood in silence, each lost in thought, feeling the weight of history around them. This was not just a search for an ancient artifact; it was a quest that might unravel the very secrets of their souls.

"Let's document everything," Redington decided, breaking the silence. "This discovery could change the world, but we must understand its power and purpose."

As they prepared their equipment, the Clavis continued to glow, casting a light that seemed to pulse with the heartbeat of the earth itself. In this hidden chamber, beneath the weight of centuries, they were not just explorers but witnesses to the unfolding mysteries of the universe.

Chapter 40

In the dim light of the ancient chamber, the team set up their equipment with methodical precision, each movement echoing off the stone walls. Redington watched Amira carefully catalog the hieroglyphs surrounding the sarcophagus. Her brow furrowed in concentration.

"The symbols here," Amira paused, tracing her fingers gently over the carvings, "They speak of guardianship and duty. It's as if the Clavis isn't just an artifact but a sentinel watching over some greater power."

Redington nodded, his mind racing with possibilities. "Does this align with the legends of the Clavis serving as a key to other realms? Perhaps it's not just about bridging physical spaces but guarding against disruptions in the cosmic balance."

Lexi, still absorbed by the aura of the artifact, listened in awe.

Amira answered, "These texts might be referencing a cycle of cosmic events. It looks like the Clavis is central to resetting or maintaining that cycle."

As the implications of their findings began to settle, a sense of urgency swept through the chamber. If the Clavis was indeed capable of influencing cosmic events, the consequences of its misuse could be catastrophic.

The low hum from the artifact grew louder, vibrating through the chamber like a warning.

Redington crouched beside the crystal sarcophagus. His eyes locked on the shimmering Clavis. "We need to understand how to interact with this safely. It's not just about unlocking it; it's about ensuring it doesn't unlock something we can't handle."

Lexi stepped closer, her camera capturing every detail of the artifact. "There must be a protocol or ritual described here. These ancients wouldn't have left such power unguarded without strict controls."

Their work was interrupted by a sudden draft of cold air sweeping through the chamber. The walls seemed to shudder, and the glow from the Clavis intensified.

Amira grabbed her notebook, flipping through pages of notes and sketches. "According to the legend, only those of pure intent can harness the

Clavis's true power. It tests the hearts of those who seek it."

Redington felt a chill run down his spine. Pure intent was a subjective measure, and each of them carried burdens and secrets that might influence their connection to the Clavis.

"Let's set up a perimeter and continue documenting everything," he suggested, his voice steady but tense. "We can't afford any mistakes. Not here, not with so much at stake."

As the night deepened outside, the team worked in shifts, monitoring the Clavis and discussing their next steps. During her watch, Lexi noticed a series of smaller symbols at the base of the sarcophagus that hadn't been recorded yet. They were subtler, almost hidden, but unmistakably deliberate.

"These could be the instructions or warnings we're looking for," she murmured, adjusting her light to get a better view.

The chamber held its breath. The only sounds are the scratching of Lexi's pen and the soft hum of the Clavis. They were on the brink of a discovery that could redefine their understanding of history and the universe.

As dawn approached, the first rays of light filtered through an opening high in the chamber wall, illuminating the Clavis in a halo of golden light. It was a new day, but for Redington and his team, it was more than that—it was the beginning of a new era in their quest, filled with as much promise as peril.

Chapter 41

As morning light spilled into the ancient chamber, casting long shadows and illuminating the dust motes in the air, Redington gathered the team for a crucial discussion. He stood before the sarcophagus, the Clavis still radiating a soft, pulsing light.

Redington began, "Based on everything we've uncovered and documented, it's clear that we're dealing with a power that could be transformative or destructive, depending on how it's used," his eyes moving from Lexi to Amira. "We need to decide our next steps very carefully."

Lexi, still poring over the newly discovered symbols, looked up. "There's mention here of a 'Guardian's Oath.' It suggests that those who seek to control the Clavis must first prove their worthiness through some form of trial or test."

Amira leaned in closer, her interest piqued. "That aligns with many ancient traditions. The trial likely involves demonstrating purity of purpose and the ability to resist personal gain."

Redington considered this. "If there's a trial, it might explain the safeguard mechanisms we've encountered. This isn't just about protecting the artifact from theft; it's about ensuring that it's used responsibly."

The team agreed to spend the rest of the day preparing for whatever the trial might involve. They set up a base camp inside the chamber, arranging their supplies and equipment to support a prolonged stay if necessary. Lexi and Amira worked on translating more of the inscriptions, hoping to find clues about the nature of the trial.

As evening approached, the chamber's atmosphere grew tense. Redington reviewed the security measures they had in place, ensuring they were alone in their discovery for now.

Finally, as they settled around the sarcophagus for a makeshift dinner, Amira cleared her throat. "I think I've found something about the trial. It's not just a test of spirit, but also of knowledge and understanding of the cosmic laws."

Lexi nodded, her gaze fixed on the Clavis. "It makes sense. This isn't just a key to physical doors but to realms of understanding and consciousness."

The discussion turned to the implications of their discovery. They speculated on the kinds of challenges they might face, from deciphering complex puzzles to confronting personal fears or illusions.

Later that night, as they took turns keeping watch, Lexi felt a strange energy emanating from the Clavis. It was as if the artifact was communicating with her, responding to her presence. She recorded her observations, her hands trembling slightly with the magnitude of what they might be about to unleash.

In the darkest hours, just before dawn, Amira, who was on watch, whispered into her recorder, "The Clavis is more than an object; it's a custodian of balance. Whoever wields it holds the power to alter not just history, but the very fabric of reality."

As the first light of dawn broke over the horizon, the team gathered once more. They were no longer just archaeologists, secret service men, and historians; they were guardians of a profound secret, standing on the threshold of a new understanding.

"We are ready," Redington declared, his voice resolute. "Today, we face the trial. We prove our worthiness to the Clavis and ourselves."

With a collective breath, the team prepared to step into the unknown, their hearts and minds open to whatever challenges awaited. They were ready to cross the threshold, test their mettle against the ancient trials, and prove they were worthy of the Clavis's secrets.

Chapter 42

As the dawn light washed over the ancient chamber, Redington and his team prepared for the trial they believed would determine their worthiness to wield the Aeternitas Clavis. The chamber felt charged, the air thick with anticipation and the silent weight of history.

Redington assembled the team around the sarcophagus. "This is more than just a test of our resolve," he explained. "It's a measure of our understanding, our integrity, and our intentions. Everything we've learned and experienced leads to this point."

Lexi, her nerves taut with the gravity of the moment, adjusted her equipment. "I've set up cameras to record everything. Whatever happens, we'll have a record."

Amira, her notes and translations at hand, nodded. "The inscriptions suggest that the trial will challenge us individually, based on our deepest fears and desires. It's designed to reveal the truth of our souls."

The first to step forward was Amira. Approaching the Clavis, she paused, taking a deep breath before placing her hand lightly upon the crystal sarcophagus. The chamber hummed softly, and a light enveloped her, casting her shadow large and stark against the ancient walls.

Amira's voice trembled as she spoke her oath. "I seek to understand, not to conquer. I come with respect, not greed." The light around her brightened, then dimmed, and she stepped back, visibly shaken but unharmed.

Next was Lexi. As she approached, the Clavis pulsed like a heartbeat under her touch. "I seek to protect, to preserve," she declared. "I hold no ill will, no desire for power." The response was immediate; a soft glow bathed her in warmth, and the chamber echoed with a sound like distant bells, signaling her success.

Redington went last. His face was stern, his resolve clear in his eyes as he laid his hands on the Clavis. "I am here to guard, to ensure balance," he intoned. The air around him grew tense, and for a moment, the outcome seemed uncertain. Then, suddenly, the tension broke like a storm clearing, and calm settled over the room.

The team exhaled in unison, and the immediate danger passed. They looked at one another, their faces reflecting a mix of relief and newfound respect. The trials had not just tested them; they had revealed the strength of their bonds and the purity of their goals.

"Now," Redington said, gathering his team, "We understand what it means to be guardians. The Clavis is not just an artifact; it's a responsibility."

As they prepared to leave the chamber, Lexi paused, looking back at the glowing Clavis. "This is just the beginning, isn't it?" she mused. "The real work starts now."

Redington agreed, "Yes, the world must never know the full power of the Clavis. It's our duty to protect it."

With a final look at the ancient device, they sealed the chamber, hiding it once again from the world. As they made their way back through the winding paths of the temple ruins, each member of the team felt the weight of their new roles as guardians of a secret that must be kept, a power that must be shielded from those who would misuse it.

Chapter 43

After sealing the ancient chamber, Redington and his team made their way back through the dense undergrowth that shrouded the temple ruins. The air was thick with the scent of earth and ancient stone, and the quiet was punctuated only by the distant calls of desert birds.

Each member of the team was introspective, lost in their own thoughts about the trials they had just undergone and the responsibilities they had assumed. Lexi broke the silence as they trudged along, her voice low and contemplative.

"The Clavis isn't just an artifact, is it? It's a test—a test of character and intent," she mused.

Amira nodded, her expression serious. "Yes, and it's shown us that it's far more than just a physical key. It's a gateway and a guardian, a filter through which only the worthy can pass."

Redington, leading the group through a particularly dense thicket, paused and turned back to face his companions. "We've all passed its tests, but the real challenge lies ahead. Protecting the Clavis is now our life's work. We must ensure it never falls into the wrong hands."

The path began to slope upward as they neared the edge of the jungle, the light filtering through the canopy becoming brighter.

As they reached a treed area, they stopped to rest, drinking from their water bottles and wiping the sweat from their brows. The clearing provided a momentary respite from the desert's heat and a chance to discuss their next steps.

"We need to set up a plan," Redington said, scanning the horizon. "A protocol for safeguarding the Clavis. It's not just about keeping it hidden; it's about making sure it's protected, even from us."

Lexi took out her notebook, ready to jot down any ideas. "We should consider forming a trust, a group dedicated solely to the protection of the Clavis. Members could be sworn in under trials similar to those we faced to ensure their purity of intention."

Amira, always the historian, added, "We might also draw from ancient societies that guarded their sacred knowledge. There are precedents in the Knights Templar, the Masons, even the ancient Egyptian priests."

The conversation grew more animated as they discussed various historical models of guardianship and protection. They debated the merits and pitfalls of each, considering how best to adapt these ancient methods to their modern needs.

As the discussion subsided, Redington looked each of his team members in the eye. "This is our life now. We are the keepers of a secret that could change the world for better or worse. It's a heavy burden, but I believe we're up to the task."

Nodding in agreement, they packed up and continued their journey out of the desert. The path led them to an overlook, where they paused to take in the view of the valley below. The sun was setting, casting a golden glow over the landscape.

"It's beautiful," Lexi whispered, almost to herself.

"Yes," Redington agreed, "And worth protecting. Not just the Clavis, but all of this." He gestured to the expanse of sand stretching out before them.

A sense of solemnity and purpose settled over the group as they stood there. They were united, not just by their adventure, but by a shared commitment to a cause greater than themselves.

The journey back to civilization was quiet, each person wrapped in their own thoughts about the future. They knew the road ahead would be long and fraught with challenges, but they were ready. For they were the guardians of the Aeternitas Clavis, and they would do whatever it took to protect it.

Chapter 44

As the team descended from the dune, the fading light cast long shadows on the sandy terrain ahead, mirroring the weight of their newfound duties. Each step they took was measured, heavy with the responsibility they had accepted as guardians of the Aeternitas Clavis. They walked in silence. Each person lost in contemplation of the future and the role they were to play in it.

"We should start by securing the Clavis temporarily," Redington finally said, breaking the silence. "Somewhere remote, yet accessible to us, and absolutely secure."

Amira nodded, pulling out a map. "I've been thinking about that. There are a few locations that might be suitable. Remote islands, underground bunkers, and even private estates with high security. We need a place off the grid, but also somewhere we can fortify against any possible threats."

Lexi chimed in, her voice determined. "And we need to set up a communication protocol among us. Something encrypted, secure. If any one of us is compromised, the rest need to know immediately."

The conversation turned tactical as they discussed various security measures that could be employed to protect the Clavis, from biometric locks to AI surveillance. They debated the merits of visibility versus obscurity, whether hiding the Clavis in plain sight or burying it away from the world was safer.

As they approached the edge of the desert, the air grew cooler, and the night began to envelop them. The stars appeared one by one, casting a celestial map above their heads. It was under this starlit dome that they pledged an oath to each other and to their cause.

"We are the shield against the darkness," Redington intoned solemnly, his hand resting on the map that lay spread out on a makeshift table they had set up with their backpacks. "From this moment forward, we act not just as individuals but as extensions of the Clavis's will—guardians of balance and protectors of the threshold."

Each member placed their hand on the map over the location they had agreed would be their temporary base. The air seemed to pulse with the energy of their commitment, a silent witness to the oath they had taken.

With the location set and their plan in motion, they made their way back to civilization. The return journey was a mix of silent reflection and strategic planning as they prepared to transition into their roles as the Clavis's guardians.

Upon their return, they set about implementing their plans. The Clavis was moved to its new, undisclosed location—a fortress of solitude and security. They established a rotating schedule for guarding the artifact, each taking turns to watch over it, ensuring it remained undisturbed.

Meanwhile, the outside world continued, unaware of the profound secret beneath its surface. The team kept up appearances, maintaining their day jobs and daily routines, but beneath the normalcy, they were ever vigilant, always watching, always ready.

Chapter 45

The first light of dawn streamed softly through the gauzy curtains as Lexi awoke, her mind still echoing with the dream of discovering the powers of the Clavis and the spectral visit from the night before. The ghostly figure of Edmund Wrightenton had imparted a grave responsibility upon her, one that intertwined deeply with the enigmatic 'Aeternitas Clavis' and the cosmic balance it guarded. Filled with a new sense of purpose, Lexi quickly dressed and made her way downstairs, driven by an urgent need to share her nocturnal encounter.

In the dining area, Redington and Lord Winston were already up, partaking in a quiet morning ritual of strong tea and contemplation. The clink of china and the soft murmur of their conversation paused as Lexi entered the room, her eyes bright with the intensity of her revelations.

"Good morning," she greeted briskly, her usual pleasantries shortened by her excitement.

Redington looked up, noticing immediately the unusual sparkle in her eye. "Morning, Lexi. You look like you've discovered something incredible."

Lord Winston also turned his attention to Lexi, his expression mixing curiosity with concern. "Indeed, you seem rather... invigorated this morning."

Without needing further encouragement, Lexi launched into her story. "I was visited by a ghost last night—Edmund Wrightenton, an ancestor in your family line," she began, her words tumbling out with eagerness. Both men sat up straighter, their skepticism suspended by the earnestness in her voice.

"He told me about the 'Vault of Veritas' and something called the 'Cosmos Dial'—an artifact that can alter reality itself. It's been hidden away because, in the wrong hands, it could cause catastrophic disruptions." Lexi paused, gauging their reaction to the fantastical elements of her account.

Redington exchanged a look with his father, a silent communication passing between them that hinted at a shared knowledge of family legends perhaps not entirely believed until now.

"The 'Aeternitas Clavis' is the key to this vault, and according to Edmund, your family has been its guardians for generations. He warned that Calponi must never find the Dial," Lexi continued, her recounting becoming more animated as she relayed the spectral warnings.

Lord Winston leaned back in his chair, stroking his chin thoughtfully. "The Cosmos Dial... Yes, I've heard whispers of it in the old family tales. It was said to be too powerful for any one person to wield. I had thought it a mere allegory."

Redington, ever the pragmatist, furrowed his brow. "A ghost, you say? It's hard to accept, but given everything we've encountered so far, I'm inclined to believe you. We need to find this key and secure the vault before Calponi even gets close."

Lexi nodded, pleased at their acceptance. "Edmund's message was clear. We should start by searching the family archives. He suggested that everything we need to understand the key's location has been preserved through symbols and artifacts here in the manor."

"Then we'll begin immediately after breakfast," Lord Winston declared, standing with a newfound vigor. "This is now more than a matter of family duty; it's a matter of global safety."

The rest of the morning was spent in the manor's vast library, where dust-laden tomes and ancient manuscripts were carefully examined. Redington, Lexi, and Lord Winston worked together, piecing together clues from cryptic marginalia and faded maps that hinted at the historical significance of their quest.

As they delved deeper into the Wrightenton family's past, the trio became increasingly aware of the gravity of their task. The 'Cosmos Dial', once a stuff of legend, was now a tangible objective that not only connected them to their ancestry but also to a looming confrontation with forces that sought to destabilize the world.

The chapter of their lives that unfolded that day was marked by a blend of historical detective work and strategic planning as they prepared to protect a legacy of cosmic proportions. Lexi felt a profound connection to the Wrightenton lineage, her role in the events not just coincidental but seemingly destined. As the shadows grew longer and the day wore on, their collective resolve hardened; they would stand guardian over the secrets of the 'Vault of Veritas', come what may.

Chapter 46

The morning sun cast long shadows across the vast library of Wrightenton Manor, where Lexi, Redington, and Lord Winston had been pouring over the ancient texts and artifacts since dawn. The air was thick with dust and the scent of old leather, a testament to the generations of Wrightentons who had presided over these archives. Each book they thumbed through and each scroll they unraveled seemed to whisper secrets of a bygone era.

Redington, methodical in his approach, meticulously examined a faded map of the estate that had been tucked away in a forgotten drawer. The map detailed not only the manor and its immediate surroundings but also several cryptic symbols that had been carelessly marked in what appeared to be a hasty afterthought. His finger traced the path from the manor to a secluded area marked with the same emblem found on the crate containing the 'Aeternitas Clavis.'

"Look at this," Redington called out, beckoning Lexi and his father over. "These symbols might be what we're looking for. If we can decipher them, they could lead us directly to the Vault."

Lord Winston leaned over the map, his eyes narrowing under the furrow of his thick brows. "These markings... they correspond to the old boundary stones on the estate. I always wondered why grandfather was so insistent on keeping those stones intact and in their original locations."

Lexi, eager and attentive, suggested, "Maybe each stone marks a part of a larger puzzle. If we visit each site, we might find physical clues or further inscriptions that help us unlock the location of the Vault."

With a plan in mind, the trio equipped themselves with the necessary tools: notebooks, cameras, and a compass. They set out into the crisp morning air, the estate sprawling before them, a land brimming with hidden secrets.

From horseback, their first stop was the nearest boundary stone, located in the old apple orchard that had once thrived with life but now stood solemn and slightly overgrown. As they approached, Lexi noticed the base of the stone was inscribed with a series of runes similar to those in Edmund Wrightenton's portrait.

Redington took several photographs while Lexi sketched the runes in her notebook. Lord Winston, meanwhile, recounted tales of his youth spent playing among these trees, unaware of the significance these stones held.

The day passed with the team uncovering similar runes on three other stones, each a considerable distance from the last, forming what seemed to be a giant circle around the estate. By the time they returned to the manor, the sun was setting, casting a golden glow over the land.

Back in the library, Lexi laid out her sketches next to the map, connecting the locations of the stones with lines that intersected right at the heart of the estate—the very place where the old Wrightenton family crypt was located.

"It looks like the intersection is pointing us to the crypt," Lexi pointed out, her finger at the center of the x marks. "Could the Vault of Veritas be underneath the crypt?"

Redington looked at Lord Winston, who had grown pale. "The crypt has always been a place of mourning, not mystery. But if that's where our journey leads, then so be it."

The next morning, armed with torches and tools, they opened the heavy doors of the crypt. The air inside was cool and musty, filled with the silence of decades. The crypt was large, housing the remains of generations of Wrightentons, but it was the floor that now interested them most. Carefully, they moved aside the old carpets that had been laid down out of respect, revealing an intricate mosaic floor underneath.

Redington cleared away the dust, uncovering a large emblem in the center of the mosaic—a perfect match to the emblem on the crate and the painting. In the very center of the emblem was a small, circular indentation—it looked just the right size to fit the 'Aeternitas Clavis.'

"This is it," Redington said, his voice echoing slightly in the stone chamber. "We need the key."

"But I thought the key was metaphoric," Lexi questioned.

The trio stood in the crypt, the weight of their discovery pressing upon them. They had found the entrance to the Vault of Veritas. Now, they needed a real key to unlock it and reveal the secrets of the Cosmos Dial. The journey ahead seemed clear, but the path to now finding a real key was fraught with danger. Calponi and his men would be arriving any moment, and they had to be quick.

Lexi turned to Redington, determination in her gaze. "Let's find that key and protect whatever lies within the Vault. We're the guardians now, and we can't let it fall into the wrong hands."

Together, they sealed the crypt and returned to the manor to plan their next move. The race was on, and they knew it was only a matter of time before they would have to defend their legacy and the world from the chaos that would ensue if the Vault were ever opened improperly. The echoes from the past had led them here, and now it was up to them to secure the future.

Chapter 47

The night was unusually still at Wrightenton
Manor. Redington, Lexi, and Lord Winston were
gathered around an old oak table strewn with
maps, ancient texts, and various artifacts,
plotting their next move. The urgency was
palpable. They knew that finding the 'Aeternitas
Clavis' was only the first step. Now, they needed
to secure the actual key to the vault.

As they strategized, the faint crackle of the
gravel driveway alerted them to unexpected
visitors. Redington peered out of the window
and spotted a sleek black vehicle making its way
toward the main entrance—Calponi's men had
arrived.

"I don't know how they got past the security,
but we need to move now," Redington
whispered, turning to Lexi and his father.
"They're here for the key."

Lord Winston's face hardened with resolve. "To the crypt. There's a secret passage in there. We can hide the maps and anything else important along the way."

The trio quickly gathered the essential items, concealing them in false bottoms and secret compartments scattered throughout the manor. With the artifacts secured, they hurried toward the crypt, the chill of the night air biting at their heels.

Inside the crypt, Lord Winston removed a brick from the wall to reveal a narrow, dark passageway. "This tunnel will take us to the old boathouse by the lake. We can lay low there."

As they navigated the cramped passage, the distant sounds of doors being forced open and shouts filled the air—Calponi's men were not wasting any time. Emerging by the boathouse, Redington looked back at the looming silhouette of the manor. Concern etched deeply on his face.

~

Meanwhile, Marco Calponi paced the grand hallway of Wrightenton Manor, frustration brewing. His men had turned the place upside down but found nothing. "Keep looking! It has to be here," he barked, his voice echoing ominously against the ancient stone walls.

~

Back at the boathouse, Lexi pulled out the map they had managed to save and spread it on an old wooden rowboat that had been stored upside down. Her finger traced the path they had marked as likely hiding spots for the key based on Edmund Wrightenton's hints.

"It has to be in the old mill," she concluded, pointing to a structure depicted on the map near a dormant waterway, not far from their current location. "The symbols align with Edmund's description, and it's one of the few places not explicitly searched yet."

Lord Winston nodded in agreement. "Then we need to be swift. Calponi will realize soon enough and turn his attention there."

Redington prepared a few makeshift weapons from the boathouse tools. "We'll go in under the cover of night. Stay quiet, and stay alert."

Under the cloak of darkness, they made their way to the old mill. The building was decrepit. Its once sturdy walls now succumbed to the ravages of time. Inside, the air was musty, filled with the scent of old wood and mold. Lexi's flashlight beam danced across the walls, finally resting on a large, rusted flour grinder.

"There," whispered Lord Winston, pointing to the base of the grinder where another emblem matching the one from the crypt was crudely etched into the stone floor. Redington and Lexi carefully moved the heavy machinery, revealing a small iron chest beneath.

Just as Redington reached for the chest, the sound of footsteps alerted them to incoming danger. Calponi's men had not been far behind.

"Take the chest and run!" Redington hissed as he and Lord Winston prepared to hold off the intruders.

Lexi, with the chest, clutched tightly, slipped out through a back window just as the mill door burst open. Calponi's men poured in, and the air was immediately filled with shouts and the clatter of a struggle.

Breathing heavily, Lexi made her way back toward the lake, the weight of the chest bearing down on her both physically and metaphorically. Every step was a mix of dread and hope—dread for her friends battling Calponi's thugs and hope that this chest contained the key to ending it all.

Reaching the boathouse, she set the chest down with a thud, her hands trembling as she prepared to open it. Inside, nestled within a velvet lining, was an intricate key, its handle fashioned like the emblem they had come to know so well.

As she held the key in her hands, Lexi knew the real battle was just beginning. The key to the 'Vault of Veritas' and the power to control reality itself was now within their grasp. But first, she needed to get back to Redington and Lord Winston, hoping against all odds that they were still all right. The night was far from over, and Calponi was not the type to give up easily. The key in her hand was not just a tool but a symbol of hope—a hope that they could still prevent disaster.

Chapter 48

Heart pounding in her chest, Lexi clutched the iron key tightly as she made her way back to the old mill. The night was oppressively silent now, the earlier chaos having settled into a menacing quiet. With every step, Lexi rehearsed her plan, going over each detail meticulously. The key felt heavier with each movement—a constant reminder of the burden she now carried.

Approaching the mill, she stayed in the shadows, using the cover of the thick bushes that lined the path. As she neared, the sight that unfolded before her was chilling. The manor's new guards—those specifically brought in to bolster security—were not just subdued but actively coordinating with Marco Calponi's men. Her heart sank; the guards were traitors.

Lexi watched from her hidden vantage point as Calponi barked orders, his men dragging a beaten but resolute Lord Winston toward a waiting vehicle. Redington was nowhere to be seen, and Lexi's worry for him knotted her stomach. She needed to act, but direct confrontation was suicide.

Mind racing, Lexi retreated silently to the crypt. The weight of the ancient key in her hand was now a symbol of lone hope. She knew what she had to do as she navigated through the woods. The moonlit path seemed to whisper caution, and each step was a silent prayer for safety.

Reaching the crypt, Lexi paused at the entrance, taking a deep breath to steady her nerves. Inside, the air was cool and still, untouched by the night's turmoil. She walked up to the mosaic floor, where the emblem awaited the return of its key. With trembling hands, Lexi inserted the key into the indentation at the center of the emblem. It fit perfectly, clicking into place with a sound that echoed ominously through the silent crypt.

The ground beneath her began to vibrate lightly at first, then more insistently. Lexi stepped back as the floor beneath the emblem started to shift, watching as a section of the mosaic floor slid away, revealing a narrow staircase spiraling down into darkness.

Lexi hesitated only for a moment before descending. The stairs led to a small, dome-shaped chamber, the walls lined with intricate carvings that glowed faintly in the dim light. In the center of the chamber stood a pedestal, upon which sat the 'Cosmos Dial,' just as Edmund Wrightenton had described. It was smaller than she had imagined, no larger than a dinner plate, but its presence was immense. Lexi could almost feel the power emanating from the artifact, a silent hum that resonated with the chamber's carvings.

She didn't have long to marvel at it—she needed to secure the Dial before Calponi realized what was happening. Lexi carefully wrapped the Cosmos Dial in a cloth she had brought and tucked it into her bag. Securing the chamber once more, she retracted the key, which automatically sealed the entrance as she ascended the stairs.

Back outside, Lexi hid the key in a crevice within the crypt, covering it with loose stone and debris. If anything happened to her, the key would be out of Calponi's reach. With the Cosmos Dial secured, she needed to find Redington and rescue Lord Winston.

Silently, Lexi made her way toward the manor, using the night's cover to avoid Calponi's men. Her mind raced with plans and contingencies, each more desperate than the last. She needed a distraction, a way to disorient Calponi's forces long enough to attempt a rescue.

As she approached, she noticed the guards' distracted focus, likely not expecting further trouble from inside the estate. Lexi found an old garden shed and quickly gathered several dry leaves and twigs, setting them alight with a small lighter that she found. She threw the makeshift firebrand toward a parked vehicle, not enough to cause harm but sufficient to cause alarm.

As predicted, the fire caught the guards' attention, and they scrambled toward the smoke, shouting and drawing Calponi's men with them. Using their momentary confusion, Lexi slipped into the house, her heart set on finding her friends and ending this night of treachery.

Each step was laden with risk, but Lexi moved with a ghost's silence, the Cosmos Dial's secure presence in her bag lending her a strange confidence. Tonight, the balance of power would shift, and she was the fulcrum.

Chapter 49

$\mathscr{L}$exi moved swiftly and silently through the shadowy corridors of Wrightenton Manor, her senses heightened and alert to any sign of Calponi's men. The chaos outside had bought her precious minutes, and she needed to use them wisely. Just as she rounded a corner near the grand staircase, she felt a sudden chill—a sensation she was beginning to recognize.

"Miss Alexandra, you carry a great burden," whispered a voice, soft and ethereal. Lexi paused and looked around, her eyes settling on the translucent figure of Edmund Wrightenton appearing before her once again.

"I need your guidance, Edmund," Lexi spoke quietly, aware of the urgency of her situation. "I have the Cosmos Dial, but I must hide it where it cannot be found."

Edmund's spectral form seemed to flicker with a knowing light. "Follow me," he instructed, gliding silently down the hallway. Lexi followed, taking her steps carefully to make as little sound as possible.

They passed through the main gallery, where Edmund stopped briefly in front of a large painting of the Wrightenton estate as it had been two centuries ago. He gestured toward the painting. "Behind this, there is a space between the walls—used by the servants of old to overhear and report on the dealings of their masters."

With a push, the painting swung forward on hidden hinges, revealing a narrow gap. Lexi peeked inside to see a small platform just wide enough to hold the Cosmos Dial.

"Place it there, but we are not done yet," Edmund instructed. After Lexi secured the artifact, they continued, moving deeper into the labyrinthine passageways of the manor.

Their next stop was a small study cluttered with the detritus of many generations. Edmund floated to a bookshelf crammed with old books. "This shelf," he said as he passed his hand through a thick tome titled The Histories of Ancient Civilizations. Lexi pulled on the book, and to her surprise, it triggered a mechanism that caused the shelf to creak open, revealing a series of peepholes that looked out over various parts of the manor.

"Through these, you can watch without being seen. Useful for ensuring your safety and monitoring your foes' movements," Edmund explained, his voice echoing slightly in the cramped space.

As they moved from room to room, Edmund showed Lexi several other secrets of the manor: hidden compartments in fireplaces, false bottoms in drawers, and even a secret exit that led to the gardens through an old, overgrown arbor.

"Your ancestors were very cautious, weren't they?" Lexi remarked, impressed by the cunning constructions.

"They had many enemies," Edmund replied somberly. "And they knew the value of secrecy."

Finally, they arrived at the library—a room Lexi had become very familiar with. Edmund stopped by a large globe dating back to the exploration age. "And here, another safeguard," he said, spinning the globe until it aligned perfectly with the North Pole. A click sounded, and a compartment opened at the base, just large enough for a small object.

"This is where you should keep the key. It is well protected and always under watch," Edmund suggested, his eyes twinkling with the wisdom of ages.

Lexi knew she would come back and place the key inside the compartment once she retrieved it. She felt a momentary relief, the weight of the cosmos seemingly lighter on her shoulders.

"Thank you, Edmund. I don't know if I could navigate all this without your help," Lexi admitted, her voice heavy with fatigue and gratitude.

Edmund's form began to fade, but his mission was accomplished. "Remember, Miss Alexandra, the greatest strength lies in knowledge and caution. Trust in the legacy you now partake in. Protect the dial, and keep the balance."

With those final words, the ghost of Edmund Wrightenton vanished, leaving Lexi alone in the vast library. She looked around, surrounded by centuries of history and secrets, now the protector of a legacy far greater than she had ever imagined.

Steeling herself for the challenges ahead, Lexi left the library to check on the chaos outside, ready to use every secret passage, every hidden nook, to her advantage. The battle for the Cosmos Dial was far from over, but now she was not just fighting with strength but with the cunning and wisdom of generations of Wrightentons whispering through the walls.

Chapter 50

The night at Wrightenton Manor was fraught
with tension, the darkness pierced intermittently
by the muffled sounds of movement and
whispered commands. After securing the
Cosmos Dial and the key, Lexi used the manor's
labyrinthine passages to move undetected,
determined to find Redington and assess Lord
Winston's situation.

She emerged from a secret panel behind a
tapestry in the east wing, nearly stumbling upon
two of Calponi's men. Holding her breath, she
waited for them to move on before continuing to
the conservatory, a place she hoped to find clues
or allies. The conservatory was empty, the
moonlight casting long shadows across the cold
stone floor. Lexi noticed a slight disturbance in
the foliage—a sign that someone might have
passed through recently. Following this trail led

her to a small, hidden door masked by dense ferns.

Pushing the door open, Lexi found a narrow, spiraling staircase leading down into the darkness. At the bottom was a small, subterranean room that historically served as a safe house during turbulent times. There, she found Redington and several members of the manor staff, including the housekeeper and the gardener. They were gathered around a dimly lit table, maps, and various communications equipment spread out in front of them.

"Lexi!" Redington whispered as she entered, relief evident in his voice. "We were starting to worry. What's the situation upstairs?"

Quickly, Lexi updated them on her spectral encounter, the hiding of the Cosmos Dial, and her evasive maneuvers through the manor's secret corridors. "The Dial and the key are safe. I've stashed them where only we can access them."

Redington nodded, processing the information. "Good work. We've managed to tap into the manor's old surveillance system here. We can see most of the main corridors and entrances. Calponi's men are thorough; they're searching everywhere."

"What about Lord Winston?" Lexi asked, her concern palpable.

Redington's face hardened. "He's being held in his study. Calponi's using him as leverage and trying to force him to disclose the location of the vault. We need to act swiftly."

The group quickly devised a plan. Using the manor's surveillance system and the network of secret passages, they would create diversions and misdirect Calponi's men, allowing Redington and Lexi to sneak into the study to rescue Lord Winston.

As they set the plan into motion, Lexi felt the weight of their precarious situation. They moved silently through the passages, emerging behind a false bookshelf in the study. Inside, they found Lord Winston, bruised but resolute, seated in a chair with his hands bound.

"Father!" Redington exclaimed softly, rushing to his side.

Lord Winston smiled weakly. "I knew you'd come. This scoundrel knows nothing of loyalty or honor."

While Redington untied his father, Lexi kept watch at the door. The sounds of the manor were muffled here, but the tension in the air was palpable.

Once Lord Winston was free, they retraced their steps through the secret passages, avoiding Calponi's men who were now scattered throughout the manor, confused by the diversions created by the staff.

Safely back in the safe house, they fortified their position, ready to withstand a siege if necessary. Lord Winston, despite his ordeal, remained composed. "We will outlast them. This manor has withstood far greater threats than Calponi."

Lexi couldn't help but feel a surge of admiration for the Wrightenton spirit as they prepared for what might come next. The manor wasn't just a home; it was a fortress, and its secrets were now her armor.

With the key and the Cosmos Dial safely hidden and their unity restored, they were ready to face whatever challenges lay ahead, fortified by the knowledge that they were not just protecting a legacy but also forging a new chapter in the storied history of Wrightenton Manor.

Chapter 51

As the dawn crept over the horizon, bathing Wrightenton Manor in a soft, golden light, the tension inside the fortified safe house was palpable. Redington, Lexi, Lord Winston, and the loyal manor staff had spent the night preparing for what they hoped would be the final confrontation with Calponi and his traitorous guards.

Redington was the first to break the silence. "Our window to act is closing. Once Calponi realizes the key and the Dial are beyond his reach, he'll become desperate, perhaps even violent."

Lord Winston, who had been coordinating their defenses, nodded solemnly. "I've made contact with an old associate at MI5. They're sending an intervention team—it's only a matter of time now."

Lexi, who had been quietly checking over the surveillance feeds, looked up. "They need to hurry. Calponi's men are getting restless—they're starting to suspect they're being played."

As if on cue, the sound of vehicles approaching filled the air. Lexi and Redington watched through the peepholes as a convoy of black SUVs stormed down the long driveway to the manor. "This is it," Redington murmured, gripping his makeshift weapon a little tighter.

From their vantage point, they saw heavily armed operatives in tactical gear dismount and begin to surround the manor. The lead operative, who Redington recognized as Commander Fitch of MI5, directed his team with precision, using hand signals to communicate silently.

Calponi was growing increasingly paranoid inside the manor, barking orders at his men to fortify their positions. Unbeknownst to him, Redington had already disabled most of their communications equipment, leaving them isolated and confused.

The first sign of MI5's assault came when smoke bombs were hurled through the ground-floor windows, filling the rooms with a disorienting fog. Shouts and the sound of scrambling feet echoed through the hallways as Calponi's men tried to regroup.

"MI5 is making their move," Lexi said, her voice low. "We need to be ready to guide them to Calponi."

Redington nodded, leading the way as they carefully navigated the secret passages to a hidden alcove above the main foyer, where they could oversee and direct the operation. They signaled to Commander Fitch, who glanced up momentarily, acknowledging their presence.

The tactical team moved with lethal efficiency, sweeping through the manor room by room. Using non-lethal force where possible, they quickly subdued Calponi's guards, using stun grenades and tasers to neutralize any resistance.

Meanwhile, Calponi, realizing the manor was lost, tried to flee through a back exit. But as he burst through the door, he found himself face to face with Lord Winston, Redington, and Lexi, who had anticipated his escape route.

"There's nowhere left to run, Calponi," Redington stated coolly, stepping forward as MI5 agents closed in behind the crime lord.

Calponi sneered, his back to the wall. "You think you've won? This isn't over, Redington."

But before he could make another move, Commander Fitch and his team had him in handcuffs. "Marco Calponi, you are under arrest for extortion, assault, and several other charges that will keep you in custody for a very long time," Fitch declared, the authority in his voice unmistakable.

As Calponi and his men were led away, the staff of Wrightenton Manor emerged from their hiding places, expressions of relief mixed with disbelief on their faces. The manor, once again, was quiet, its halls free of intruders.

Lord Winston placed a hand on Redington's shoulder, a grateful smile on his face. "Well done, son. And you, Miss Alexandra, have proven yourself a true protector of Wrightenton's legacy."

As the MI5 team began their cleanup operation, Lexi looked around at the relieved faces of the staff and the agents working efficiently. The danger had passed, but the adventure, she knew, was far from over. The Cosmos Dial was safe, but its secrets and responsibilities were now hers and Redington's to bear.

As the sun rose higher, casting light into the dark corners of the manor, Lexi felt a new chapter beginning. She was ready to face whatever challenges lay ahead, with Redington by her side and the spirit of Wrightenton Manor watching over them. The siege was over, but the journey of the Cosmos Dial was just beginning.

Chapter 52

As the dust settled on the tumultuous events at Wrightenton Manor, the household slowly returned to a semblance of normalcy. The absence of Calponi and his men, now in the custody of MI5, left a palpable relief hanging in the air. Yet, for Lexi, the adventure was far from over. The Cosmos Dial, securely hidden within the manor's cryptic passageways, beckoned to her with an almost sentient urgency.

That night, as Lexi lay in her guest room under the soft, luxurious linens, her mind buzzed with unresolved questions about the Dial. Despite her exhaustion, sleep was slow to come, and when it did, it pulled her into a vivid, immersive dream—a memory not her own, yet intimately connected to her spirit.

Lexi found herself standing in a lush, verdant forest that felt both ancient and alive with whispered secrets. She was dressed in robes that hinted at a time centuries past, her hands adorned with intricate silver jewelry that gleamed with symbols of the celestial bodies. She cradled the Cosmos Dial in her hands, which radiated a soft, pulsating light.

She was not alone. Around her stood a circle of individuals, each robed and masked, representing the various elements of nature— earth, air, fire, water, and ether. They were the Guardians of the Dial, and she, a Keeper, was entrusted with its protection and the maintenance of cosmic balance.

An elder, his mask carved to resemble the spiraling galaxies above, stepped forward. His voice was both a whisper and a command, filling the space with its resonance. "The Cosmos Dial governs not just time but the very laws that bind the universe. With it, you, the Keeper, must oversee the harmony of the stars and ensure the delicate balance of nature is maintained."

Lexi, within the dream, nodded solemnly, her gaze fixed on the mesmerizing depths of the Dial. It shimmered, displaying an ethereal map of the cosmos, with stars and planets aligning in a dance of ancient geometry.

"The Dial interfaces with the cosmic laws," the elder continued, "It can amplify the natural order or disrupt it, should the Keeper falter. The harmony of the stars keeps the earthly realm in balance. Misuse, therefore, cannot be afforded."

As the ceremony progressed, Lexi felt an overwhelming connection to the cosmos. The Dial in her hands seemed to pulse in sync with her heartbeat, and she understood intuitively how to manipulate its surface to open gates between dimensions, heal corrupted lands, and even bend time to revisit past or future possibilities.

But with great power came great responsibility. The elder's warnings echoed in her mind: "Beware the lure of the Dial, for its gifts are not without cost. Each use draws on the cosmic balance itself. You must always act in wisdom."

Lexi awoke with a start, the images and sensations of the dream lingering in her mind like echoes of a forgotten melody. The room was bathed in the pale light of dawn, and for a moment, she could still feel the cool weight of the Cosmos Dial in her hands.

She sat up, her head spinning with the revelations of her dream. It wasn't just a dream; it was a memory, a past life where she had been the Keeper of the Dial. The responsibilities it entailed were enormous, and the powers it held were beyond comprehension. She realized then that her connection to the Dial was deeper than she had ever imagined.

As she made her way to the breakfast room, the need to discuss these revelations with Redington and Lord Winston was urgent. She knew they had to understand the full scope of what they were dealing with. The Cosmos Dial wasn't just a powerful artifact—it was a pivotal element in the cosmic tapestry, capable of altering the very fabric of reality.

Today, she would start by sharing her dream, her past life, and the urgent need to understand more about the Cosmos Dial. Their journey was not just about protecting an artifact but safeguarding the harmony of the entire cosmos.

Chapter 53

$\mathcal{L}$exi gathered with Redington and Lord Winston in the main study, the morning light casting serene patterns across the room filled with ancient tomes and artifacts. Each face showed traces of the recent ordeal but also a readiness to understand deeper mysteries— particularly how the Cosmos Dial related to the profound journey of the soul.

As they settled, Lexi began, her voice steady yet filled with awe. "Last night, I had a dream— or rather, a memory from a past life. I was a Keeper of the Cosmos Dial, responsible for maintaining the cosmic balance and harmony of the stars. But there's more to it, much more."

Lord Winston leaned forward, intrigued. "Go on," he prompted.

"The Dial," Lexi continued, "Is not just a tool for managing cosmic events. It's deeply connected to the evolution of the soul. It records and influences the journey of souls across lifetimes, ensuring that each cycle of life and rebirth serves the greater harmony of the universe."

Lord Winston, always the scholar, stroked his chin thoughtfully. "That aligns with ancient texts from various cultures. They speak of devices or artifacts that interact with the spiritual plane, guiding the soul's progression toward enlightenment."

Lexi nodded. "Exactly. The Cosmos Dial doesn't just affect the physical world but also the spiritual plane. It ensures that souls learn the lessons they are meant to in each lifetime, guiding them through experiences designed to achieve growth and balance."

She paused, recalling more details from her dream. "Each turn of the Dial can influence soul paths, aligning them with cosmic laws that govern their next incarnation. It's about learning and evolving through every life until they are ready to transcend the cycle—until they are ready for Nirvana, or whatever one might call the ultimate spiritual graduation."

Redington looked thoughtful. "So, the misuse of the Dial could disrupt not just earthly balance but the spiritual evolution of countless souls?"

"Indeed," Lexi confirmed. "If someone with ill intentions, like Calponi, were to manipulate the Dial, it could cause chaos not only here but in the fabric of the spiritual world. It could stall or warp the soul's natural progression, trapping it in cycles it would normally evolve past."

Lord Winston leaned back, his eyes wide with the realization of the stakes. "Then it's imperative that we not only protect the Dial but also master its operations. We need to ensure it's used wisely to aid in the spiritual advancement of souls as intended."

While Lord Winston and Lexi were drawn deeper into the historical and mystical significance of the Dial, Redington found himself grappling with the weight of it all.

As they convened in the main hall, preparing to delve further into their research, Redington appeared unusually pensive. Lexi noticed his distant gaze as she laid out several ancient manuscripts they had discovered in the hidden library.

"Redington, are you alright?" Lexi asked, her voice laced with concern.

He paused, looking up from the scattered papers. "I've been thinking about everything we've uncovered," he began, his voice hesitant. "About the Dial, its powers, its responsibility... and I'm not sure I'm the right person for this. This isn't just another case or a mystery to solve—it's about cosmic balance and spiritual journeys. It's far beyond the usual 'bad guy' scenarios I handle."

Lord Winston set aside a heavy tome he had been perusing. "I understand your concerns,

Ferguson. This does seem out of our usual realm. But your role in this isn't just coincidental; you're here because you're needed."

Redington shook his head, the decision clear in his eyes. "I think my being here might actually complicate things further. I'm a man of action, not of... spiritual contemplation. My real job is in New York, dealing with tangible threats, not cosmic ones. I think it's best if I return."

Lexi felt a pang of disappointment. "But we've just started to uncover the capabilities of the Dial. We need all hands on deck, and your perspective has always grounded us."

He smiled faintly at her, appreciative of her words but resolute. "And I'll always be a call away, ready to provide that grounding. But think about it—my skepticism, my discomfort with these concepts... it might cloud our goals here. You and my father have a handle on this. My staying might just hold you back."

Lord Winston nodded slowly, understanding the practicality of Redington's words. "If that's your decision, I won't stop you. You've already helped immensely, and as you said, New York might benefit from having you back, especially if other, more earthly threats arise."

Redington left the room to gather his belongings, his steps echoing solemnly through the hallways of Wrightenton Manor. As he ascended the grand staircase to his temporary quarters, the weight of the decisions made in the study lingered heavily in his mind. He had always been a man of action, dealing with concrete threats that could be seen, analyzed, and dismantled. The intangible, almost mystical responsibilities associated with the Cosmos Dial were out of his comfort zone, and he felt a profound sense of relief mixed with a twinge of guilt as he packed his suitcase.

The room was filled with the few personal items he had brought for the stay—nothing that spoke of permanence. As he zipped his bag shut, his gaze lingered on a small, leather-bound notebook resting on the bedside table. It was a journal he had started upon his arrival at the manor, initially meant to detail his investigation and findings. Now, it contained questions and reflections on cosmic laws and the spiritual ramifications of the Dial—topics he never imagined would fill its pages.

With his bag in hand, Redington took one last look around the room that had been his haven during this bizarre, enlightening, and tumultuous investigation. He made his way back downstairs, each step resolute yet heavy with unresolved thoughts.

Lexi and Lord Winston were waiting for him in the main hall, their faces a mixture of understanding and sadness. Redington approached them, his expression composed.

"Take care of this place," he reiterated, his voice firmer now that his decision was final. "And of yourself, Lexi. This manor, the Dial—it's in good hands with you both."

Lexi walked with him to the front of the manor, where a sleek, black car awaited. The early morning air was crisp, and the silence between them was thick with unspoken words—mutual respect for each other's paths and the roles they had come to accept.

As Redington slid into the car, he offered Lexi a final nod—a silent promise to be there should they ever need him. The engine hummed to life, and as the car drove away, winding down the long driveway flanked by ancient oaks, Lexi felt the mantle of her responsibilities settle firmly on her shoulders.

The manor seemed quieter now, almost reflective of the void Redington's departure had left. She and Lord Winston turned almost simultaneously and walked back into the heart of the manor. Their steps echoed in the empty hall, a stark reminder of the solitude that their monumental task imposed.

Back in the study, surrounded by relics of the past and the omnipresent weight of the future, Lord Winston opened another ancient scroll. "The Cosmos Dial isn't just our burden; it's our privilege," he mused, his voice imbued with a newfound determination. "We'll honor Redington's contributions by continuing our work with as much passion as he showed."

Lexi nodded, her resolve steeling. "We'll protect it, learn from it, and use it wisely. Not just for us but for the balance of everything. For every soul that's still on its journey."

With Redington's pragmatic skepticism now absent, Lexi and Lord Winston were free to delve deeper into the metaphysical aspects of their guardianship. The task was daunting, the scope immeasurable, but they were prepared to rise to the occasion, guided by the wisdom of the past and the uncertain promises of the future.

The echoes of the manor's long history whispered through its walls, reminding them that while the players might change, the game of cosmic balance continued. And they were now its principal guardians, standing watch over not just an artifact but the very fabric of cosmic order.

Chapter 54

That night, as the shadows of evening stretched across the grounds of Wrightenton Manor, Lexi retreated to her room, the weight of the day's conversations heavy on her mind. The stillness of the manor offered little comfort, and as she drifted into sleep, her thoughts tangled with the unresolved mysteries of the Cosmos Dial.

Lexi found herself in a vast library that seemed timeless and ethereal, its shelves towering with ancient scrolls and books glimmered with subtle, otherworldly light. The air was thick with the scent of sandalwood and old parchment, and the silence was profound, punctuated only by the soft flutter of turning pages.

Standing before her was a figure bathed in a radiant, multicolored light—Archangel Raziel, the Keeper of Secrets and the Patron of Mysteries. His presence was both awe-inspiring and comforting, and he held in his hands an ancient tome that Lexi instinctively knew to be the Book of Raziel, the Sefer Raziel HaMalakh.

"Welcome, Seeker of Truth," Raziel's voice echoed in the vastness, rich and melodious. "You have been drawn here by your soul's quest for understanding—the fundamental essence of why a soul journeys through the earthly plane."

Lexi stepped forward, her heart full of questions. "Why am I here? And what is the purpose of the Cosmos Dial in the journey of a soul?"

Raziel smiled a gesture that seemed to light up the entire room. "The Cosmos Dial is a tool, one of many, created to guide the souls through their cosmic lessons. Each turn aligns the soul's path with the experiences it needs to embrace its potential and to evolve."

He opened the tome to a page that shimmered with golden text. "This is one of the sacred texts—the Book of Secrets. It complements the knowledge found in the Book of Enoch and guides those who seek to understand the celestial mechanics behind their soul's journey."

As Lexi peered at the page, words and images began to make sense. The text explained how each soul's journey was interconnected with cosmic laws that governed the universe. It detailed the role of the Cosmos Dial in maintaining this order, ensuring that each soul could fulfill its destiny through lessons learned on Earth.

"The purpose of a soul's Earthly visitations is to acquire knowledge—knowledge that is essential for its spiritual evolution," Raziel continued. "Each life is a chapter in the grand book of a soul's existence. The experiences, challenges, and joys all culminate in the soul's progression toward enlightenment or what some may call Nirvana."

Lexi listened, fascinated and overwhelmed by the depth of understanding being offered. "And the books?" she asked, gesturing to the tome.

"These texts, including the Book of Enoch, provide the context and the clarity for those who guide and teach the souls. They are not just books but repositories of divine wisdom, detailing the structure of spiritual laws and the pathways to higher realms."

Archangel Raziel closed the tome and looked deeply into Lexi's eyes. "Your role, as a Keeper of the Dial, is not just to protect it but to use the knowledge it offers to aid in the harmonious progression of souls. But remember, with great power comes great responsibility. You must ensure that this knowledge does not fall into the wrong hands, for its misuse could lead to chaos not just on Earth but across the spiritual planes."

Lexi awoke with a start, the morning light streaming through her window. The dream had felt so real and vivid that she could still feel the weight of the tome in her hands. She now understood her role not just as a guardian of the Cosmos Dial but as a steward of the knowledge it represented. The journey of her soul, and indeed the journeys of all souls, was intricately linked to the cosmic balance that the Dial helped maintain.

Filled with a new sense of purpose, Lexi rose from her bed, determined to discuss her vision with Lord Winston. They needed to understand fully the Dial's role not just in the cosmic order but also in the spiritual evolution of every soul it influenced.

Today, they would begin a deeper exploration—not just of the physical but of the spiritual implications of their guardianship. The Cosmos Dial was more than an artifact; it was a means to understanding the profound structure of the universe and the soul's place within it.

Chapter 55

As the new day dawned over Wrightenton Manor, Lexi met with Lord Winston in the study, the morning light illuminating the ancient scrolls and books that surrounded them. With the revelations from her dream still vivid in her mind, Lexi was eager to share her newfound understanding with Lord Winston, who was equally prepared to delve deeper into the mystical aspects of the Cosmos Dial.

"Lord Winston," Lexi began, her voice tinged with excitement and gravity, "Last night, I had a vision. Archangel Raziel appeared to me, revealing the deeper purpose of the Cosmos Dial. It's not just a regulator of cosmic balance but a guide for the soul's journey across lifetimes."

Lord Winston looked intrigued yet cautious. "A remarkable vision, indeed. And does this vision suggest a way for us to use the Dial safely, to perhaps even harness its capabilities without risking the chaos we fear?"

Lexi nodded, her resolve clear. "Yes, he showed me the Book of Secrets and spoke of the Dial's role in aligning soul paths. We need to learn how to interact with the Dial—not to manipulate it but to understand its indications and guide its adjustments subtly."

Encouraged by her assurance, Lord Winston proposed an experimental approach. "Let's try to connect with the Dial on a spiritual level. Perhaps, like in your dream, we can induce a meditative state to see beyond the physical and perceive its operations in the cosmic fabric."

They moved to the room where the Cosmos Dial was secured. The chamber was cool and dimly lit, with the Dial itself resting on a pedestal, its surface shimmering slightly in the half-light.

"First, we must clear our minds," Lexi instructed as they sat before the Dial. "Let go of all earthly concerns and focus on your breathing. Imagine your consciousness expanding, reaching out to the cosmos where the Dial resonates."

Lexi closed her eyes, her breathing deep and even. She envisioned her mind as a vast, star-filled sky, each star a fragment of knowledge or memory. Slowly, she felt her consciousness extend toward the Dial, her thoughts mingling with the whispers of cosmic winds.

As they both drifted deeper into meditation, a profound silence enveloped them. Lexi could feel, more than see, the presence of Lord Winston in her expanded consciousness, his spiritual signature calm and steady.

Suddenly, Lexi's mind was catapulted beyond the confines of the manor, soaring through the astral planes. She perceived the Cosmos Dial not as a physical object but as a brilliant node of energy, a nexus of cosmic ley lines that intersected at multiple dimensions.

She saw the Dial's influence radiating outwards, threads of light touching different lives, different souls—each thread a pathway of soul progression, a line of fate being gently guided toward enlightenment. The vision was overwhelming but enlightening, revealing the intricate web of cosmic balance that the Dial controlled.

Beside her, in this out-of-body experience, she sensed Lord Winston's awe and his dawning understanding of their role as not just protectors but facilitators of cosmic harmony.

Together, they observed how subtle shifts in the Dial could alter the energy flows and how careful adjustments could bring harmony where there was discord. The knowledge flowed not through words but through direct perception, an intuitive understanding imprinted directly onto their souls.

Gradually, they retracted their consciousness, pulling back from the cosmic expanse into the confines of the manor. As they opened their eyes, the room seemed the same yet transformed—a space that they now knew was connected to the vastness of the universe.

"We've just scratched the surface," Lexi said, her voice filled with wonder and a hint of caution. "But we must tread carefully. The balance we observed is delicate, and our interventions must be thoughtful and minimal."

Lord Winston nodded in agreement, his mind still reeling from the experience. "We have been given a great tool and a greater responsibility. We will use the Dial, but we will do so with wisdom, safeguarding not just the earth but the spiritual journey of countless souls."

As they left the chamber, both felt a renewed sense of purpose. They were no longer merely scholars and protectors of an ancient artifact but active participants in a cosmic ballet, dancing to the rhythm of the universe itself, guided by the ancient wisdom of the Cosmos Dial.

Chapter 56

Under the dim light of the early dawn, Lexi and Lord Winston convened once more in the library of Wrightenton Manor. The air was thick with the scent of old books and whispered secrets, the weight of their previous discoveries still lingering as they prepared to delve deeper into the mysteries of the Cosmos Dial.

Lord Winston adjusted the heavy tome on the table, opening to a page marked with ancient symbols. "Today, we attempt to bridge the knowledge of earth and the cosmic truths, to explore the deeper connections facilitated by the Dial," he announced, his voice resonant with a mix of excitement and solemnity.

Lexi, feeling the gravity of their task, nodded. "Let's focus on the Tree of Knowledge, the concept of dual realms—Heaven and the Underworld—and how the Dial might connect them."

They positioned themselves around the concealed chamber where the Cosmos Dial was hidden, not to unearth it but to connect with it spiritually as they had before. This time, Lexi introduced a new element to their ritual—a small, intricately carved falcon feather cloak draped over the back of her chair, a symbolic nod to Freyja, the mythical being known for traveling between worlds.

As they entered a meditative state, Lexi envisioned the Tree of Knowledge—a massive, sprawling tree with roots deep in the earth and branches stretching upwards into the heavens. The Cosmos Dial appeared in her vision as a radiant beacon at the base of the tree, its pulsing energy acting as a conduit between the earth and the astral planes.

"The Dial," Lexi spoke aloud within her trance, "It's not just a tool but a bridge. It connects the physical and the spiritual, offering a pathway between the realms."

Lord Winston, sharing in the vision, added, "And it governs the laws that maintain the balance between these realms. It ensures that actions within one have repercussions in the other, embodying the cosmic laws of karma— good and evil, right and wrong."

As their shared vision deepened, the figure of Freyja appeared, cloaked in her falcon feathers, majestic and powerful. She approached the Tree of Knowledge and spoke in a voice that resonated through the cosmos.

"The Cosmos Dial, when used with wisdom, can teach you the secrets of the universe. It can show you how the forces of good and evil shape the destinies of all living beings," Freyja explained, her eyes reflecting the vastness of the worlds she traversed.

She gestured to her cloak. "Like my falcon cloak, which lets me fly between worlds, the Dial can help you navigate these realms. But beware, for such journeys are fraught with peril for those who are unprepared or wield the Dial for selfish gains."

Freyja extended her hand toward the Cosmos Dial, which now glowed with an intense light. "The laws governing this artifact are ancient and must be respected. The balance between good and evil, light and dark, is delicate. Misuse of the Dial could lead to chaos not just on Earth, but across all realms."

As her words echoed in their minds, Lexi and Lord Winston felt the overwhelming responsibility of their guardianship. The Dial was more than a keeper of balance; it was a guardian of the cosmic law itself.

Gradually, the vision faded, and Lexi and Lord Winston found themselves back in the library, the falcon cloak still draped over the chair, now seeming ordinary yet imbued with the essence of their experience.

"We have much to consider," Lord Winston remarked thoughtfully. "Our role is not just to protect the Dial but to understand it—to ensure we never tip the balance it so carefully guards."

Lexi nodded in agreement, her mind still racing with the images of the Tree and Freyja. "We'll document everything. Every vision, every lesson from Freyja. We mustn't lose any piece of this knowledge."

As they prepared to document their experiences, both felt a renewed sense of purpose. The Cosmos Dial was their bridge to understanding not only the laws of good and evil but the very fabric that wove the universe together. With great power came great responsibility, and they were determined to meet this challenge with wisdom and courage. The journey ahead was uncertain, but they were no longer just scholars of the past; they were now navigators of the cosmic realms.

Chapter 57

As night enveloped Wrightenton Manor, Lexi retired to her room, her mind swirling with the cosmic revelations and mythical visions she had encountered. The gravity of her responsibilities, combined with the ancient wisdom imparted by Freyja, left her both exhilarated and exhausted. Seeking solace in sleep, she hoped for a night of rest. Instead, she found herself plunged into another profound dream, one that would further expand her understanding of the Cosmos Dial and its intricate connection to universal laws.

Lexi found herself in an ethereal courtroom, the walls and floors made of clouds, the sky above a vivid tapestry of twilight hues. Seated before her was an assembly of celestial beings, their forms shimmering with starlight. In the center of this assembly stood an imposing figure holding a gavel made of pure radiant light. This figure, Lexi intuitively knew, was the Arbiter of Cosmic Law.

"Welcome, Keeper of the Dial," the Arbiter's voice boomed in the expanse. "You are here to learn about the Law of Sevens, a fundamental cosmic principle that governs the progression and crisis of all that exists."

Lexi listened intently as the Arbiter began to elucidate the law. "The universe operates on a rhythm of sevens—seven days of creation, seven-year cycles of growth and decay, seven stages of spiritual awakening. Each cycle of seven marks a progression in complexity and understanding and each is punctuated by a crisis or a threshold that must be crossed."

"The Law of Crisis," the Arbiter continued, "Is tied to the Law of Sevens. At each seventh interval, a crisis occurs—a turning point where old structures are tested and new levels of consciousness are achieved. This law ensures that nothing remains static; everything is pushed toward evolution, toward greater harmony."

As the Arbiter spoke, visions flashed before Lexi's eyes: planets aligning every seven years, civilizations reaching peaks of crisis and rebirth at seven-century intervals, and individuals facing life-changing decisions in the seventh year of decisive phases of their lives.

"These crises are not punishments but opportunities," the Arbiter emphasized. "They are cosmic catalysts designed to elevate. The

Cosmos Dial, which you guard, is a tool to foresee and manage these crises, to help guide souls through their thresholds of transformation."

The dream shifted, and Lexi found herself holding the Cosmos Dial in a vast library, each book a record of cosmic laws and events. She opened a tome to a page titled "The Application of the Law of Sevens." Here, detailed annotations described how the Dial could be calibrated to predict upcoming crises, both large and small, and suggestions on how to use these crises for positive change.

"You must use the Dial not to avert the natural crises but to prepare for them," the Arbiter's voice echoed around her. "Help those you guide to embrace these challenges, to grow stronger and more enlightened through them."

Lexi awoke, the morning light streaming through her window. The dream was vivid in her mind, each detail etched with clarity. She now understood that her role was not just to protect the Dial but to utilize it in alignment with cosmic rhythms to assist in the navigation of life's inevitable crises under the Law of Sevens.

Where is Sophea when you need her? She would know what to do.

Armed with this new knowledge, Lexi met Lord Winston at breakfast, eager to share her insights. "The Cosmos Dial is more than a guardian of balance; it's a guide through the universe's rhythmic pulses of challenge and change. We can help those touched by its influence to not only anticipate their personal and collective crises but to use them as stepping stones," she explained passionately.

Lord Winston, intrigued and inspired by her description, agreed. "Then let us begin a detailed study of historical cycles and their crises. We'll map them against the Law of Sevens and see how we might apply this knowledge practically."

Chapter 58

In the tranquility of Wrightenton Manor's oldest library, Lexi and Lord Winston spread out their maps and historical chronicles across the grand oak table that dominated the room. The morning light streamed through the stained-glass windows, casting colorful patterns that danced over the ancient texts and scrolls—an apt metaphor for the dynamic interplay of light and shadow that governed cosmic laws.

Lord Winston, his eyes reflecting a scholar's zeal, adjusted his glasses and pointed to a series of charts that outlined significant historical events. "Look here, Lexi. Each of these pivotal moments in history corresponds to the seventh year of a decade. Wars, revolutions, great discoveries—all precipitated by underlying crises that, I believe, were forecasted by cosmic rhythms."

Lexi, her mind abuzz with the revelations from her dream, nodded. "The Cosmos Dial acts much like a conductor's baton, not causing the music but allowing us to anticipate the next note, the next inevitable pulse of change."

She walked over to the Cosmos Dial, which lay central among the scrolls, its surface alive with a soft, internal luminescence. "If we can tune into this 'music,' perhaps we can prepare ourselves better for the crises it heralds."

Turning her attention to the intricate device, Lexi began adjusting its dials under Lord Winston's watchful eye. A pattern began to emerge as she aligned the symbols representing different cosmic laws. The dial's hands moved with precision, pointing to specific dates and times that had historical significance.

"This is extraordinary," Lord Winston murmured, scribbling notes feverishly as each alignment revealed more insights. "It's as if the Dial is not just measuring time but the quality of time—the emotional, spiritual, and physical currents that flow through humanity."

"Let's test it," Lexi proposed, her voice charged with determination. "If we select an upcoming date that the Dial identifies as a 'pulse point,' we can observe what happens and perhaps even intervene to mitigate any negative impacts."

Lord Winston agreed, and they chose a date— a few weeks into the future—that the Dial indicated would be significant. They decided they would watch carefully to see what crisis might unfold and how they might use their foreknowledge to turn a potential negative into a positive outcome.

As the weeks passed, Lexi and Lord Winston monitored global events closely. When the chosen date arrived, a major economic downturn began to unsettle global markets—a ripple effect that started in a small, usually insignificant stock market but had the potential to cause widespread financial distress.

Using their understanding of the Dial's warning, they contacted financial experts and charitable organizations to prepare. They set up funds to help those most affected and provided information that helped stabilize the markets more quickly than would have normally been possible. Their discreet interventions allowed them to guide the crisis toward a more benign resolution, preventing what could have been a severe global recession.

In the aftermath, as they reviewed their actions and the outcomes, Lexi felt a profound connection to the Cosmos Dial's purpose. "We didn't change what was destined to happen," she reflected aloud, "But we helped manage it, soften it. It's about stewardship, not control."

Lord Winston, looking over the charts and the data they had collected, nodded in agreement. "Indeed, the Dial guides us to understand that every crisis is a moment of potential transformation. By anticipating these moments, we can act to support positive change and growth, rather than mere survival."

Lexi and Lord Winston became more adept at reading the Cosmos Dial's signals as they continued their work. They documented their findings and methods, creating a guide for future keepers of the Dial. Their legacy would not just be one of guardianship over a powerful artifact but of mentorship to a future where humanity could more harmoniously ride the rhythmic pulses of cosmic change.

Chapter 59

In the serene twilight that enveloped Wrightenton Manor, Lexi found herself in the grand library, surrounded by ancient manuscripts that whispered secrets of cosmic lore and soul evolution. As she and Lord Winston prepared to delve deeper into their understanding of the Cosmos Dial, Lexi's mind was drawn to the teachings revealed in her recent visionary experiences—specifically, the progression of the soul through its many lifetimes.

"Lord Winston," Lexi began, her voice echoing slightly in the high-ceilinged room, "It seems that the Cosmos Dial doesn't just balance cosmic forces; it appears to mirror the journey of the soul itself. From its naive beginnings to its ultimate enlightenment."

Lord Winston adjusted his spectacles, intrigued. "Do elaborate, Lexi. How do you perceive this alignment?"

Lexi spread out a series of diagrams and charts across the table, each representing different stages of soul development. "Consider the Dial not just as a timekeeper of the cosmos but as a marker of spiritual progression. Each major division on its face can be seen as a stage in the soul's journey." She pointed to a paper with the stages a soul must endure to reach Nirvana.

Reading the first stage, "Newbie, 1-5 lifetimes. At the first marker, the soul is a Newbie," Lexi pointed at the initial segment of the Dial. "These souls are like infants, instinctually navigating the physical world. Their stories are simple, focusing on survival and sensory experiences—akin to a seed sprouting in sunlight, purely reactive and adapting to immediate stimuli."

Moving her finger to the next section, she continued, "Child, 5-1000 lifetimes. Here, we have the Child stage. These souls revel in the physicality of the world. They explore and discover, experiencing life through the joys and pains of the body. Their narratives are rich with physical adventures and sensory discoveries."

She moved her finger down again, "Teenager, 1001-5000 lifetimes. As the Dial progresses, it reaches the Teenager phase. Souls in this segment are vibrant with vitality and energy. They are adventurers and challengers, testing limits and learning about the consequences of their actions, both physically and energetically."

"Next, the Adult souls, 5001-10,000 lifetimes," Lexi indicated a more complex series of engravings on the Dial, "Engage in intellectual and philosophical pursuits. They seek deeper understanding, grapple with cognitive challenges, and start to touch upon meditation and philosophical wisdom."

"Finally, the Geriatrics, 10,000 plus lifetimes," she said, her voice softening. "These are the souls nearing the end of their soulular cycles. They deal with supermental lessons and delve into the purposes of existence. Their experiences are profound, often touching on cosmic awareness and deep spiritual insights."

Lord Winston, deeply moved by the description, added, "And the Dial, in its wisdom, guides each soul not randomly but with purpose—to ensure that each crisis or turning point they encounter is ripe for their current stage of spiritual development."

Lexi nodded, "Exactly. And with each full turn of the Dial through these stages, a soul moves closer to its graduation—its liberation and ultimate union with the divine, marked by wisdom and blissful energy."

As Lexi sat down, she added, "The practical application of this knowledge," Lexi mused, "Is profound. By understanding where a soul might be on this Dial, we can predict and assist in navigating the crises it faces. We could use the Dial not to alter destiny but to provide guidance and enlightenment at critical junctures."

Lord Winston looked at the Dial with newfound respect. "Then let us continue our studies, Lexi. Let's map out these stages against historical events and personal journeys, perhaps even our own. We have a tool that can offer not just knowledge but wisdom, and with great wisdom comes the responsibility to use it judiciously."

As they settled down to document their findings, the room filled with an aura of sacred duty. The Cosmos Dial, central to their research, glimmered faintly under the moonlight streaming through the windows. It was no longer just an artifact but a beacon of spiritual navigation, a guide through the eons of soul development.

This understanding transformed their mission at Wrightenton Manor from guardians of a mysterious artifact to shepherds of souls across their cosmic journeys. Each tick of the Dial was a step in a soul's path, and Lexi and Lord Winston were now its vigilant overseers, committed to aiding those souls in their quest for enlightenment and eventual transcendence.

Chapter 60

As the golden hues of dusk settled over Wrightenton Manor, Lexi stood by the grand window in the study, her eyes gazing out at the sprawling gardens that whispered secrets of centuries past. The recent discoveries and the deepening understanding of the Cosmos Dial had both excited and overwhelmed her, and she found herself wishing for the presence of her friends, Isabella, Kesia, and Sophea, who were still in Nepal.

Unknown to Lexi, at that very moment, Sophea was meditating in a small, serene garden in Kathmandu, her senses attuned to the subtle energies that connected all things. As Lexi's wish echoed through the cosmic web, it resonated with Sophea, who had always been sensitive to the needs of her friends. She opened her eyes, a decisive glint in them, and immediately knew it was time to journey to Wrightenton Manor.

"Ladies," Sophea called out to Isabella and Kesia, "I have heard a call from Lexi. She needs us. The energy of the Cosmos Dial beckons, and it's our time to aid in its guardianship."

Isabella and Kesia, now both well-versed in spiritual and cosmic matters, did not hesitate. They understood the importance of the summon and quickly made arrangements for their departure.

A few days later, Lexi was in the library when she heard the sound of a car approaching. Rushing to the window, she saw her three friends appear from the vehicle, their faces alight with the joy of reunion and the seriousness of their purpose.

Lexi rushed out to greet them, embracing each in turn. "I can't believe you're here," she exclaimed, her heart full of gratitude. "I hoped, but didn't truly expect..."

"We heard your call, and the Dial's energy guided us," Sophea explained, her voice calm and soothing. "It's time for us to assist you and Lord Winston in understanding and protecting this incredible artifact."

Lord Winston greeted the newcomers warmly, appreciating their swift response and readiness to help. Having the staff take care of their luggage, he led them to the study, where the Cosmos Dial was securely hidden, and began to explain their findings about the soul's journey, the Law of Sevens, and their experiences with the Dial.

Sophea, with her background in anthropological studies, played the part of one who was particularly fascinated. "This aligns with many ancient beliefs and practices around the world. It's not just about spiritual evolution but about how deeply interconnected our physical reality is with these cosmic principles."

Kesia, who had been training in energy healing at the monastery, added, "And it's about how we can apply this knowledge to help people navigate their lives better—understanding their crises and challenges as part of a larger, cosmic narrative."

That evening, under the starlit sky, the group sat in the garden, the Dial among them, pulsating softly with a light that seemed to breathe in sync with the earth itself. They each shared their experiences and insights, weaving a tapestry of ideas that enriched their collective understanding.

Sophea led a meditation that focused their energies on the Dial. As they attuned themselves to its frequency, they experienced a collective vision of the Dial's place in the cosmic lattice, seeing how it could potentially influence the energetic threads that connected life forms across the universe.

"We are stewards of this cosmic instrument," Sophea concluded as the vision faded, "And we must use it wisely to maintain balance and harmony, not just on Earth but in the broader cosmos."

Over the next few days, Lexi, Lord Winston, Isabella, Kesia, and Sophea developed a plan to monitor the influences of the Dial, create educational programs to share their understanding with others responsibly, and research historical alignments and their outcomes.

As they worked, the sense of being a part of something much larger than themselves grew. Wrightenton Manor had become more than a home or a repository of ancient artifacts—it was now a center of cosmic guardianship, a place where the harmony of the universe was being actively maintained.

This new journey together had just begun, but each of them knew that the path they walked was carved by the stars themselves, guided by the ancient, pulsating heart of the Cosmos Dial.

Chapter 61

The tranquil atmosphere of Wrightenton Manor, now buzzing with the new guardians and their explorations into the cosmic mysteries of the Cosmos Dial, was abruptly pierced by the sharp ring of a telephone.

One of Lord Winston's servants entered the room and announced, "It is for Miss Constantine."

Lexi, deep in discussion with Isabella over an ancient celestial map, excused herself and walked briskly to the main hall to answer the call.

"Lexi here," she answered, her tone shifting to one of concern as she recognized the caller.

"Lexi, it's Redington," came the response, his voice tense and laced with urgency.

Lexi's heart skipped a beat.

"Listen, I've got troubling news. Marco Calponi isn't just sitting quietly in custody. He's making moves from behind bars."

Lexi's grip on the phone tightened. "What kind of moves?"

Redington sighed heavily. "He's somehow communicated with his contacts in the underworld—the mob. There's talk of a vendetta against you and your companions at the Manor. They're not just coming after you with conventional means. They want the Dial, Lexi."

Her heart raced at the implications. "To use it for what?"

"Destruction," Redington replied grimly. "They believe the Dial can be used to cause massive disruptions, both physical and spiritual. If they get their hands on it, we could be looking at chaos that has not been seen in centuries. And from what the informants are saying, they think nothing of crossing lines between our world and darker realms to get what they want."

Lexi paced the length of the phone cord, processing the information. "How did this alliance even come about?" she asked, her mind reeling at the complexity and danger of their situation.

Sophea said from behind Lexi, "The underworld thrives on power and fear, and Calponi has been a master at manipulating both. Now, he's promising them a share of the Dial's powers, painting it as a tool to extend their influence beyond imaginable limits."

Lexi turned to Sophea as she put Redington on speaker, "And the celestial part?"

Sophea added, "He's got some warlocks and other dark practitioners rallying around him. They're fringe elements, mostly cast out from any legitimate magical community, but desperate and dangerous enough to cause real trouble."

"We need to prepare. We can't let them reach the Manor, much less the Dial," Lexi stated, her voice firm despite the sinking feeling in her stomach.

Redington declared, "I agree. I'm coming back, Lexi. I've got some contacts who might help us understand more about what we're up against, and I'll bring reinforcements. We need to fortify the Manor, physically and, I guess, spiritually."

"Thank you, Redington. Be careful," Lexi replied, a mix of gratitude and fear in her voice.

After hanging up, Lexi and Sophea gathered their other companions in the study. Lexi relayed the conversation to them, her expression serious and commanding attention. "We have a significant threat on our hands, one that involves not just the physical security of the Manor but also its spiritual sanctity."

Isabella, Kesia, and Lord Winston listened intently, each processing the gravity of the situation. Sophea was the first to speak, "We'll need to set up protections—both magical and mundane. Lord Winston, I'll need you to contact your old allies, experts in ancient barriers and seals."

Kesia nodded, "I'll focus on the spiritual defenses. We can set up wards and enchantments that will alert us to any breaches or dark energies attempting to infiltrate the Manor."

Isabella added, "And I'll help coordinate our physical defenses. We need to ensure that all entry points are secure, and I suggest we set up even more surveillance around the perimeter."

Feeling the weight of her leadership, Lexi concluded, "We stand on the brink of a confrontation that tests not just our strength but the very principles we aim to protect with the Cosmos Dial. Let's prepare. We will defend this place and the Dial with everything we've got."

As the group dispersed to begin their preparations, the Manor transformed from a place of scholarly pursuit into a fortified stronghold. Lexi looked out across the estate, her resolve hardening. The coming days would bring their greatest challenge yet, and she was ready to meet it head-on.

Chapter 62

As the sun dipped below the horizon, casting long shadows across the sprawling grounds of Wrightenton Manor, the estate braced for an impending siege. The once-quiet halls and rooms buzzed with activity as Lexi and her companions orchestrated their defenses against the dark alliance that threatened them.

The manor's physical security was tightened under Lord Winston's coordination. Surveillance cameras were installed at strategic points, covering every possible angle of approach. The ancient wooden doors were reinforced, and the windows were fitted with unbreakable glass. Every entry point was secured with both high-tech security systems and old-world craftsmanship that made use of the manor's architectural strengths.

Kesia, with her profound knowledge of spiritual energies, thanks to her time with her friend Luna, began crafting an intricate network of wards and protective spells. She painted sigils with consecrated chalk at every doorway, window, and chimney. "These are not just physical barriers," she explained as she worked. "They're woven with spells to alert us to dark energies and to weaken any who bear ill intentions."

Sophea and Isabella focused on the mystical defenses. They contacted allies known for their expertise in ancient barriers and protective magics. Soon, the manor was surrounded by a subtle, almost imperceptible shield—a shimmering barrier that could repel dark magic and prevent spiritual intrusions.

Just as the final preparations were underway, a sleek black car rolled up the gravel drive, and Redington stepped out, his expression grim but determined. He was not alone; accompanying him were two figures Lexi recognized as renowned mystic defenders, specialists in combatting dark arts and underworld connections.

"Redington, you made it," Lexi greeted, relief evident in her voice as they met at the front steps.

"I told you I'd bring reinforcements," Redington replied, clapping a reassuring hand on her shoulder. "These are the best in their fields. If Calponi thinks he can breach these walls, he's in for a rude awakening."

Inside the manor, Redington introduced his companions: Mara, an expert in arcane countermeasures, and Jothan, a strategist known for his experience with supernatural conflicts. Together, they joined the rest of the group in the main study to finalize their plans.

Mara immediately set to work, enhancing Kesia's wards with her own powerful runes. "These will not only alert us but also sap the strength of any who come bearing malice toward this place," Mara explained, her hands moving deftly over the surfaces she enchanted.

Jothan spread out one of the detailed maps of the estate and surrounding areas. "Our best strategy is to control the engagement zone. We'll funnel them through the north approach— it's the most defensible with the least cover for an approaching enemy."

Lexi nodded, taking in his advice and feeling a surge of confidence with these new allies by her side. "And if they breach the outer defenses?"

"Then we fall back to the inner sanctum," Jothan said, pointing to the fortified central chamber where the Cosmos Dial was now secured behind layers of magical and physical protections. "We make our stance there."

As night fell, the manor settled into a tense quiet. Lexi walked the corridors, her thoughts a whirlwind of scenarios and possibilities. She stopped by the window, looking out at the protective barriers that shimmered faintly in the moonlight, and felt a momentary peace. They were as prepared as they could be.

Turning from the window, she returned to the study, where her friends and allies were gathered, making final checks on their equipment and spells. They were a formidable team, each member ready to defend not just the manor and the Dial, but also the principles they stood for—the balance of the cosmos and the protection of all souls from the darkness that sought to disrupt their journeys.

The night would be long, and the battle fierce, but Lexi knew that together, they could face anything. With the Cosmos Dial at the heart of their defense, they stood ready to maintain the harmony of the universe against the chaos that threatened to engulf it. The stage was set, and the defenders of Wrightenton Manor were prepared for the siege that would soon begin.

Chapter 63

As darkness enveloped Wrightenton Manor, an oppressive silence settled over the estate, broken only by the occasional rustle of leaves in the brisk night wind. Lexi and her team were in a state of high alert, their senses tuned to any hint of disturbance. The atmosphere was charged with anticipation, each member ready to defend their charge against the impending onslaught.

It began subtly. The air grew colder, and the light from the candles flickered as if agitated by an unseen breath. Kesia, who was monitoring the network of wards, was the first to sense the intrusion.

"The outer barrier has been breached," she announced tensely, her eyes fixed on the glowing symbols that formed a protective ring around the manor. "Something powerful."

Redington checked his weapon—a specially crafted firearm loaded with rounds blessed by ancient rites. He looked over at Lexi, nodding once with grim determination. "Positions, everyone," he commanded, his voice low but carrying clearly through the tense air.

No sooner had they taken cover than the shadows around the manor began to churn and coalesce. Dark figures emerged from the tree line, their forms barely human, twisted by dark magics and sinister intent. They advanced slowly, testing the remaining barriers and probing for weaknesses.

Mara and Sophea chanted in unison, strengthening the shields and repelling the first wave of shadowy figures. The air crackled with magical energy, and the ground at the manor's boundaries scorched where the dark entities tried to pass.

Isabella, positioned at the upper window with a crossbow, took aim and let loose a volley of enchanted bolts. Each found its mark, causing several demonic attackers to dissolve into wisps of shadow. However, for every figure that fell, two more took its place, pressing forward with relentless determination.

Suddenly, a low, menacing growl echoed through the night, and a new wave of creatures joined the fray—beasts from nightmares, their eyes glowing with malevolence. Redington fired, his rounds disintegrating several beasts, but the battle was far from over.

"Stay focused!" Jothan yelled over the din of combat, directing the defenders to adjust their positions as the attackers began to flank the manor's western wing.

In the midst of chaos, Lexi remained centered, her thoughts clear. She drew upon the Cosmos Dial's energy, channeling it to bolster their defenses. The Dial hummed softly, its glow intensifying as if responding to her call. The air around the manor shimmered momentarily, and the next assault by the shadow beings seemed to falter, their movements becoming sluggish, their forms less substantial.

"We have them now!" Kesia shouted, her hands weaving a complex spell that sent waves of radiant energy pulsating across the battlefield. The shadow beings shrieked, their forms destabilizing under the assault of pure, radiant magic.

But the enemy was cunning. From the dark woods, a figure detached itself from the shadows—taller, more imposing than the others. It walked forward, a staff in hand that pulsed with a dark energy that seemed to absorb light itself.

"This one is different," Sophea warned, her voice urgent. "It's a conduit of dark power, maybe a warlock or worse."

Lexi realized they needed to end this quickly. "Focus all attacks on that leader," she commanded. Her allies responded, concentrating their fire and magical attacks on the figure.

With a concerted effort, a barrage of magical and physical attacks converged on the warlock. Under the relentless assault, the figure halted, its shield flickering under the onslaught. With a final, desperate push, Redington fired a blessed round directly into the heart of the shadowy warlock. With a scream that echoed like a death knell through the night, the figure exploded in a burst of dark energy.

As the echo of the explosion faded, so too did the intensity of the assault. The remaining shadow figures, leaderless and directionless, retreated into the darkness from which they had emerged. The defenders of Wrightenton Manor stood down, their chests heaving with exertion, their faces lit by the glow of victory yet shadowed by the knowledge of the dark forces they had just repelled.

"We held them off," Lexi said, her voice a mix of relief and fatigue as she looked around at her companions. "Thanks to each of you. But this might only be the beginning."

Lord Winston, leaning heavily against the wall, nodded in agreement. "We must remain vigilant. Calponi's allies in the underworld might regroup for another assault. We need to strengthen our defenses and perhaps even go on the offensive."

As dawn broke over Wrightenton Manor, the night's battle was over, but the war for the Cosmos Dial was just beginning. They had defended their sanctuary this time, but the shadow of the underworld loomed large, promising that peace would be fleeting. The guardians of the Dial prepared for what was to come, fortified by their unity and the cosmic justice they had sworn to uphold.

Chapter 64

As the first light of dawn cast its pale glow over the battle-scarred grounds of Wrightenton Manor, the defenders gathered in the main hall, weary but resolute. The night's events had proven the severity of the threat they faced—not only from earthly foes but also from darker, more sinister forces aligned with Marco Calponi.

Looking older and more tired than the night before, Lord Winston addressed the group with a grave expression. "Last night was a stark reminder of the dangers we face. We were prepared yet barely held our ground. We must use this time wisely to fortify our defenses and perhaps consider a more proactive strategy."

Lexi nodded in agreement, feeling the weight of her responsibilities more acutely than ever. "We need to understand more about our enemies. Who they are, what drives them, and how they plan to strike next. Knowledge will be our greatest weapon."

Redington, who had spent the early morning hours scouting the perimeter for any signs of lingering threats, added, "I've reached out to my contacts. We should have intelligence reports coming in soon. We'll know better what to prepare for."

Sophea, who had been quietly meditating in a corner, spoke up. "The Dial is not just a beacon for us. It's a beacon for them. They felt its power last night when we used it to bolster our defenses. We can assume they will come harder and stronger now."

Kesia, rubbing her temples after a night of casting spells, suggested, "We should consider using the Dial in a more controlled manner. Maybe even camouflage its energy signature to mask its exact location."

Mara, the arcane expert, quickly sketched a few symbols on a piece of paper. "I can create a series of arcane dampeners that will diffuse the energy signature. It will give us a cloak of sorts, a mystic veil to hide behind."

Lord Winston took the lead on physical fortifications. "We've held them off once with what we had. Now, let's make it impregnable. Automated defenses, enhanced surveillance, and maybe even some drone reconnaissance."

As the team planned, Lexi returned to the Cosmos Dial, her thoughts deep and conflicted. She reached out, touching the cold metal, feeling its ancient power thrum beneath her fingers. Closing her eyes, she whispered a plea for guidance.

The air around her shimmered, and a vision coalesced. She saw a dark tide rising, led by a figure cloaked in shadow—a warlock of immense power, his eyes burning with a malevolent light. Behind him, legions of shadowy creatures surged forward, more organized and potent than the ones they had faced.

Lexi's eyes snapped open. "They will come again, led by a warlock. Not just to test us, but to overwhelm us."

Recognizing the need for more support, Lexi proposed reaching out to potential allies. "We need more than just us to hold the line. There are others who stand against the darkness. We should call them here, make a stand together."

Lord Winston agreed, his voice firm. "I will contact the Order of Light. Their knights are skilled in both combat and mystical warfare. We'll offer them sanctuary and a cause."

As they each set about their tasks, the Manor transformed once more, not just into a fortress but into a beacon of hope—a rallying point for all who would stand against the encroaching darkness. Lexi stood at the window, looking out at the rallying forces, her heart both heavy and hopeful. They were outnumbered and outmatched but not outwitted or out spirited.

The Cosmos Dial, central to their defense, glowed softly under the morning light, a reminder of the cosmic balance they fought to preserve. As allies began to arrive, drawn by the promise of a noble stand, Lexi felt the first stirrings of hope. Here, at Wrightenton Manor, they would stand for the Dial, humanity, and the cosmic order itself. The storm was approaching, but they were ready to meet it together.

Chapter 65

As the day wore on, Wrightenton Manor began transforming from a stately home into a veritable fortress of the mystical and the martial. The upcoming conflict loomed large but so did the burgeoning sense of unity among those gathered under its ancient roofs. Allies from various corners of the globe and realms of existence trickled in, each bringing unique strengths and capabilities to fortify the manor's defenses.

By late afternoon, the once-quiet grounds buzzed with activity. Members of the Order of Light established training grounds on the west lawn, clad in shimmering armor that reflected the sun's rays in brilliant patterns. Their calming and authoritative presence brought a new level of discipline to the preparations.

In the shaded groves to the north, Redington's contacts from the urban shadows—hackers, informants, and street-savvy fighters—rigged surveillance systems and set up communication networks that would alert them to any physical intrusion.

Kesia and Mara worked together to weave an intricate network of magical defenses, layering wards, and protective spells that shielded the manor and created a sanctuary space for those who might need respite from the dark energies they were preparing to combat.

Lexi and Lord Winston convened inside the manor with Jothan and Isabella to map out their battle strategy. They had spread out a large parchment map of the estate and surrounding lands on the massive oak table that dominated the library.

Jothan, with a tactician's precision, pointed to key locations. "If they breached the north wing last time, it's because they perceived it as a weak point. We'll turn it into a trap. Here and here," he indicated two points, "We'll set up decoys that mimic the energy signature of the Dial."

Isabella, taking notes, added, "And I'll coordinate with the Order to station their most powerful mystics there. Any force trying to penetrate will meet a surprise they won't recover from."

Lord Winston, meanwhile, focused on alliances. "I've reached out to the Elemental Guilds. The Fire Guild has expressed their readiness to assist, and the Water Guild may not be far behind. Their mastery over their respective elements will be crucial."

Sophea and Mara oversaw the calibration of the Cosmos Dial itself, ensuring its energies were attuned not just for defense but also for alerting them to breaches in the cosmic balance. "If we can predict their moves even a few minutes beforehand, we'll have the advantage," Sophea explained as her hands moved deftly over the ancient runes encircling the Dial.

Mara nodded, her eyes alight with the challenge. "I've modified the Dial to send a pulse through the ley lines if it detects a surge in dark energy. It will give us a heads-up and weaken any incoming spells."

The group took turns having naps throughout the day.

As dusk fell, the manor settled into a wary peace. Lexi walked the perimeter with Redington, reviewing the final placements of guards and magical traps. "Do you think we're ready?" she asked him, her voice tinged with both hope and anxiety.

Redington looked around, taking in the sight of the well-prepared grounds and the determined faces of their allies. "We're as ready as we can ever be, Lexi. You've done an incredible job rallying everyone, setting the stage not just for tonight but for whatever comes after."

Lexi nodded, feeling the truth of his words. This was more than just a battle; it was a prelude to a greater war, a setup for the deeper mysteries and challenges they would face."

As they returned to the manor, the first stars appeared in the twilight sky, and the Cosmos Dial began to emit a soft, pulsating glow—a reminder of the power they were sworn to protect and the inevitable forces drawn to its light.

Tonight, Wrightenton Manor was not just a home nor merely a fortress. It was a beacon of light and hope, a rallying point for all who stood in defense of the cosmic order. The stage was set, the players were ready, and the night ahead promised to be a pivotal chapter in the ongoing saga of the Cosmos Dial.

Chapter 66

The night cloaked Wrightenton Manor in darkness, thick and oppressive as if to mirror the weight of the looming confrontation. Inside, the glow of candlelight and the hum of magic being woven into the air provided a stark contrast to the shadowy unease outside. Lexi stood by a window in the main hall, her gaze piercing the darkness, watching for the first signs of the assault she knew was coming.

The silence of the night was shattered by a low, rumbling growl that swept across the fields like a harbinger of doom. Kesia, stationed at the northern watchtower with her mystical sensors, was the first to react. "They're here," she broadcasted over the communications network, her voice a mix of calm and alertness.

From the wooded edges of the estate, shadowy figures emerged, not walking but almost flowing over the ground, their forms blurry and indistinct. Behind them, larger, more formidable shapes took form—beasts of nightmare conjured from the underworld's darkest depths.

Redington met the first wave head-on alongside Mara and a squadron of the Order's knights. The clash was titanic, the sound of magic and might clashing against claw and fang echoing through the night. Mara's runes flared brightly, sapping the strength of their adversaries and causing disarray in their ranks.

At the eastern flank, Isabella and Jothan orchestrated a volley of enchanted arrows and mystical barriers that turned the ground into a quagmire for the advancing foes. Each step they took drained them further, their dark energies being siphoned off and dispersed into the night.

As the battle raged, a new figure appeared on the field—another warlock leader, his presence chilling the very air around him. He raised his staff, and a wave of dark energy surged forth, aimed directly at the manor's heart.

Sophea, sensing the incoming threat, channeled her counter-spells through the Cosmos Dial. The Dial absorbed the dark wave, its glow intensifying before redirecting the energy back at the warlock, creating a shockwave that knocked him and his immediate forces off their feet.

Despite their initial successes, the defenders soon realized they were being herded into a trap.

"They're splitting us up, using the lesser minions to corral us," Jothan yelled over the din of battle. "Regroup! Focus on the warlock!"

Understanding the tactical shift necessary, Lexi signaled for a retreat toward the manor. The grounds, imbued with Kesia's protective spells, would provide a narrower battleground that could limit the effectiveness of the enemy's numbers.

Back at the manor, Lord Winston and the remaining mystics had prepared the last line of defense. The ground was etched with sigils, the air thrummed with latent energy ready to be unleashed, and the very stones of the manor were imbued with protective magic.

As the retreating defenders made their way back, they fell into formation, a solid wall of steel and spellcraft facing the oncoming tide. The warlock, recovering from his setback, advanced once more, his eyes ablaze with hatred and dark power.

With a defiant roar, the defenders unleashed their full might. The Cosmos Dial, central to their defense, glowed like a beacon, its energy pulsating through the ley lines laid out by Mara and Sophea. The clash was monumental, light against dark, hope against despair.

In the heart of the battle, Lexi found herself face to face with the warlock. With a cry that melded fury and determination, she drew upon the Dial's power, channeling it through her being. Light swirled around her, forming a shield and a spear of pure radiance.

Lexi struck with a final push, fueled by the collective will and power of all the defenders. The spear of light pierced through the darkness, finding its mark. The warlock screamed, a sound of ultimate defeat, as his form dissipated, his dark energies unraveling into nothingness.

As the last of the shadows were banished and the creatures of nightmare retreated, the sky began to lighten with the first hints of dawn. Exhausted but victorious, the defenders of Wrightenton Manor gathered in the main hall, their faces weary but alight with the joy of survival and triumph.

"We did it," Lexi breathed out, her eyes meeting those of her companions. "But this is only the beginning. As long as the Cosmos Dial exists, it will attract those who crave its power."

Lord Winston, stepping forward, placed a hand on her shoulder. "Then we will be ready, Lexi."

Chapter 67

The dawn at Wrightenton Manor was tinged with the dual relief and weariness of the night's hard-won battle. As the first rays of sunlight pierced the lingering shadows, they cast long, golden streaks across the battered but unyielded grounds of the estate. Inside, the defenders, though exhausted, shared in the brief respite that victory afforded them. Yet, the air was thick with the unspoken knowledge that this respite could be fleeting.

The group gathered around the long oak table for a debriefing in the majestic library, strewn with maps and remnants of hastily conjured defenses. Lord Winston, his face showing lines of fatigue, addressed the group.

"We have held them off, but this victory, while significant, is but a pause in the storm that seeks to engulf us. We must use this time wisely," he declared, his voice resonating with a mix of caution and determination.

Lexi nodded, feeling the weight of Lord Winston's words. "We need to understand more about the forces aligned against us. The Dial is not just a target; it's a beacon that draws power and conflict to it."

Redington, leaning against the mantle, chimed in with a tactical perspective. "We've seen what they're capable of, and we've measured our own strengths and weaknesses. Now's the time to shore up our defenses, yes, but also to think about allies. We can't face the next wave alone."

Lord Winston, who had been coordinating the manor's physical defenses, added, "I've reached out to other historical and mystical preservation societies. They have resources, both scholarly and arcane, that could aid us. Plus, their vested interest in protecting such artifacts could make them invaluable allies."

Kesia, still vibrant with the remnants of last night's magical exertions, suggested, "We should also consider sending emissaries to the Elemental Guilds. Their mastery of natural forces could provide us with offensive and defensive capabilities."

Sophea, who had been quiet, said, "And let's not forget the power of knowledge. The more we understand about the Cosmos Dial from historical records, the better we can predict and counteract attempts to misuse it."

Lexi, feeling a surge of purpose, responded affirmatively. She knew the importance of each task and the role they played in the broader defense of the Dial. The Manor began to buzz again, not with the chaos of battle but with the ordered hustle of preparation and fortification.

Later that day, as the sun reached its zenith, Lexi took a moment for herself in the manor's ancient gardens. The flowers and trees seemed unaware of the nocturnal tumult, blooming proudly in the daylight. It was here that she felt a momentary peace, a connection to the world that wasn't fraught with cosmic wars and mystical vendettas.

Yet, even this peace was interrupted by the soft chime of the Cosmos Dial, resonating gently through the fabric of the manor. Lexi stood and went inside to the Dial, its surface glowing under the touch of sunlight. She laid a hand upon it, feeling the pulse of cosmic energy that coursed through its ancient mechanisms.

As she touched the Dial, visions flickered before her eyes—echoes of potential futures, some filled with light and others shadowed by darkness. The Dial was showing her the stakes, the myriad paths that lay ahead, dependent on their actions and choices.

With a deep breath, Lexi stepped back, the visions fading as she withdrew her hand. She knew what needed to be done, and she was prepared to lead her companions through whatever challenges came next.

As she took a deep breath, her resolve was clear. They would fortify, they would ally, and they would learn. The Cosmos Dial was their responsibility, not just to protect but to understand. And understand it they would, for the sake of all realms connected by its power.

The battle had been won, but the war, the war for the soul of the cosmos, was just beginning. Lexi and her allies were ready to meet it head-on, armed with knowledge, power, and a profound commitment to maintaining the cosmic balance. The journey to "Wisdom of a Soul" was underway and promised to be as arduous as it was enlightening.

Chapter 68

As the late afternoon sun cast long shadows over the grounds of Wrightenton Manor, the atmosphere was one of busy preparation and strategic collaboration. Lexi and her companions were fully engaged in forging alliances and strengthening their defenses, aware that the respite provided by their recent victory might be short-lived.

Inside the study, Isabella worked diligently at her communications setup, reaching out to various historical and mystical preservation societies. Her efforts were met with keen interest; the threat to the Cosmos Dial had galvanized a network of allies, each bringing their unique resources and expertise to the table.

Meanwhile, Kesia and Lord Winston set off to meet representatives from the Elemental Guilds. Their journey took them deep into the heart of

an ancient forest where the Earth Guild resided.
The guild, recognizing the severity of the threat,
agreed to lend their power, promising to send
earth elementals to fortify the manor's defenses.

Back at the manor, Sophea, and Redington
delved into the arcane library, unearthing scrolls
and tomes that contained forgotten spells and
wards. They worked together to weave these
into the existing magical fabric of the manor,
creating a strengthened lattice of protection that
was both complex and potent.

Using her deep knowledge of arcane
countermeasures, Mara assisted by setting up
mystical dampeners that cloaked the manor's
location from those who might seek it through
magical means. Her spells were intricate,
designed to mislead and confuse any dark
practitioners who attempted to pinpoint the
Dial's energy signature.

Outside, Jothan oversaw the construction of
physical fortifications. He directed the
placement of enchanted artillery—cannons that
could fire bursts of elemental energy designed to
disrupt and disorient any invading forces.

By evening, the manor resembled a command
center, bustling with activity. Lexi called a
meeting with all key members of their newly
formed alliance. They gathered around the large
table in the main library, maps and plans spread
out before them.

"Thank you all for your swift actions and the
strengths you bring to our cause," Lexi began,

her voice firm. "We have built a formidable defense, but we must be prepared for anything. Our enemies are diverse and determined."

Redington introduced the tactical plan. "We've established surveillance on all approaches and reinforced all potential weak points. Additionally, our new allies from the preservation societies are setting up further wards and offering relics that will enhance our mystical defenses."

Kesia reported on the support from the Elemental Guilds. "The Earth Guild will reinforce the physical structure of the manor. The Fire Guild has sent salamanders that can be summoned in case of attack, and the Water Guild is creating barriers that can flood the grounds on command to hinder any ground assault."

Sophea added, "And from the arcane texts, Lord Winston and I have resurrected old wards that will alert us to any breaches in our magical defenses. We will know the moment they attempt to cross."

As night fell, the manor settled into a watchful peace. After a short cat nap, Lexi walked the perimeter, reviewing every defense, every spell, and every alliance they had forged. The night air was cool, carrying with it the scent of the impending autumn, and the rustle of the leaves seemed to whisper secrets of ancient magic and battles fought long ago.

In the quiet of the night, Lexi felt a profound connection to the Cosmos Dial, its presence a constant hum in her mind. She knew that the battle they had won was only the first of many. But she also knew they were no longer alone; they had created a network of might and magic that spanned across realms and disciplines.

Standing under the stars, Lexi felt the weight of the Dial's destiny, and her own, interlinked with the fate of the cosmos. The coming days would test them all, but she was ready—to lead, to defend, and to preserve. The stage was set not just for a battle but for a saga that would echo through the ages as they stood on the brink of "Wisdom of a Soul." The night might be long, but the light of their resolve burned fiercely against the darkness.

Chapter 69

With Wrightenton Manor transformed into a bastion of both ancient wisdom and modern defenses, Lexi felt a brief moment of calm settle over the estate. The air was crisp with the onset of night, and the newly installed defenses hummed softly in the background, a testament to the rigorous preparations they had undertaken. The allies had gathered, each bringing their unique strengths to fortify the Manor against the impending darkness.

The unusual stillness of the evening did little to ease the tension that hung in the air. Lexi, walking through the Manor's corridors, felt the eerie calm as a stark contrast to the flurry of activity that had consumed their last few days. She knew this lull was deceptive, a mere pause before the chaos likely to unfold.

Isabella joined Lexi as she inspected the perimeter defenses from a high balcony. "It's too quiet," Isabella murmured, echoing Lexi's thoughts. "Like the deep breath before the plunge."

Lexi nodded, her gaze scanning the horizon. "We're ready for them, whatever comes. The Elemental Guilds have fortified the grounds and set traps that will harness the natural forces should our enemies dare to attack."

Back inside, Jothan and Redington poured over tactical maps, their discussion a low buzz. "We've got the physical and magical realms covered," Jothan pointed out, tracing lines that represented their defensive strategies. "But we need to be adaptable. Our enemies have shown both cunning and brute force."

Redington, examining a series of reports from his scouts, added, "The underworld's reach is long. We should expect surprises. Calponi's influence has not waned with his imprisonment; if anything, it has deepened."

In the library, Sophea and Mara were deep in concentration, enhancing the mystical wards around the Manor. Each rune they inscribed pulsed with energy, creating a network of power that would alert them to any breach. "These wards are linked directly to the Cosmos Dial," Mara explained. "Any significant disruption will resonate through these, giving us an early warning."

Kesia, working alongside them, infused the barriers with elemental energies. "Fire to cleanse, water to soothe, earth to shield, and air to discern," she intoned, her hands moving rhythmically as she bound the elements to their will.

Later, as dusk turned to night, Lexi stood before the Cosmos Dial, its surface glowing under the soft light of the moon filtering through the windows. The Dial was more than just a relic; it was a conduit for immense cosmic powers, and Lexi felt both its allure and its burden.

She was joined by Lord Winston, who regarded the Dial with a mix of reverence and concern. "This Dial has the power to change the very fabric of reality," he said quietly. "We must be judicious in its use. It is not only a weapon but a beacon of balance."

Lexi touched the Dial, feeling the familiar hum of energy. "I know," she responded. "We will use it to protect, not to provoke. Its power is immense, but so is our responsibility."

As the night deepened, the defenders took their positions. The Manor was silent, save for the soft murmurs of the last-minute checks. Each person knew their role, and each one prepared to defend not just the Manor and the Dial but also the ideals they stood for.

From the vantage point of the main tower, Lexi surveyed the grounds, her companions at her side. They were warriors of light in a world that threatened to be consumed by darkness. The stakes were higher than they had ever been, and as they waited for the battle to begin, they found strength in their unity.

"This is the calm before the storm," Lexi said to her allies, her voice steady and sure. "But no matter what happens tonight, we stand together. For the Dial, for the Manor, and for the future of all realms connected by its power."

The air was charged with potential, with the imminent clash of cosmic forces. The night might bring battle, but Wrightenton Manor stood ready, a steadfast beacon of light against the encroaching darkness. The defenders were prepared, come what may, to protect the ancient artifact that bound them together and to face whatever challenges the darkness brought to their doorstep. The storm was about to break, and they were ready to meet it head-on.

Chapter 70

Under the cloak of night, the tension at Wrightenton Manor reached a crescendo as the first signs of the enemy's approach stirred the defenders into heightened alertness. The distant sounds of movement—rustling leaves and the soft thud of stealthy footsteps—heralded the onset of the anticipated assault.

Jothan, coordinating the defense from the ground, responded with practiced calm. "Understood. Archers and elementalists to the east wall. Let's soften their approach."

Mara and Kesia, stationed at strategic points along the eastern defenses, unleashed the first wave of countermeasures. Streams of fire mingled with gusts of razor-sharp wind tore through the advancing ranks, disrupting their formation and sowing chaos.

As the battle intensified, a dense fog began to roll across the fields, unnatural and cloying. Through the mist, the silhouette of a formidable figure emerged—the third warlock leader, his staff glowing with a malignant light. He raised his staff, and the ground before him roiled as shadowy tendrils rose to form a phalanx of spectral warriors.

Sophea, sensing the surge of dark magic, initiated the mystical barriers they had prepared. "Activate the ley-line defenses now!" she declared. The ground around the manor lit up with luminous runes, creating a barrier that pulsed against the dark magic, diminishing the potency of the warlock's creations.

The battle grew fiercer as elemental forces clashed. The Earth Guild's elementals, massive beings of stone and soil, rose from the earth, their forms interlocking to form bulwarks against the invaders. Meanwhile, the Fire Guild's salamanders breathed streams of fire, creating a blazing no-man's-land that incinerated anything that dared cross.

Redington, moving through the ranks, provided strategic oversight and direct support where needed. His presence bolstered the morale of the defenders, and his actions were as precise as they were lethal.

Amidst the chaos, Lexi focused on a subtler aspect of the battlefield. Utilizing her affinity for spirits, she summoned spectral scouts to infiltrate the enemy lines and gather intelligence.

What they discovered was troubling—the warlock was not merely leading a physical assault but was also attempting to weaken the manor's spiritual defenses through a dark ritual.

"Lexi, we need to disrupt his ritual," Kesia reported, urgency clear in her voice. "It's amplifying their power and could potentially breach our inner sanctum."

Lexi nodded, formulating a quick plan. "Mara, Sophea, with me. We're going to need a focused strike to break his concentration and disrupt the ritual."

Gathering a small, elite team, Lexi led them through a concealed passage that allowed them to flank the warlock's position. Emerging from the shadows, they confronted the warlock, who was encircled by dark energies and deep in concentration.

The sudden appearance of Lexi and her team caught him off-guard, disrupting his incantations. Mara quickly erected a shield to block a retaliatory strike while Sophea launched a barrage of cleansing light to purify the area.

Lexi, seizing the moment, advanced toward the warlock. With a shout, she channeled the pure energy of the Cosmos Dial through her being, her arms glowing with radiant power as she struck at the heart of the dark ritual.

With a deafening crack, the ritual circle shattered, the backlash of energies knocking the warlock off his feet and dispelling the shadowy warriors he had summoned. The fog began to lift, and the dark energies that had overwhelmed the field started to dissipate.

"We've broken their main offensive," Lexi gasped, exhausted but exhilarated. "Now to push them back for good."

With the warlock's defeat, the morale of the invading forces crumbled. Jothan capitalized on this shift, rallying the defenders for a final push. "Drive them back! For the Manor, for the realms!" he cried.

The defenders surged forward, their spirits lifted by the breaking of the ritual. The battle lines shifted rapidly, and soon, the enemy was in retreat, harried by the relentless counterattacks of Wrightenton's guardians.

As dawn approached, the remnants of the dark army fled into the shadows from whence they had come, leaving behind the echo of their defeat. Wrightenton Manor stood strong, its defenses unbreached, its guardians victorious but vigilant.

The night had tested them all, but it had also proven the strength of their alliances and the power of unity against darkness. As they regrouped to assess and repair, there was a shared sense of accomplishment—and the knowledge that the war was far from over, but for now, they had won a crucial battle.

Chapter 71

As the first light of dawn washed over Wrightenton Manor, it illuminated the signs of the night's fierce battle. Scorch marks adorned the once-pristine walls, and the ground was littered with remnants of dark magic and elemental fury. Yet, despite the destruction, there was a pervasive sense of triumph among the defenders. They had faced a formidable foe and emerged victorious, albeit not without cost.

Lexi and Lord Winston walked through the grounds, surveying the damage and cataloging repairs needed. The physical scars were evident, but there were deeper, less visible impacts to consider—the emotional and spiritual toll on their allies and the grounds themselves, still vibrating with the residual energy of the battle.

"Structurally, the Manor held up well, thanks to the Earth Guild's elementals," Lord Winston observed, making notes on a clipboard. "But we'll need to cleanse and reconsecrate the grounds. There's still a dark taint marring the ley lines."

Kesia, overhearing the conversation, nodded in agreement. "I can feel the disturbances in the flow of energy. We'll need to perform several rituals to restore the balance and ensure no lingering malevolence takes root."

Mara was setting up a makeshift infirmary inside the Manor to tend to the wounded. While their physical injuries were treatable, the psychic shocks sustained during the battle by those sensitive to magical forces required more delicate handling.

Mara applied her knowledge of arcane healing, using light magic to soothe the auras of the afflicted. "The body heals much faster than the spirit," she explained to a young knight of the Order, who had been overwhelmed by the warlock's dark energies. "Rest here, and let the light mend what has been broken."

Later in the day, Lexi convened a meeting with all key defenders and allies in the Manor's main hall. The mood was somber yet hopeful as they discussed not only the battle's outcomes but also the lessons learned and strategies for future encounters.

Redington, who had been instrumental in organizing the physical defenses, shared his insights. "We underestimated their ability to corrupt and use the land against us. Next time, our perimeter defenses need to be not only stronger but also more resilient against magical subversion."

Jothan added, "The surveillance tech helped, but we were blind in areas where their magic dampened our electronics. We need a hybrid system of tech and magic for better coverage and integration." Then, he outlined the tactical adjustments required based on the night's experiences. "Our response was reactive. We need predefined response scenarios for future engagements that integrate our magical and physical capabilities more seamlessly."

Lexi listened intently, her mind already racing with plans and contingencies. "This battle was a test," she addressed the room, her voice resonant with authority and conviction. "We learned much, and we will continue to adapt. Our enemies will not rest, and neither will we. We must be proactive, not just in defense but in strengthening our bonds with allies and understanding our enemies' motivations."

After the meeting, Lexi retreated to the room where the Cosmos Dial was securely housed. She approached the ancient artifact, its surface still humming softly with the power it had wielded to help turn the tide of battle. Lexi placed her hand on the Dial, feeling the pulse of cosmic energy.

"Show me," she whispered, her eyes closing as she sought guidance for the path ahead.

Visions flickered before her, scenarios of possible futures, each branching out from the decisions they would make in the coming days.

The Dial's visions were cryptic, but one message was clear: the battle for the Cosmos Dial was far from over. There were darker forces at play, and the stakes were higher than they had ever imagined.

As Lexi opened her eyes, her resolve hardened. She would prepare Wrightenton Manor not just to defend but to be a beacon of hope and a bastion of power against the darkness. The coming days would require her to gather all her strength and wisdom, for the challenges ahead were daunting, but she knew they would not face them alone.

Chapter 72

In the wake of the recent battle, the atmosphere at Wrightenton Manor was one of cautious vigilance. The victory, though significant, was not lost on anyone as merely the precursor to greater challenges that lay ahead. Lexi, fully aware of the escalating threat, initiated plans to deepen their alliances and fortify the Manor's mystical and physical defenses.

Lexi arranged a series of meetings with the leaders of the allied forces that had come to their aid. Each meeting aimed to cement the bonds forged in battle and to outline a framework for mutual defense and intelligence sharing. The leaders of the Earth and Fire Guilds, impressed by the Manor's strategic importance and Lexi's leadership, pledged their continued support.

"The Earth Guild will fortify the grounds, making them unyielding to dark forces," declared the Earth Guild's elder, his voice echoing like rolling stones. "And our elementals will stand guard, merging with the very soil to shield this place."

The Fire Guild's representative, a fiery woman with hair like molten lava, added, "Our flames will light the dark corners where evil seeks to hide. No shadow shall fall upon this Manor without our knowing."

Back at the Manor, Sophea, and Mara focused on enhancing the ley lines that intersected beneath the estate. Using the Cosmos Dial as a focal point, they conducted rituals that purified and amplified the ley energies, creating a protective aura that would act as a first line of defense against magical intrusions.

Working alongside them, Kesia devised a series of sentinel spells that would alert them to any malicious magical activity. "These sentinels will not only warn us of incoming threats but also weaken any magical force directed against the Manor," Kesia explained as she wove the complex web of enchantments.

Redington and Isabella, realizing the need for improved surveillance, implemented a dual magical and technological observation system. Enchanted scrying mirrors were installed alongside state-of-the-art surveillance cameras, providing comprehensive coverage of the Manor's surroundings.

"We'll see them coming, by magic or by might," Redington assured Lexi as they inspected the new installations. "And we'll be ready."

With the physical and magical preparations underway, Lexi also organized training sessions for the Manor's defenders. These sessions, led by Jothan and the knights of the Order of Light, were intense and rigorous, combining physical conditioning with strategic combat exercises.

"The next time we face our enemies, it will not just be as defenders but as warriors prepared to strike back," Jothan proclaimed, his voice resolute.

During a routine patrol of the outer grounds, one of Kesia's elemental scouts detected an anomaly—a faint but distinct pulsation of dark energy seeping through a crack in one of the newly reinforced ley lines. Alerted to the potential breach, Kesia and Sophea investigated the site.

"This isn't just a residual effect from the battle," Sophea noted, her expression grave as she examined the crack. "It's a deliberate attempt to weaken our defenses from within. Someone or something is testing our barriers."

That evening, under a moonlit sky, Lexi convened a council with her top advisors and allies in the Manor's ancient stone circle, a site of power used by the defenders to enhance their connection to the cosmic energies.

"We are not just fighting a war of defense but a war of attrition," Lexi stated, her voice echoing slightly off the standing stones. "Our enemies are probing for weaknesses, and we must respond not only with strength but with cunning."

The group discussed various strategies, from counter-espionage to preemptive strikes against known enemy strongholds. The decision was made to send out scouts—both physical and astral—to gather intelligence on the dark forces amassing against them.

As the meeting concluded, the allies placed their hands together, each pledging their commitment to the defense of Wrightenton Manor and the protection of the Cosmos Dial. The energy of their united spirits pulsed through the stone circle, sending ripples of power into the surrounding lands.

Standing at the center, Lexi felt the weight of her responsibilities and the strength of the bonds that united them. "Together, we will turn the tide," she vowed. "Not just for us, but for all who stand in the shadow of darkness."

With the Manor fortified, allies rallied, and strategies set, Lexi and her companions prepared for the challenges ahead. The shadows might gather, but Wrightenton Manor would stand as a beacon of light, ready to face whatever came from the darkness. The stage was set for a confrontation that would determine the fate of realms, both earthly and celestial.

Chapter 73

In the still hours before dawn, with the world outside shrouded in darkness and a palpable silence enveloping Wrightenton Manor, Lexi found herself in the ancient chapel that had served the estate's various inhabitants for centuries. Here, amidst the aged stone and stained glass that depicted scenes of celestial intervention, Lexi sought solace and guidance.

Lexi knelt at the weathered altar, her hands clasped tightly together, her eyes closed as she focused her thoughts and opened her heart to the divine. She began the invocation with a voice that was both steady and filled with reverence.

"Archangel Raziel, keeper of secrets and divine wisdom, I seek your guidance in this hour of need," Lexi intoned, the flickering candlelight casting soft shadows across the chapel. "Reveal to me the path that we must walk to protect the sacred balance and to thwart the darkness that seeks to usurp the Cosmos Dial's power."

As she spoke, the air around her seemed to thicken. The candles flickered more intensely, and a gentle warmth filled the space, a sign of Raziel's presence. The archangel did not appear in a physical form, but his voice, clear and resonant, echoed through the chapel.

"Lexi Constantine, your plea has been heard," Raziel's voice enveloped her, imbued with calm authority. "The path you seek is fraught with peril but also ripe with potential. You must prepare not only your defenses but your spirit and those of your allies."

"The new warlock you face is but a pawn in a greater scheme. Seek out the Heart of Tenebris, a source of his dark power. It lies hidden, guarded by shadows within the Forest of Whispers. Securing it will weaken your foe's influence."

Lexi listened intently, her mind racing as she absorbed Raziel's words. "How will we find this Heart within such a place, steeped in deception and danger?" she asked, her voice a whisper of concern.

"Use the Cosmos Dial, not as a shield but as a beacon. Its light can pierce the shadows that protect the Heart. Trust in those who wield the elements, for they will be crucial in this endeavor. And remember, the purest light is born from the darkest shadow. Embrace the light

within you and your allies to guide your way,"
Raziel advised.

As the presence of Raziel receded, leaving a
lingering sense of power and purpose, Lexi rose
from her knees, fortified by the archangel's
guidance. She left the chapel with a clear
direction and convened a meeting with her
closest advisors as the first light of dawn crept
across the sky.

Gathering in the library, Lexi shared her
divine encounter. "We have a new objective—
the Heart of Tenebris. It's the key to diminishing
the warlock's power. We'll need to organize a
strike team immediately. Kesia, Sophea, and
Mara, you will accompany me. Redington,
manage the defenses here with Lord Winston."

Familiar with the arcane energies, Kesia
suggested, "The Forest of Whispers is
ensorcelled to mislead and confuse. We should
consult with the Air Guild for clarity of thought
and the Fire Guild for illumination."

Sophea nodded in agreement, adding, "And I
will prepare protective prayers to shield us from
the dark energies that pervade the forest."

Redington, though concerned, understood his
role. "We'll keep the Manor secure and continue
gathering intelligence. Be careful, Lexi. This
Heart seems like more than just a power
source—it's a beacon of darkness."

With the team assembled and their roles
defined, preparations began at a frenetic pace.

Lexi and her team equipped themselves with the necessary artifacts and weapons. Each enchanted to counteract the dark magics they would face.

As they set out for the Forest of Whispers, the weight of their task was palpable, but so was their determination. Led by Lexi's newfound clarity and the guidance of Archangel Raziel, they felt prepared to face whatever lay ahead.

Back at the Manor, Redington, and Lord Winston watched the team depart, their expressions a mix of resolve and concern. "They carry with them the hopes of all who stand in the light," Winston murmured, turning to reinforce the Manor's defenses.

The quest for the Heart of Tenebris was more than a mission; it was a pivotal moment in the battle against darkness, a step closer to the ultimate confrontation that Lexi knew was inevitable. As they ventured into the shadowed forest, the battle for balance continued, each step guided by the wisdom of the archangel and the courage of the defenders.

Chapter 74

The journey to the Forest of Whispers was fraught with an oppressive sense of foreboding. The forest itself, a sprawling expanse of gnarled trees and perpetual twilight, seemed to absorb not just light but sound, giving the impression of a world removed from time and reality. Lexi and her team, each attuned to the energies of their mission, proceeded with a mixture of caution and resolve.

As they crossed the threshold of the forest, the air grew noticeably colder, and a suffocating silence enveloped them. Kesia, who led the way with her staff glowing softly with protective runes, whispered, "The forest disorients senses and magics alike. Keep close and maintain visual contact at all times."

Mara, carrying a lantern enchanted with fire from the Fire Guild, provided the only source of reliable light, casting eerie shadows that danced mockingly around them. "The light wards off weaker spirits, but be wary of illusions," she cautioned, her eyes scanning the dark recesses between the trees.

Isabella, clutching a satchel of charms and wards, periodically set down protective markers that emitted a faint hum, creating a breadcrumb trail of energy they could follow back if needed.

Not long into their trek, the team encountered their first obstacle. Shadowy figures, barely discernible from the darkness around them, began to materialize. They moved with a chilling grace, their forms blurring at the edges, making them difficult to target.

"Stand back," Mara commanded, drawing a sword imbued with celestial light. With a deft swing, she cleaved through the nearest shadow, its form dissipating into a cloud of dark mist. "These are minor guardians. The Heart must be close."

As they delved deeper, the encounters became more frequent and intense. Kesia's spells illuminated the path, revealing traps and illusions that sought to lead them astray. "This place is alive with malice," she noted, dispelling a particularly vicious hex that had almost ensnared Mara.

Lexi, sensing the increasing malevolence, paused to consult the Cosmos Dial. She focused on channeling its energies. The Dial emitted a pulse of light, which cut through the gloom and highlighted a narrow path through the undergrowth. "This way," she said, her voice firm despite the ominous atmosphere.

The team followed, with Sophea reinforcing their rear guard.

Eventually, the forest began to open up into a clearing dominated by an ancient, twisted tree. Beneath its sprawling canopy, a dark crystal pulsed with a sinister energy—the Heart of Tenebris. It was encased in a thicket of thorns that seemed to writhe with a life of their own.

Mara stepped forward, examining the barrier. "These thorns are imbued with dark magic. I can weaken them, but it will take time and leave me vulnerable."

Lexi nodded. "Do it. Kesia, Sophea, cover her. I'll prepare the ritual to extract the Heart."

As Mara began her incantation, the air around them crackled with dark energy. Shadows converged on the clearing, drawn by the disruption of their sanctum. Kesia and Sophea worked in tandem, casting barrier spells and prayers and repelling the encroaching darkness.

With Mara's efforts weakening the thorn barrier, Lexi approached the Heart, her sword ready. She chanted a series of ancient words, her voice clear and resonant. The ground trembled, and the thorns retracted, revealing the dark crystal.

Lexi reached out, her hands enveloped in a protective aura and grasped the Heart. It thrummed with malevolent power, but she held firm, severing its ties to the dark energies. With a final, piercing scream from the forest, the connection was broken.

"Retreat!" Lexi shouted as the clearing began to collapse on itself. The team hurried back along the path they had come, the forest now shrieking in fury at the theft of its dark heart.

They emerged from the Forest of Whispers just as the sun rose, casting light over a world that seemed far removed from the dark horrors within. The Heart of Tenebris was secured, a significant blow to their enemies, and a critical advantage gained for the forces of light.

As they made their way back to Wrightenton Manor, each member of the team felt the weight of what they had achieved—and the cost at which it had come. The battle was far from over, but they had won an important victory today.

Chapter 75

With the Heart of Tenebris safely extracted from the Forest of Whispers, the journey back to Wrightenton Manor was tense, marked by the vigilant watchfulness of Lexi and her team. The forest's angry howls had faded into an unsettling quiet as if the very land mourned the loss of its dark centerpiece.

Upon their return, the Manor's atmosphere was one of cautious optimism. The Heart, now contained within a crystal lattice crafted by Mara, pulsated with a subdued yet ominous glow. The containment chamber, designed to suppress its malignant energies, was set up in the Manor's deepest vault, guarded by an array of spells and physical barriers.

Lexi convened a meeting in the library with all key allies and mystic defenders present. "The Heart of Tenebris is more than a source of dark power. It's a demonic key," she explained. "A key to understanding—and potentially countering—the warlock's plans."

Taking the lead on the mystical investigation, Kesia employed various divination tools to probe the Heart. With each spell cast and rune read, the Heart revealed shadows of its past manipulations and hints of its future intentions. "This object has been used to orchestrate chaos far beyond our lands," Sophea announced grimly. "Its reach is extensive, but so is its vulnerability."

Sophea, working alongside Kesia, added, "It's tethered to ley lines that extend across the continent. If we can decode its network, we can potentially sever the warlock's control over many dark creatures and cursed sites."

Jothan and Redington, focusing on the tactical implications, discussed the potential of using the Heart as bait. "If we can lure key figures of the enemy's forces into a trap using the Heart as bait, we could decimate their leadership in one fell swoop," Jothan proposed, his eyes scanning the maps laid out before him.

Redington nodded, his mind racing through scenarios. "We'll need airtight defenses and a plan for quick extraction. If we play this right, we could turn the tide of this war."

Recognizing the need for a united front, Lexi called for a council of all allied forces the following day. Leaders and representatives from the Elemental Guilds, the Order of Light, and various mystical preservation societies convened at the Manor. Each was briefed on the nature and potential of the Heart of Tenebris.

The Fire Guild's representative, a fiery-haired sorceress named Elara, suggested an elemental seal. "We can forge a seal combining all four elemental powers to contain and neutralize the Heart's energy, making it safe to use without risk of corruption."

The Water Guild proposed a purification ritual, which would cleanse the Heart and potentially allow it to extract its raw energies for use in reinforcing the Manor's defenses.

Under the vaulted ceilings of the Manor's ancient ritual chamber, a grand ceremony was held. Lexi, accompanied by the elemental masters, initiated the ritual. The Heart was placed at the center of a sigil-marked floor, surrounded by channels carved for the elemental energies.

As the ritual progressed, the Heart's dark glow diminished, replaced by a pulsating light that grew brighter and purer with each incantation and offering. The air was thick with the power of the elements—flames danced, water flowed, air swirled, and stones shifted.

When the ritual concluded, the Heart, now radiant with cleansed energy, ceased its ominous pulsations. "It is done," Elara declared, her voice echoing powerfully. "The Heart is now a beacon of balance, not malice."

As the allies celebrated their success, Lexi felt a profound sense of accomplishment and hope. The cleansed Heart could now be used to fortify the ley lines against dark intrusions, potentially turning the Manor into a stronghold against any future assaults.

However, Lexi knew that their victory, significant as it was, represented just one battle in a much larger war. The warlock and his forces would not sit idle, and the dark powers behind him were still a looming threat. But for now, Wrightenton Manor stood stronger and more united than ever, a testament to the power of collaboration and the enduring strength of the light.

With the dawn breaking over the horizon, Lexi looked out across the Manor's grounds. Her resolve hardened like the newly fortified ley lines. The battle for balance was far from over, but they were ready—with new wisdom, new allies, and a newfound power in the Heart of Tenebris.

Chapter 76

*A*s the newly purified Heart of Tenebris began its role as a bastion of balance within Wrightenton Manor, the shadowy forces that had once thrived under its dark influence found themselves disoriented and weakened. However, the relative peace following the Manor's victory was not to be mistaken for the end of the conflict. Far from it, the forces of darkness were merely regrouping, their malevolent intent as strong as ever.

Deep in the hidden recesses of the Shadow Realm, the warlock, his form barely held together by dark magics, convened with his closest advisors—a cabal of necromancers and demonologists. His failure to secure the Heart had not gone unpunished; his masters in the darker planes had seen to that.

"We must retaliate," he hissed, his voice a blend of fury and pain. "The Heart was our key to unleashing the Nether Gates. Without it, our plans are compromised."

A demonologist, her eyes glowing with a fiendish light, stepped forward. "There is another way, master. The Ancients spoke of the Obsidian Scepter, a relic capable of magnifying dark energies independently of the Heart. It lies hidden, guarded by the Sphinx of Lycarnos."

The warlock considered this, his mind turning over the new possibilities. "Prepare the expeditions," he commanded. "We cannot afford further delays. The Manor and its defenders must not disrupt our efforts again."

Back at Wrightenton Manor, unaware of the dark plans being woven against them, Lexi and her team focused on integrating the Heart's energies with the Manor's ley lines. The process was intricate, requiring the precise alignment of magical energies with the natural earth forces.

Sophea, tasked with overseeing the integration, worked closely with Mara and Kesia. "The ley lines are responding well to the Heart's influence," Sophea reported during their daily briefing. "Its energy is promoting harmony and enhancing our defensive spells."

However, Redington, ever the strategist, cautioned against complacency. "We should prepare for their next move," he advised. "The enemy will have learned from their defeat. They'll come at us harder and more cunningly."

Lexi, taking Redington's advice to heart, convened a strategy session focused on anticipating and countering the dark forces' next likely steps. During the meeting, Jothan introduced intelligence gathered from their mystical scouting networks.

"There's chatter in the shadow networks about an Obsidian Scepter," Jothan revealed. "It's reputed to be powerful enough to open and control the Nether Gates without the Heart."

Lexi grasped the severity of this new threat. "Then we must secure the Scepter before they do. It would be catastrophic should it fall into their hands."

Determined to stay one step ahead, Lexi planned a two-pronged approach. While part of her team would continue to fortify the Manor and explore further uses of the Heart, she would lead an expedition to retrieve the Obsidian Scepter.

"We'll need every advantage we can get," Lexi stated as they prepared for the journey. "Kesia, Sophea, you'll come with me. Mara, you and Lord Winston hold the fort. Ensure the Manor remains impenetrable."

As preparations for the new quest were underway, the Manor bristled with activity. Lexi and her chosen team equipped themselves with artifacts and weapons suited to their formidable task. They studied maps and ancient texts, plotting their course to the Sphinx of Lycarnos, where the Scepter was rumored to be hidden.

Lord Winston, although remaining behind, gave Lexi a reassuring nod. "We've withstood much, and we'll withstand more. Go with confidence. We'll keep the home fires burning."

As Lexi, Kesia, and Sophea left Wrightenton Manor at dawn, the air crisp and the sky a clear blue, they felt the weight of their responsibility. The journey ahead promised to be perilous, but the stakes were too high to consider failure.

Back at the Manor, Mara and Lord Winston watched them depart, their expressions a mixture of concern and determination. "May the light guide them," Mara whispered, turning back to her duties.

The quest for the Obsidian Scepter had begun, a race against dark forces that sought to unravel the fabric of reality. Lexi and her team were ready to face whatever challenges lay ahead, armed with knowledge, magic, and the unyielding spirit of Wrightenton Manor's defenders. The shadows might gather, but the light was on the move.

Chapter 77

Lexi, Sophea, and Kesia set out at the break of dawn, their path leading them toward the fabled Sphinx of Lycarnos, guardian of the Obsidian Scepter. The journey was expected to be perilous, traversing lands that were steeped in ancient magics and dark legends.

The terrain gradually shifted as they ventured further from Wrightenton Manor, from verdant woodlands into a harsher landscape of craggy hills and mist-shrouded valleys. Kesia, adept at navigating enchanted landscapes, used her divining tools to steer them clear of natural obstacles and magical traps that seemed to sprout increasingly as they neared their destination.

"The land itself resists our passage," Kesia observed, scanning the thick fogs that rolled eerily around them. "It's as if the very earth knows of our quest and seeks to thwart us."

Midway through their journey, the trio encountered a grove that was home to a congregation of elemental spirits. These spirits, wary of intruders, initially reacted with hostility. Sophea, drawing on her diplomatic skills and the residual goodwill from the Elemental Guilds, parleyed with the spirits, explaining their quest and the danger the Obsidian Scepter posed to the world.

Moved by Sophea's earnestness and the clear purity of their intentions, the spirits agreed to grant them safe passage through their domain. One, a sprite named Thalor, even offered to guide them through the labyrinthine forest that lay ahead.

With Thalor's guidance, they navigated the complex pathways of the forest, avoiding its myriad dangers. The sprite's presence seemed to calm the more restless spirits of the wood, allowing the team safe passage where many had failed before.

As they emerged from the forest, the iconic silhouette of the Sphinx of Lycarnos came into view, perched ominously on a cliff overlooking the Sea. The sight of it, even from a distance, was enough to instill a mix of awe and fear in the hearts of the travelers.

Approaching the Sphinx was no simple task; the path was littered with riddles and traps, each designed to test the wisdom and purity of those who dared seek the Scepter. Lexi, leading her companions, approached the Sphinx with a mixture of reverence and resolve.

"Who seeks the Scepter of Shadows?" the Sphinx intoned, its voice echoing against the cliffs.

"I, Lexi, guardian of Wrightenton, accompanied by my allies," Lexi responded confidently, stepping forward. "We seek to protect the realms from darkness that threatens to consume them."

The Sphinx regarded them for a moment before posing its riddle, a complex puzzle of logic and lore that twisted their minds and tested their resolve. After a tense and thoughtful pause, Lexi gave her answer, which pleased the ancient guardian.

Impressed by her wisdom and the purity of her intent, the Sphinx allowed them to approach the altar where the Obsidian Scepter lay. However, it warned, "The Scepter possesses a dark will of its own. Only one with a heart both brave and pure can wield it without falling to its corruption."

Lexi approached the altar, her heart steady, her mind clear of doubt. As she reached out and touched the Scepter, a surge of dark energy coursed through her, testing her spirit and resolve. With a strong will and the support of her allies' protective magic, she overcame the initial onslaught of the Scepter's corruptive influence.

With the Scepter secured, Lexi, Kesia, and Sophea made their way back to Wrightenton Manor. The journey home was less hindered, and the Scepter's power was now contained and tempered by Lexi's strength and the purity of their mission.

As they neared the Manor, the sense of an impending larger battle loomed over them. With the Obsidian Scepter in hand, they were a significant step closer to thwarting the dark forces arrayed against them.

Chapter 78

$\mathcal{A}$s Lexi, Kesia, and Sophea approached Wrightenton Manor with the Obsidian Scepter securely in their possession, the atmosphere at the manor was one of intense anticipation. The return of the expedition team with the artifact was not just a victory—it was a harbinger of the potential turning of tides in the ongoing battle against darkness.

Upon their arrival, the trio was greeted with a mixture of relief and eager curiosity. Lexi presented the Scepter to the assembly of allies, who were gathered in the main hall, their faces lit by the glow of the artifact now purified of its malevolent will.

Kesia, alongside Mara and Sophea, immediately set to work integrating the Scepter's energies with the Manor's existing defenses. The artifact, once a tool for opening the Nether Gates, was repurposed to strengthen the ley lines that Sophea and Mara had been fortifying.

In the ritual chamber, under the detailed supervision of Mara and Kesia, a series of enchantments were woven around the Scepter. These enchantments were designed not only to harness its power but to ensure it could not revert to its former dark purpose.

"By binding the Scepter's power thus, we effectively turn it against its creators," Mara explained as her hands traced complex sigils in the air. "It will now serve as a beacon of light, its energy pulsing through the ley lines, cleansing and protecting."

Later, in a strategic council held in the war room, Jothan laid out the updated defense plans. "With the Scepter's power now allied to our cause, we can fortify the Manor against both physical and spiritual assaults. However, we must be proactive. The enemy will not remain idle, knowing that we have turned one of their key assets against them."

Lexi, taking the lead in the discussion, proposed a series of preemptive strikes. "We have the advantage, and we should use it. Targeted strikes against known enemy strongholds could disrupt their plans and give us more time to prepare for the inevitable counterattack."

That evening, Lexi took a moment to walk the grounds of the Manor, the weight of the

Scepter's presence on her mind. The air felt lighter, the usual oppressive sense of impending doom somewhat alleviated by the artifact's reconfigured energies.

She was joined by Redington, who had been coordinating the Manor's physical security enhancements. "It's a rare piece of good news," he commented, watching the sunset paint the sky in hues of gold and crimson. "But I'm wary of relying too much on a single asset, even one as powerful as the Scepter."

Lexi nodded, her thoughts aligning with his. "It's a powerful tool, but it's not a cure. We'll need more than the Scepter if we're to end this threat permanently. Our next steps must be carefully planned."

Later that night, Lexi found herself drawn to the chapel where she had first prayed for guidance from Archangel Raziel. As she knelt before the altar, the Scepter beside her began to glow softly, resonating with the sacred space.

Her prayer was simple: "Guide us forward." As she prayed, visions flickered before her eyes—a tapestry of potential futures, each thread illuminated by the light of the Scepter. In these visions, she saw battles won and lost, allies gained and sacrificed, and dark forces gathering with renewed fury.

Yet, amidst these swirling possibilities, a constant remained—the light of the Scepter, a beacon in the darkness, guiding their way. With a renewed sense of purpose, Lexi rose from her prayers, her resolve hardened.

The next day dawned with Lexi and her allies ready to enact their new strategies. The Manor buzzed with activity as plans were set into motion, each person driven by a shared goal—to leverage the newfound power of the Obsidian Scepter to finally turn the dark tide threatening to engulf their world.

As they prepared for the challenges ahead, Lexi knew that the path would be fraught with danger. But with the Scepter's light to guide them, the defenders of Wrightenton Manor stood ready to face whatever darkness lay ahead, united and stronger than ever.

Chapter 79

With the Obsidian Scepter now a beacon of protective power, Lexi's strategy shifted from purely defensive to proactive engagement. The Manor's council had agreed on a series of precise, calculated strikes against key enemy positions, aiming to disrupt the dark forces' infrastructure and diminish their capability to mount a significant offensive.

In the library, the map of the region was laid out, dotted with markers indicating known enemy strongholds and suspected supply lines. Lexi, alongside Jothan and Redington, coordinated with the allied leaders via magical communication to finalize their plans.

"Our first target will be the Shadow Nexus," Lexi declared, pointing to a location deep within the enemy territory marked by a swirling dark emblem. "It's a focal point for their magical communications and artifact trafficking. Destroying it will cripple their coordination."

The Fire Guild and Earth Guild representatives were tasked with leading the assault, using their elemental prowess to breach the Nexus defenses. Equipped with the reconfigured Scepter, Kesia would provide support by reinforcing the allied troops' magical shields and disrupting enemy spells.

Leading a contingent of the Manor's best physical combatants, Redington prepared for a ground assault. "We'll strike under the cover of night. Stealth and speed are our allies here," he briefed his team.

As night fell, the allied forces moved out, the elements themselves seeming to shield their movements. The Earth Guild caused the ground to swallow up noise around their troops, while the Fire Guild obscured their advance with a dense, magically induced fog.

Reaching the outskirts of the Shadow Nexus, they encountered minimal resistance—most likely due to Kesia's disruption spells, which confused and disoriented the enemy sentinels. Mara, leading the magical assault team, quickly set up a perimeter as Sophea began to channel the Scepter's energy into the ground.

With a profound boom that shook the earth, the foundations of the Shadow Nexus began to crumble. Fire and earth converged in a spectacular display, tearing apart the dark fortifications as Lexi and Redington led the charge into the heart of the Nexus.

Inside the Nexus, chaos reigned. The dark mages and their minions were caught off guard, their dark spells backfiring or fizzling out in the wake of the Scepter's purifying influence. Lexi, wielding a sword of radiant light, cut through the shadowy figures that attempted to regroup and mount a defense.

With the main defensive spells neutralized, the allied forces quickly secured the Nexus. The capture of enemy artifacts and intelligence would provide the Manor's forces with not only additional magical resources but also crucial information about the enemy's plans and infrastructure.

As the allied forces returned to Wrightenton Manor with their spoils of war, the mood was one of jubilant relief. The victory at the Shadow Nexus had been a significant blow to the enemy, proof that the tide was turning in their favor.

In the aftermath, Lexi convened with her advisors to discuss the implications of their victory. "We've struck a significant blow today," she acknowledged, "But we must remain vigilant. The enemy will retaliate, and we must be ready to counter."

Lord Winston, reviewing the captured artifacts and documents, added, "These will give us insight into their network. We'll need to decipher these quickly and prepare for the next phase of our offensive."

The success of the mission reinforced the allies' resolve to continue their aggressive posture. Plans were drawn for further strikes, each designed to exploit the weaknesses revealed by the intelligence gathered during the Nexus raid.

As Lexi looked over the maps and listened to her advisors strategize, she felt a mix of hope and the heavy burden of leadership. The war was far from over, and each victory brought its own set of challenges and decisions. But for now, Wrightenton Manor stood strong—its walls a bulwark against the darkness, its leaders a beacon of hope for their allies.

The battle for balance continued, with each side adapting and evolving in response to the other's moves. Lexi knew that the days ahead would require even more courage and cunning. The journey to "Wisdom of a Soul" was proving to be as perilous as it was pivotal.

Chapter 80

Following their triumphant raid on the Shadow Nexus, the allies at Wrightenton Manor enjoyed a brief period of strategic advantage. However, the darkness was far from defeated, and unsettling signs soon began to emerge that hinted at a deeper, more ominous counterstrategy by their adversaries.

While the scholars and mages at the Manor pored over the captured documents and artifacts, they uncovered disturbing references to the "Draconis Veil," a mythical dark artifact believed to amplify malevolent magics and potentially capable of opening rifts between worlds. The implications of such another artifact falling into enemy hands were dire.

"We must assume they are searching for the Draconis Veil," Lexi stated during a high-level meeting. "If they were willing to risk so much for the Obsidian Scepter, the Veil might be their ultimate goal."

Reports from the Manor's scouts and magical sensors indicated a marked increase in dark forces' movements along the ley lines, particularly toward the ancient ruins known as the Cradle of Shadows, reputed to be the last known location of the Draconis Veil.

Redington, analyzing the patterns, noted, "They're mobilizing quicker than anticipated. It's not just small scouting parties; these are organized battalions. They're definitely up to something big."

Understanding the urgency of the situation, Lexi convened her council to plan a preemptive strike to either recover or neutralize the Draconis Veil before the enemy could.

"The Cradle of Shadows is heavily warded and notoriously treacherous," Mara cautioned. "It's believed that the ruins themselves are alive and not fond of visitors."

Despite the risks, the consensus was clear— waiting was not an option. They would have to confront the enemy there and ensure the Veil did not become a tool of darkness.

With the decision made, Lexi and her team began preparations. She sent messages to all allied factions requesting additional support. The Fire Guild and Earth Guild promised to send reinforcements, while the Air Guild offered to provide aerial surveillance.

Kesia, tasked with leading the ground assault, coordinated with Mara to design a series of protective wards and offensive spells tailored to the unique threats of the Cradle of Shadows.

On the eve of their departure, Lexi gathered her closest advisors and strike team for a final briefing. "This mission will be dangerous, potentially more so than any we've undertaken," she admitted, her expression grave. "The Cradle is not merely a place, but a test—one we must pass."

Redington, equipped with maps and recon data, outlined their approach strategy. "We'll split into three teams. One to breach, one to secure, and one as reserve. We'll need to be flexible and adapt quickly to whatever the Cradle throws at us."

Later, alone in the guest room, Lexi reviewed the ancient texts describing the Cradle of Shadows. The myths spoke of it as a place where reality was thin, where the past and present blurred. She knew that they were not just going into a physical location but into a confrontation with the unknown.

As she set aside the texts and prepared her gear, Lexi felt a resolve settling over her. They were the bulwark against the encroaching darkness, the defenders of realms seen and unseen. The weight of her responsibility was immense, but so was her determination.

As dawn broke, the convoy of allies set out from Wrightenton Manor, the early morning light casting long shadows across the assembled force. Lexi rode at the front, her gaze fixed on the horizon.

The journey to the Cradle of Shadows would be fraught with peril. The battle for the Draconis Veil was not just a confrontation with the enemy but potentially a defining moment in the ongoing war between light and darkness.

As they rode out, the Manor behind them stood silent and watchful, a steadfast sentinel in an ever-shifting landscape of power and prophecy. The echoes of darkness were all around, but so too were the whispers of hope—carried on the winds that swept across the land, heralding the coming storm.

Chapter 81

The journey to the Cradle of Shadows was fraught with an ominous tension that permeated the air, thickening as Lexi and her team ventured deeper into the uncharted territories. The landscape around them gradually transformed from the familiar woodlands of the Manor to the bleak, barren fields that bordered the ancient ruins known as the Cradle.

As they neared their destination, the environment grew increasingly hostile. Thick fogs rolled in unexpectedly, obscuring sight lines and distorting sounds, while the ground beneath their feet became treacherous with hidden crevices and sudden, steep declivities.

"The Cradle is protecting itself," Sophea murmured, her eyes narrowing as she scanned their surroundings with a mix of wariness and academic fascination. "It's not just the physical barriers. There are spells at work here designed to turn back the unwary."

Their first encounter was not with the enemy but with the Cradle's own defenses. Animated statues, remnants of an ancient civilization that once revered dark energies, sprung to life, attacking the team with a ferocity that belied their weathered appearances. Kesia and Mara worked in tandem, countering the animated assault with bursts of elemental magic—fire to shatter, earth to bind.

"Keep moving!" Lexi commanded, leading the charge as they made their way through the gauntlet of guardians. Each step forward was hard-won, the Cradle's defenses unyielding and relentless.

Finally, they reached the heart of the Cradle— a vast, open courtyard surrounded by towering monoliths, at the center of which stood an altar. There, shrouded in a pulsating aura of darkness, was the Draconis Veil, its presence a palpable weight in the air.

"It's more powerful than we anticipated," Lexi observed, her expression grave as she surveyed the artifact. "Taking it won't be easy. We need to neutralize its defenses first."

No sooner had they formulated a plan than the enemy struck, a coordinated attack that seemed to emerge from the shadows themselves. Dark mages, accompanied by hordes of shadow creatures, launched a ferocious assault, intent on overwhelming Lexi's team.

The battle was chaotic, with Lexi and her allies pushed to their limits. The Fire Guild's warriors unleashed torrents of flame, carving swathes through the enemy ranks, while the Earth Guild's elementals fortified their position, making a stand at the altar.

Kesia focused on the Veil and chanted an ancient incantation to disrupt the artifact's dark aura. "Cover me!" she yelled over the din of battle, her voice barely audible as she concentrated on her spell.

With the enemy's focus divided between reclaiming the Veil and combating Lexi's forces, an opportunity presented itself. Sophea, utilizing a rare artifact from the Manor's vaults, amplified Kesia's spell, sending a shockwave of purified magic through the courtyard.

The effect was immediate and dramatic. The Veil's dark aura faltered, its hold on the surrounding energies waning as the spell took effect. Seizing the moment, Lexi surged forward, the Obsidian Scepter in hand, and claimed the Veil.

With the Veil secured, Lexi called for a retreat. "Fall back!" she commanded, leading her team out of the Cradle as the enemy regrouped for another assault. The retreat was as perilous as the approach, but the team's spirits were buoyed by their success.

Back at Wrightenton Manor, the Veil was placed in a specially prepared containment field, and its energies are to be studied and hopefully repurposed for the light. The victory was celebrated, but Lexi knew this was only a reprieve.

In the quiet that followed the celebration, Lexi reflected on the journey ahead. The acquisition of the Draconis Veil had shifted the balance of power. The dark forces would not sit idly by, and Lexi needed to prepare for the next phase of the conflict.

"The battle continues," she told her council. "Let's use this time wisely. Strengthen our defenses, deepen our alliances, and remain vigilant. The darkness is persistent, but we will be ready."

As the Manor settled down for the night, the stars above seemed to shine a little brighter, a silent testament to the enduring spirit of those who defended the light. The road ahead was fraught with dangers, but Lexi and her allies faced it united, their resolve unbroken.

Chapter 82

Lexi's eyes fluttered open to the muted sounds of a gentle rain pattering against the windowpane, the scent of damp earth filling the air. She lay still for a moment, her mind foggy and disoriented, struggling to reconcile the vivid intensity of her dreams with the stark, simple reality of her surroundings—a small, sparsely furnished room in Nepal where she had been recuperating from a severe bout of flu.

As her vision cleared and her senses returned, Lexi became aware of three worried faces hovering over her. Isabella, Kesia, and Sophea were seated beside her bed, each displaying a mix of relief and concern.

"You're awake! Oh, Lexi, you had us worried sick," Isabella exclaimed, her voice a mix of scold and sigh, relief washing over her features as she took Lexi's hand.

Lexi tried to sit up, her head spinning slightly as she did. "How long...?" she managed to ask, her voice hoarse and weak.

"Three weeks," Sophea replied softly, handing Lexi a glass of water. "You collapsed with a fever. We thought it was just exhaustion, but then you didn't wake up..."

As Lexi's memories of the last few days—or what she had perceived as days—returned, she recounted the vivid dreams of battles, the Obsidian Scepter, the Draconis Veil, and the relentless onslaughts of dark forces. With each detail she shared, her friends exchanged looks of astonishment.

"It was all so real," Lexi murmured, the confusion evident in her eyes. "We were defending Wrightenton Manor, using artifacts... The Scepter, the Veil... We won, or I think we did. It felt like we did."

Kesia, always the pragmatic one, considered this carefully. "Holy Hannah, Lexi, dreams can be a manifestation of our fears and hopes. But given the detail and the consistency with what we know of the dark forces, it might have been more—a vision, perhaps, sent as a warning or a premonition."

Sophea, who had delved deeply into spiritual and mystical studies, nodded thoughtfully. "Dreams, especially those experienced under fever, can tap into a deeper consciousness. They might reveal not just fears but paths—potential futures we might face. It's possible the Cosmos

Dial was communicating with you, through the
veil of your unconscious mind."

Chapter 83

*L*exi's convalescence at the monastery in Nepal was marked by a profound sense of disorientation. Her mind, still reeling from the vivid dreamscapes of battles and artifacts, struggled to reconcile with the quiet, meditative life she had been leading before her illness.

"Hey, wasn't I in London? I know I was in New York?" Lexi's weak voice carried a mix of confusion and concern as she surveyed her surroundings—the simple, sparse room starkly different from the grandeur of Wrightenton Manor in her dreams.

"No, Lexi, you returned here a few weeks ago," Isabella responded gently, trying to anchor her friend to the present reality. "You mentioned feeling overwhelmed and needing a retreat. You wanted to reconnect with your spiritual roots here at the monastery before you fell ill."

As Lexi grappled with this information, another wave of fatigue washed over her, and she drifted back into a restless sleep. It was here, in the boundary between wakefulness and dreams, that she encountered Archangel Raziel once again. His presence was both majestic and comforting, a stark contrast to the chaotic energies of her previous dream.

"Alexandra," Raziel's voice resonated with a clarity that transcended the dream, "The vision you experienced was more than a mere illusion wrought by fever. It was a revelation of the delicate balance that governs all."

Raziel continued, his tone imbued with the gravity of his words, "The celestial realm operates under a mandate to maintain equilibrium between good and evil, knowledge and power. The battles you witnessed, the artifacts you encountered—these are metaphors for the struggles that every soul must navigate."

He gestured expansively, and the dream space around them shimmered, revealing scenes of ethereal beauty juxtaposed with shadowy turmoil. "Each artifact represented one of the nine gifts of the Spirit—prophecy, healing, miracles, and others. Through these gifts, souls learn, grow, and choose their paths."

"The earthly experiences you undergo are crucial," Raziel explained as the visions shifted to show myriad human interactions—joy, suffering, learning, and healing. "These experiences forge your spirit, preparing it for higher duties and eventual ascension. Your dream of the Manor was an allegory, teaching you about the power of unity, the necessity of struggle, and the importance of guardianship over the spiritual and the material."

Lexi listened, mesmerized by the unfolding wisdom. "Why show me this, Raziel? Why now?" she asked, her voice a whisper in the celestial vastness.

"To prepare you, Lexi. The challenges ahead are not just battles against external darkness but also internal enlightenment. You are to be a guardian of balance—not just at a mythical Manor, but within your own soul and in the wider world."

With a final, all-encompassing glance, Raziel's form began to fade, his last words echoing in the dream, "Remember, Lexi, balance is not achieved by suppressing one force for another, but by navigating and harmonizing all. The path is arduous but noble."

Lexi awoke with a start, the morning sun casting gentle rays through the small window. The dream's vividness and Raziel's message lingered in her mind, imbuing her with a newfound purpose. She rose, her body still weak, but her spirit invigorated, and joined her friends in the tranquil gardens of the monastery.

Gathered with Isabella, Kesia, and Sophea, Lexi shared her visionary encounter. As she spoke of balance, the spiritual gifts, and the allegorical battles, her friends listened intently, each absorbing the implications in their own way.

"We are all on our paths, but together, we share a journey," Lexi concluded, her gaze sweeping over the serene landscape. "Let's use the wisdom of this vision to guide us in our actions and choices to better ourselves and, through us, the world."

The rest of the day was spent in contemplative discussion and peaceful meditation. The monastery, a nexus of spiritual energy, seemed the perfect crucible to forge their resolve and prepare for the challenges that lay ahead.

As they retired for the evening, the stars overhead twinkled with a celestial wink—a reminder of Raziel's presence and the ongoing guidance from the realms beyond, ensuring that their paths were aligned with the cosmic balance. Lexi reflected on the profound journey she had undertaken, not just in this lifetime but across countless incarnations. Each experience, whether filled with joy or sorrow, had been a stepping stone toward a greater understanding of her soul's purpose.

Lexi had learned that the journey of a soul is not measured by material success or earthly accomplishments but by the depth of wisdom gained and the love cultivated along the way. Every life, every trial, and every triumph had served to refine her spirit, bringing her closer to the ultimate truth—that all souls are interconnected, each playing a vital role in the vast tapestry of existence.

The knowledge she had acquired was not just for her personal growth but was meant to be shared to uplift others and help guide them on their own journeys. Understanding that the true essence of life is found in the balance of giving and receiving, of learning and teaching, Lexi embraced her role as both a student and a teacher in the eternal dance of souls.

As she gazed at the night sky, she felt a deep peace settle within her, knowing that every step she had taken was guided by the unseen hand of destiny. The lessons learned were now woven into the fabric of her soul, a testament to the endless pursuit of enlightenment and the unwavering quest for the divine.

At that moment, Lexi realized that the journey was far from over. The knowledge she had gained was merely a glimpse of the infinite wisdom that awaited her. With a heart full of gratitude and a soul attuned to the cosmic rhythms, Lexi closed her eyes, ready to rest and dream of the many adventures yet to come, knowing that she was forever connected to the Source of all that is.

Prayer to Archangel Raziel,

Raziel, divine protector of knowledge, I am ready for your blessing. Please remove any blocks that I may have and open my ability to see, hear, feel, and understand the spiritual secrets of the celestial and earthly worlds that you are about to share, thank you for empowering me with your deeper spiritual insights.

Acknowledgments

First and foremost, I wish to express my deepest gratitude to the divine muse that whispers through the breeze and guides the pen with an unseen but ever-felt presence. The journey of writing Knowledge of a Soul has been transformative, and it is with a humble heart that I offer thanks to those who have walked with me on this path.

To my family and friends—your unwavering support and endless encouragement have been the pillars upon which this project has rested. Your belief in my vision, even when the road was obscured by the fog of doubt, helped illuminate the way forward. I am eternally grateful for your love and patience.

I extend my sincere appreciation to my literary agent and the wonderful team at Maximilian Enterprises, especially my editor, whose keen insights and suggestions helped refine and sculpt this narrative into its final form. Your dedication to this story has been a beacon of professionalism and passion.

A special thank you goes to the cultural consultants and historians who provided invaluable expertise that enriched the authenticity and depth of the story's setting and characters. Your contributions have been integral to the soul of this book, ensuring accuracy in the midst of creative interpretation.

To the artist who crafted the cover and the visual representations within these pages, your talent has given Knowledge of a Soul a face that mirrors its spirit—thank you for your remarkable artistry.

My gratitude extends to the academic and spiritual communities whose works on mythology, theology, and philosophy have informed and inspired the conceptual foundations of this novel. Your research and writings were crucial in weaving the intricate tapestry of this story.

I must acknowledge the contributions of artificial intelligence in this creative process, specifically OpenAI's ChatGPT, which provided assistance with initial brainstorming, factual verification, and even some aspects of narrative structuring. This technology has opened up new avenues for creativity that were previously unimagined.

And finally, to you, the reader—thank you for embarking on this journey through the pages of Knowledge of a Soul. It is for you that these words have been woven into a story meant to entertain, enlighten, and inspire. May you find a reflection of your own journey within this narrative.

May we all continue to learn, to grow, and to understand the deeper narratives that guide our souls through the cosmos of collective experience.

With all my gratitude,
Dr. Constance

Footnotes & Bibliography

Footnotes

- The concept of "the balance of light and darkness" is explored in various mythologies across the world, symbolizing the dual nature of existence. This theme is central to the narrative structure of Knowledge of a Soul.

- The reference to "Archangel Raziel" and his role as the keeper of secrets and divine mysteries is rooted in Kabbalistic teachings, where Raziel is believed to have given the book of Sefer Raziel HaMalakh to Adam, the first human.

- The description of the "Obsidian Scepter" is inspired by historical artifacts and the symbolic use of obsidian in ancient and mystical practices. Obsidian is often associated with protection and prophecy in various cultures.

- The "Draconis Veil" is a fictional artifact created for the purposes of this novel. Its properties and lore are inspired by traditional narratives about dragons and veils found in various cultures, symbolizing power and mystery.

- The "Ritual of the Silver Light" mentioned is an amalgamation of various historical ritualistic practices aimed at purification and protection. The ritual is fictional but draws on elements common to many traditions.

Bibliography

Mythological Sources:

Campbell, Joseph. The Hero with a Thousand Faces. Pantheon Books, 1949.

Hamilton, Edith. Mythology: Timeless Tales of Gods and Heroes. Little, Brown and Co., 1942.

Graves, Robert. The Greek Myths. Penguin Books, 1955.

Philosophical and Theological Texts:

Kaplan, Aryeh. Sefer Yetzirah: The Book of Creation. Weiser Books, 1997.

Pagels, Elaine. The Gnostic Gospels. Random House, 1979.

Smith, Huston. The World's Religions. HarperOne, 1991.

Cultural and Historical Studies:

Eliade, Mircea. Shamanism: Archaic Techniques of Ecstasy. Princeton University Press, 1964.

Frazer, James George. The Golden Bough: A Study in Magic and Religion. Macmillan, 1890.

Armstrong, Karen. A History of God: The 4,000-Year Quest of Judaism, Christianity and Islam. Ballantine Books, 1993.

Artificial Intelligence and Creativity:

Du Sautoy, Marcus. The Creativity Code: Art and Innovation in the Age of AI. Harvard University Press, 2019.

McCormack, Jon and d'Inverno, Mark. Computers and Creativity. Springer, 2012.

General References:

National Geographic. Treasures of the Earth: Need, Greed, and a Sustainable Future. National Geographic Books, 2010.

History Channel. Documentary series on ancient civilizations, broadcast 2005-2010.

The Author

Dr. Constance Santego

Dr. Constance Santego is an esteemed author, educator, and holistic healer whose work spans across several disciplines including spiritual wellness, ancient mythologies, and personal development. With a doctoral degree in Natural Medicine, Constance has dedicated her life to exploring the intersections of spirituality, health, and human consciousness.

Born and raised in a small town steeped in folklore and surrounded by nature, Constance developed an early fascination with the stories and rituals that define different cultures. This curiosity blossomed into a lifelong pursuit of knowledge, leading her to travel extensively, in places as diverse as Greece, England, Mexico, and Spain.

Constance's academic journey is complemented by her practical experience in the healing arts. She is a certified Reiki Master, a practitioner of many modalities, and has conducted numerous workshops on meditation, energy healing, and mindfulness. Her holistic practice aims to integrate the body, mind, and spirit to foster well-being and spiritual growth.

Literary Contributions

Dr. Santego is the author of several books that explore spiritual themes through a blend of narrative fiction and insightful commentary. Her works often weave together elements of ancient myths with modern existential questions, creating a rich tapestry that resonates with readers seeking deeper understanding of themselves and the universe.

Knowledge of a Soul, her latest novel, continues this tradition by exploring the themes of balance, power, and transformation. It draws heavily from her scholarly research into mythological stories and her experiences in mystical practices. Through her narrative, she invites readers to contemplate the cosmic balance of light and darkness, and the individual's role within this eternal dance.

Future Projects

Dr. Santego is currently working on her next book, which promises to delve deeper into the spiritual journeys of historical figures across various cultures. She continues to contribute to academic nonfiction, sharing her insights on holistic health and spiritual wellbeing.

Constance lives in a serene lakeside town, where she enjoys her family time, herbal gardening, and writing. Her life's work reflects her passion for bringing light and healing into the world, guiding others through their spiritual journeys with compassion and wisdom.

Also Available

Play the game Ikona and test
your Virtues and Sins
For additional information on
Constance Santego's wide range of
Motivational Products, Coaching Sessions,
Spiritual Retreats,
Live Events and Educational Programs
Go to
www.ConstanceSantego.ca

Follow me on:
Instagram - Constance_Santego &
Facebook - constancesantegoo
YouTube Channel - Constance Santego
Subscribe and receive free information &
Meditations